To Kill A Mockingbird
and other plays

Edited by Sadler & Hayllar

Copyright © R. K. Sadler and T. A. S. Hayllar 1996

All rights reserved.
Except under the conditions described in the
Copyright Act 1968 of Australia and subsequent amendments,
no part of this publication may be reproduced,
stored in a retrieval system, or transmitted in any form or by any means,
electronic, mechanical, photocopying, recording or otherwise,
without the prior permission of the copyright owner.

First published 1996 by
MACMILLAN EDUCATION AUSTRALIA PTY LTD
627 Chapel Street, South Yarra 3141
Reprinted 1998

Associated companies and representatives
throughout the world

National Library of Australia
cataloguing in publication data

To kill a mockingbird and other plays.

   ISBN 0 7329 3566 0.

   1. College and school drama. 2. Children's plays, English.
   I. Sadler, R. K. (Rex Kevin). II. Hayllar, T. A. S. (Thomas Albert S.).

822.00809283

Typeset in Baskerville and Avant Garde by
Superskill Graphics, Singapore

Printed in Malaysia

Illustrated by Ian Forss and Andrew Plant
Cover design by the Modern Art Production Group
Cover photograph courtesy of Austral International

To Kill a Mockingbird (screenplay)
WARNING:
This screenplay is not to be performed either by professionals or amateurs. The amateur and stock rights to *To Kill a Mockingbird* **(dramatised by Christopher Sergel) are controlled exclusively by The Dramatic Publishing Company, P.O. Box 109, Woodstock, IL 60098.**

Contents

Preface   v

1 **To Kill a Mockingbird**   2
   Screenplay by Horton Foote
   Drama activities   65

2 **Adam's Ark**   76
   by Harold Hodgson
   Drama activities   140

3 **The Hood, the Sad and the Cuddly**   146
   by Robin George
   Drama activities   167

4 **Dracula**   174
   adapted by Tom Hayllar
   Drama activities   208

5 **The Cowpokes of Calico**   212
   by Bill Condon
   Drama activities   221

6 **Possible Changes**   226
   by Vashti Farrer
   Drama activities   237

Acknowledgements   242

Preface

A problem facing English and drama teachers of the middle and upper secondary students is that there are very few collections of plays that meet the needs of today's teenagers. *To Kill a Mockingbird and Other Plays* directly addresses this problem. The plays allow teenagers to confront issues and use their imaginations as they empathise with a wide range of characters from the present and the past.

Humour and excitement, conflict, tension and suspense are all here for the acting. Some of the plays raise social, moral and emotional issues that will help students understand their surroundings in the widest sense.

In the collection there are six complete scripts covering a wide range of genres: film, stage and radio scripts, including science fiction, real life drama, farce, Gothic horror and melodrama. Innovative and creative drama activities accompany each play. Large casts, with usually more than twelve characters, allow for maximum class participation.

The inclusions of the complete screenplay of *To Kill a Mockingbird* provides a unique opportunity to compare the three written and visual texts: novel, screenplay and film. Much enjoyment can be derived from studying this academy award winning screenplay.

1

To Kill a Mockingbird

screenplay by HORTON FOOTE

To Kill a Mockingbird
screenplay by HORTON FOOTE

adapted from the novel *To Kill a Mockingbird* by HARPER LEE

THE film, *To Kill a Mockingbird*, starring Gregory Peck as Atticus Finch was first released in 1962. Gregory Peck as the kind and quietly spoken Alabama lawyer won an Academy Award for his performance. The film condemns the evils of racial prejudice in the deep South.

Horton Foote's adaptation of *To Kill a Mockingbird* for the screen also won him an Academy Award. He was later to win another Academy Award for his original screenplay *Tender Mercies*. He very much enjoyed adapting the novel for the screen and says of his experience, 'I felt I understood the world of Harper Lee's novel and its people. The town of the novel was not unlike the town I was born and brought up in, and the time of the novel, the depression era of the 1930s, was a period I had lived through.'

Harper Lee

CAST

ATTICUS FINCH	Gregory Peck
SCOUT FINCH	Mary Badham
JEM FINCH	Phillip Alford
DILL HARRIS	John Megna
SHERIFF HECK TATE	Frank Overton
MISS MAUDIE ATKINSON	Rosemary Murphy
MRS DUBOSE	Ruth White
TOM ROBINSON	Brock Peters
CALPURNIA	Estelle Evans

JUDGE TAYLOR	Paul Fix
MAYELLA EWELL	Collin Wilcox
BOB EWELL	James Anderson
STEPHANIE CRAWFORD	Alice Ghostley
BOO RADLEY	Robert Duvall
GILMER	William Windom
WALTER CUNNINGHAM	Crahan Denton
MR RADLEY	Richard Hale
WALTER CUNNINGHAM, JR	Steve Condit
REVEREND SYKES	Bill Walker
NARRATION (JEAN LOUISE FINCH)	Kim Stanley

CREDITS

PRODUCED by Alan J. Pakula
DIRECTED by Robert Mulligan
SCREENPLAY by Horton Foote, adapted from Harper Lee's novel *To Kill a Mockingbird*
DIRECTOR OF PHOTOGRAPHY: Russell Harlan, A.S.C.
MUSIC by Elmer Bernstein
ART DIRECTORS: Alexander Golitzen and Henry Bumstead
FILM EDITOR: Aaron Stell, A.C.E.
COSTUMES by Rosemary Odell

A Universal presentation of a Pakula-Mulligan, Brentwood Productions Picture

FADE IN.
EXTERIOR: MAYCOMB, ALABAMA. DAYBREAK.

It is just before dawn, and in the half-light cotton farms, pinewoods, the hills surrounding Maycomb, and the Courthouse Square are seen. A young woman's voice is heard.

Jean Louise (*Voice over*) Maycomb was a tired old town, even in 1932 ... when I first knew it. Somehow, it was hotter then. Men's stiff collars wilted by nine in the morning. Ladies bathed before noon and after their three o'clock naps. And by nightfall they were like soft teacakes with frosting from sweating and sweet talcum. The day was twenty-four hours long, but it seemed longer. There's no hurry, for there's nowhere to go and nothing to buy . . . and no money to buy it with. Although Maycomb County had recently been told that it had nothing to fear but fear itself.

(*The Finch house and yard are seen. It is a small frame house, built high off the ground and with a porch in the manner of Southern cottages of its day. The yard is a large one, filled with oaks, and it has an air of mystery about it in the early morning light.*)

That summer, I was six years old.

(**Walter Cunningham**, *a thin, raw-boned farmer in his late fifties, comes into view. He is carrying a crokersack full of hickory nuts. He passes under the oak tree at the side of the house.* **Scout**, *six, dressed in blue jeans, drops from one of its branches to the ground. She brushes herself off and goes toward* **Mr Cunningham**.)

Scout Good morning, Mr Cunningham.

Cunningham Mornin' Miss.

Scout My daddy is getting dressed. Would you like me to call him for you?

Cunningham No, Miss . . . I . . . don't care to bother.

Scout Why, it's no bother, Mr Cunningham. He'll be happy to see you. Atticus. (**Scout** *hurries up the steps and opens the door.*) Atticus, here's Mr Cunningham.

(**Scout** *steps back onto the porch as* **Atticus** *enters.* **Walter Cunningham** *seems ill at ease and embarrassed.*)

Atticus Good morning, Walter.

Cunningham Good morning, Mr Finch. I . . . didn't want to bother you none. I brung you these hickory nuts as part of my entailment.

Atticus (*Reaching for the sack of nuts*) Well, I thank you. The collards we had last week were delicious.

Cunningham (*Gesturing, and then turning to leave*) Well, good morning.

Atticus Good morning, Walter.

(**Atticus** *holds the sack of nuts.* **Scout** *is on the steps behind him.* **Scout** *leans on Atticus' shoulders as they watch* **Mr Cunningham** *leave.*)

Scout, I think maybe next time Mr Cunningham comes, you better not call me.

Scout Well, I thought you'd want to thank him.

Atticus Oh, I do. I think it embarrasses him to be thanked.

> (**Atticus** *turns and puts the sack on the porch and starts for the front yard to get the morning papers.* **Scout** *follows after him.*)

Scout Why does he bring you all this stuff?

Atticus He is paying me for some legal work I did for him.

Scout Why is he paying you like this?

Atticus That's the only way he can . . . he has no money.

> (**Atticus** *comes back to the porch as* **Scout** *follows. He picks up the newspaper and reads.*)

Scout Is he poor?

Atticus Yes.

Scout Are we poor?

Atticus We are indeed.

Scout Are we as poor as the Cunninghams?

Atticus No, not exactly. The Cunninghams are country folks, farmers, and the crash hit them the hardest.

> (**Calpurnia**, *in her late fifties, appears at the screen door.*)

Calpurnia Scout, call your brother. (*She goes back inside.*)

Scout Atticus, Jem is up in the tree. He says he won't come down until you agree to play football for the Methodists.

(**Atticus** *walks toward the tree. In a treehouse, high up in the tree, sits* **Jem**. *He is ten, with a serious, manly little face. Right now, he is scowling.*)

Atticus Jem . . . Son, why don't you come on down and have your breakfast? Calpurnia has a good one . . . hot biscuits.

Jem No Sir. Not until you agree to play football for the Methodists.

(**Atticus** *is looking up at* **Jem**. **Scout** *is swinging in the tyre swing.*)

Atticus Oh, no, Son. I can't do that. I explained to you I'm too old to get out there. After all, I'm the only father you have. You wouldn't want me to get out there and get my head knocked off, would you?

Jem I ain't coming down.

Atticus Suit yourself.

(**Atticus** *turns and starts for the kitchen door as he reads the newspaper.* **Jem** *moves out from behind the covering and watches.* **Scout** *starts to go across the street and stops by the tree.* **Miss Maudie Atkinson**, *a strong, warm-hearted woman, keenly interested in* **Atticus** *and the children, is working on her flowers in her yard across the street.*)

Maudie Good morning.

Scout Good morning, Miss Maudie.

Maudie What's going on over there?

Scout I'm having a terrible time, Miss Maudie. Jem is staying up in that tree until Atticus agrees to play football for the Methodists, and Atticus says he's too old.

Jem Every time I want him to do something . . . he's too old . . . He's too old for anything.

Maudie He can do plenty of things.

Atticus (*Entering the yard from the house and walking over*) You be good, children, and mind Cal. Good morning, Maudie.

Maudie Good morning, Atticus.

(*Church bells ring.*)

Jem He won't let me have a gun. He'll only play touch football with me . . . never tackle.

Maudie (*Glancing in Atticus' direction, then looking at* **Jem**) He can make somebody's will so airtight you can't break it. You count your blessings and stop complaining . . . both of you.

(**Atticus** *continues on out of the yard.* **Miss Maudie** *walks away.* **Scout** *climbs up into the tree.*)

Scout Jem, he is pretty old.

Jem I can't help that.

(*He swings down to the lower limb in disgust and looks down into Miss Stephanie Crawford's collard patch next door. A boy,* **Dill**, *is sitting among the collards. Sitting down, he is not much higher than the collards. He has a solemn, owlish face, a knowledge and imagination too old for his years. He looks up at* **Jem**.)

Dill (*Tentatively*) Hey . . .

Jem Hey, yourself.

Dill (*Standing up*) I'm Charles Baker Harris. I can read. You got anything needs reading, I can do it.

Jem How old are you? Four and a half?

Dill Going on seven.

Jem Well, no wonder then. Scout's been reading since she was born and don't start to school till next month. You look right puny for goin' on seven.

Dill I'm little, but I'm old. Folks call me Dill. I'm from Meridian, Mississippi, and I'm spending two weeks next door with my Aunt Stephanie. My mama works for a photographer in Meridian. She entered my picture in the 'Beautiful Child Contest' and won five dollars. She gave the money to me and I went to the picture show twenty times with it.

(**Scout** *and* **Jem** *climb down from the treehouse.* **Scout** *climbs into the tyre swing as* **Jem** *leans against the tree facing* **Dill**.)

Scout Our mama's dead, but we got a daddy. Where's your daddy?

Dill I haven't got one.

Scout Is he dead?

Dill No.

Scout Well . . . if he's not dead, you've got one, haven't you?

(**Jem** *turns to* **Scout**.)

Jem Hush, Scout.

(**Jem** *motions to her with his head as* **Scout** *whispers.*)

Scout   What's happened, what's up?

(**Calpurnia** *enters with a shirt, and starts to dress* **Scout**.)

Dill, this is Calpurnia.

Calpurnia   Pleased to know you, Dill.

Dill   Pleased to know you. My daddy owns the L and N Railroad. He's going to let me run the engine all the way to New Orleans.

Calpurnia   Is that so?

(**Calpurnia** *exits.* **Jem** *turns away.* **Scout** *finishes putting on her shirt.*)

Dill   He says I can invite . . . anybody . . .

Jem   Shhh!

(**Mr Radley**, *in his seventies, a regal, austere man, walks by.* **Scout** *and* **Jem** *see him and become very subdued, as if they were afraid. Their attention leaves* **Dill**, *and he senses this and looks at them to see what is happening.*)

There goes the meanest man that ever took a breath of life.

Dill   Why is he the meanest man?

Jem   Well, for one thing he has a boy named Boo that he keeps chained to a bed in that house over yonder. (*Points to the house.*) See, he lives over there.

(*Moving shot: As they start to move out of the yard,* **Scout** *follows behind them. They go down the sidewalk past Miss Stephanie's house, north to the Radley house.*)

Boo only comes out at night when we are asleep and it's pitch-dark. When you wake up at night you can hear him. Once I heard him scratching on our screen door, but he was gone by the time Atticus got there.

(*They are standing by a light pole now, staring at the Radley house and yard. The house is low and was once white with a deep front porch and green shutters. But it darkened long ago to the colour of the slate-grey yard around it. Rain-spotted shingles droop over the eaves of the veranda. Oak trees keep the sun away. The remains of a picket fence drunkenly guard the front yard. A 'swept' yard that is never swept, where Johnson grass and rabbit tobacco grow in abundance. Dill's eyes have widened. He is becoming truly intrigued.*)

Dill   Wonder what he does in there?

Scout   I wonder what he looks like?

Jem Well, judging from his tracks, he's about six and a half feet tall. He eats raw squirrels and all the cats he can catch. There's a long, jagged scar running all the way across his face. His teeth are yellow and rotten. His eyes are popped. And he drools most of the time.

Dill Aw, I don't believe you.

(**Miss Stephanie**, *Dill's aunt, comes up behind them. She is in her late fifties – a spinster and the neighbourhood gossip. She comes up without their hearing her. She has a habit of half-shouting when she talks.*)

Stephanie Dill, what are you doing here?

Dill My Lord, Aunt Stephanie, you almost gave me a heart attack.

Stephanie Dill, I don't want you playing around that house over there. There's a maniac living there and he's dangerous.

Jem See? I was just trying to warn him about Boo, and he wouldn't believe me.

Stephanie Well, you'd just better believe him, Mr Dill Harris.

Jem Tell him about the time Boo tried to kill his papa.

Stephanie Well, I was standing in my yard one day when his mama come out yelling, 'He's killing us all.' Turned out that Boo was sitting in the living room cutting up the paper for his scrapbook, and when his daddy come by, he reached over with his scissors, stabbed him in his leg, pulled them out, and went right on cutting the paper.

(*Dill's eyes are popping with excitement.*)

They wanted to send him to an asylum, but his daddy said no Radley was going to any asylum. So they locked him up in the basement of the courthouse till he nearly died of the damp, and his daddy brought him home. And there he is to this day, sittin' over there with his scissors . . . Lord knows what he's doin' or thinkin'.

EXTERIOR: FINCH YARD. DAY.

Jem *is swinging in the tyre swing. In the distance the town clock is heard to strike five.*

Jem Come on, Scout, it's five o'clock. (*Jumps from the swinging tyre and starts to run out of the yard.*)

Dill Where are you going?

Scout It's time to meet Atticus.

(*She runs after **Jem**; **Dill** follows her.*)

(*Moving shot: They run down the street.*)

Dill Why do you call your daddy 'Atticus'?

Scout 'Cause Jem does.

Dill Why does he?

Scout I don't know. He just started to when he began talking.

(*They run up the street toward town.* **Jem** *slows down.*)

Jem Mrs Dubose is on her porch. (*He gestures to* **Dill**.) Listen, no matter what she says to you, don't answer her back. There's a Confederate pistol in her lap under her shawl and she'll kill you quick as look at you. Come on.

(*They walk cautiously on and start to pass the* **Dubose** *house. It is an old and run-down house. It has steep front steps and a dogtrot hall.* **Mrs Henry Lafayette Dubose** *sits on the front porch in her wheelchair. Beside her is a Negro girl,* **Jessie**, *who takes care of her.*)

Scout Hey, Mrs Dubose.

Mrs Dubose (*Snarling at the children*) Don't you say 'hey' to me, you ugly girl. You say 'good afternoon' to me. You come over here when I'm talking to you.

(**Scout**, **Jem**, *and* **Dill** *keep on going. They are made very uncomfortable by her. They see* **Atticus** *coming and run toward him.*)

Jem Atticus, this is Dill. He's Miss Stephanie's nephew.

Atticus How do you do, Dill.

Mrs Dubose Listen to me when I'm talking to you. Don't your daddy teach you to respect old people? You come back here, Jean Louise Finch . . .

Atticus (*Taking the children and walking over to her porch*) Good afternoon, Mrs Dubose. My, you look like a picture this afternoon.

(*The children are trying to hide behind* **Atticus**. *They begin to giggle nervously at each other.*)

Scout (*Whispering*) He don't say a picture of what.

Atticus (*Turning to look at the yard*) My goodness gracious, look at your flowers. Did you ever see anything more beautiful? (*He gestures with hand holding hat.*) Mrs Dubose, the gardens at Bellingrath have nothing to compare with your flowers.

Mrs Dubose Oh, I don't think they're as nice as last year.

Atticus Oh, I can't agree with you.

Jem (*Whispering*) He gets her interested in something nice, and she forgets to be mean.

(*The three children are standing behind* **Atticus**. **Atticus** *hits* **Jem** *with his hat.*)

Atticus I think that your yard is going to be the showplace of the town.

(*The children giggle.*)

Well, grand seeing you, Mrs Dubose.

(*He puts on his hat. They start on.*)

INTERIOR: SCOUT'S ROOM. NIGHT.

She is undressed and in bed. **Atticus** *is seated on the bed.* **Scout** *is reading to him from* Robinson Crusoe.

Scout 'I had two cats which I brought ashore on my first raft, and I had a dog . . .' (*Holds the book to her face and looks at* **Atticus**.) Atticus, do you think Boo Radley ever comes and looks in my window at night? Jem says he does. This afternoon when we were over by their house . . .

Atticus (*Interrupting*) Scout, I told you and Jem to leave those poor people alone. I want you to stay away from their house and stop tormenting them.

Scout Yes Sir.

Atticus (*Looking at his pocket watch*) Well, I think that's all the reading for tonight, honey . . . it's getting late.

(*She closes the book and he sits up and takes the book and puts it on the table.*)

Scout What time is it?

Atticus Eight-thirty.

Scout May I see your watch?

(*He gives it to her. She opens the case and reads the inscription.*)

'To Atticus, my beloved husband.' Atticus, Jem says this watch is going to belong to him some day.

Atticus That's right.

Scout Why?

Atticus Well, it's customary for the boy to have his father's watch.

Scout What are you going to give me?

Atticus Well, I don't know that I have much else of value that belongs to me. But there's a pearl necklace . . . and there's a ring that belonged to your mother . . . and I've put them away . . . and they're to be yours.

(**Scout** *stretches her arms and smiles.* **Atticus** *kisses her cheek. He takes his watch and gets up. He covers her and puts out the lamp.*)

Good night, Scout.

Scout Good night.

Atticus Good night, Jem.

Jem (*From his room*) Good night.

(**Atticus** *goes out.*)

INTERIOR: JEM'S ROOM. NIGHT.

Jem *pulls the covers over himself in the darkness.*

INTERIOR: SCOUT'S ROOM. NIGHT.

Scout *lies in bed, thinking.*

Scout Jem?

Jem (*Off camera*) Yes?

Scout How old was I when Mama died?

Jem (*Off camera*) Two.

Scout And how old were you?

Jem (*Off camera*) Six.

Scout Old as I am now?

Jem (*Off camera*) Uh huh.

Scout Was Mama pretty?

Jem (*Off camera*) Uh huh.

EXTERIOR: FRONT PORCH. NIGHT.

Atticus *is on the front porch. He can hear the children's conversation.*

Scout (*Off camera*) Was Mama nice?

Jem (*Off camera*) Uh huh.

Scout (*Off camera*) Did you love her?

Jem (*Off camera*) Yes.

Scout (*Off camera*) Did I love her?

Jem   (*Off camera*)   Yes.

Scout   (*Off camera*)   Do you miss her?

Jem   (*Off camera*)   Uh huh.

>(*There is silence.* **Atticus** *listens to the night sounds.* **Judge Taylor**, *seventy-five, comes up on the porch.*)

Judge   Evening, Atticus.

Atticus   Evening, Judge.

>(*The* **Judge** *walks over to him and pulls up a chair as he starts to sit.*)

Rather warm, isn't it?

Judge   Yes, indeed.   (*Fans himself with his hat.*)

Atticus   How's Mrs Taylor?

Judge   She's fine . . . fine. Thank you.   (*A pause.*)   Atticus, you heard about Tom Robinson?

Atticus   Yes Sir.

Judge   Grand jury will get around to chargin' him tomorrow. (*A pause.*)   I was thinking about appointing you to take the case. Though I realise you're very busy these days with your practice. And your children need a great deal of your time.

Atticus   Yes sir.   (*Reflects thoughtfully.*)   I'll take the case.

Judge   I'll send a boy for you tomorrow when his hearing comes up.   (*The* **Judge** *rises.*)   Well, I'll see you tomorrow, Atticus.

Atticus   Yes Sir.

Judge   And thank you.

Atticus   Yes Sir.

>(**Judge Taylor** *leaves. Again there is silence.* **Atticus** *rocks and listens to the night sounds.*)

EXTERIOR: FINCH PORCH. THE NEXT MORNING.

Jem, **Dill**, *and* **Scout** *enter through the door.* **Dill** *turns to* **Jem**.

Dill   Hey, Jem, I bet you a 'Grey Ghost' against two 'Tom Swifts', you won't go any farther than Boo Radley's gate.

Jem   Aw . . .

>(*They start down the steps,* **Jem** *in the lead.*)

Dill   You're scared to, ain't you?

Jem I ain't scared. I go past Boo Radley's house nearly every day of my life.

Scout Always running.

(**Jem** *and* **Dill** *turn to her.* **Jem** *shoves her.*)

Jem You hush up, Scout. (*Starts wheeling a rubber tyre.*) Come on, Dill.

Scout Me first, me first . . . me first.

(**Jem** *stops with the tyre and turns to* **Scout**.)

Jem You've gotta let Dill go first.

Scout (*Jumping up and down angrily*) No, no, me first.

Dill Oh, let her go.

Jem Scout, be still. All right, get in.

(**Jem** *takes hold of the tyre and* **Scout** *gets inside it.*)

Hurry up.

Scout All right.

Jem You ready?

Scout Uh huh. Let her go.

(*When she is inside,* **Jem** *suddenly pushes it with all his might.*)

(*Moving shot: It leaves the sidewalk, goes across the gravel road to the sidewalk in front of the Radley place, through the gate, up the Radley sidewalk, hits the steps of the porch, and then rolls over on its side.* **Dill** *and* **Jem** *watch this with helpless terror.* **Scout**, *dizzy and nauseated, and unaware of where she is, lies on the ground.*)

Jem (*Yelling frantically*) Scout, get away from there. Scout, come on.

(**Scout** *raises her head and sees where she is. She is frozen with terror.*)

Scout, don't just lie there. Get up!

(**Jem** *runs to* **Scout**, *seated on the ground in front of the house.*)

Let's go.

(*He gets his sister by the hand, then looks up at the house, drops her hand, runs up the steps to the front door, touches it, comes running down, grabs the tyre, takes his sister by the hand, and starts running out of the yard.*)

Run for your life, Scout. Come on, Dill!

(*Moving shot: They run out of the yard, up the sidewalk to their own yard.* **Dill** *runs fast behind them. When they get to the safety of their yard, they are all exhausted and fall on the ground.* **Jem** *is elated by his feat of touching the Radley house.*)

Now who's a coward? You tell them about this back in Meridian County, Mr Dill Harris.

(**Dill** *looks at* **Jem** *with new respect.*)

Dill I'll tell you what let's do. Let's go down to the courthouse and see that room they locked Boo up in. My aunt says it's bat-infested, and he almost died from the mildew. Come on. I bet they got chains and instruments of torture down there. Come on!

(**Dill** *runs out of the yard, as* **Jem** *and* **Scout** *reluctantly follow.*)

EXTERIOR: COURTHOUSE SQUARE. DAY.

A group of four idlers sit lounging under some live oak trees. They watch with eagle eyes whatever happens on the square and in the courthouse.

Dill, *followed by* **Scout** *and* **Jem**, *come by them.*

One of the men, **Hiram Townsend**, *recognises* **Scout** *and* **Jem**. *He is in his seventies and is dressed in work clothes.*

Hiram Jem Finch?

Jem Yes Sir.

Hiram If you're looking for your daddy, he's inside the courthouse.

Scout Thank you, Sir, but we're not looking for . . .

(**Jem** *gives her a yank and a look and she shuts up, and they go on.*)

Jem Thank you, Mr Townsend, Sir.

(*They go toward the courthouse.*)

Dill What's your daddy doin' in the courthouse?

Jem He's a lawyer and he has a case. The grand jury is charging his client today. I heard somethin' about it when Judge Taylor came over last night.

Dill Let's go watch.

Jem Oh, no, Dill . . . He wouldn't like that. No, Dill . . .

(**Dill** *goes into the courthouse.* **Scout** *and* **Jem** *seem worried about following but reluctantly decide to.*)

INTERIOR: COURTHOUSE HALL.

The three children enter. They look around.

Dill Where's your daddy?

Jem He'll be in the courtroom. Up there.

(*Moving shot:* **Dill**, **Scout**, *and* **Jem** *solemnly climb the stairs to the second floor.*)

Dill, wait a minute.

(*There is a small foyer here and a door leading into the courtroom. They go up to the courtroom door.*)

Dill Is that the courtroom?

Jem Yeah. Ssh!

Dill (*Trying to look into the keyhole*)   I can't see anything.

Jem Ssh!

Dill You lift me up so I can see what's going on.

Jem All right. Make a saddle, Scout.

(**Jem** *and* **Scout** *make a packsaddle with their arms and* **Dill** *climbs up and peers in the glass at the top of the door.*)

Dill Not much is happening. The judge looks like he's asleep. I see your daddy and a coloured man. The coloured man looks to me like he's crying. I wonder what he's done to cry about?

(**Dill** *gets so absorbed in watching that he stops talking.* **Scout** *and* **Jem** *begin to feel the strain of holding him up.*)

Scout What's going on?

Dill There are a lot of men sitting together on one side and one man is pointing at the coloured man and yelling. They're taking the coloured man away.

Jem Where is Atticus?

Dill I can't see your daddy now, either. I wonder where in the world . . .

Atticus (*Coming out of a side door and coming toward them*)   Scout. Jem. What in the world are you doing here?

(*They whirl around, dropping the startled* **Dill**.)

Jem Hello, Atticus.

Atticus What are you doing here?

Jem We came down to find out where Boo Radley was locked up. We wanted to see the bats.

Atticus I want you all back home right away.

Jem Yes Sir.

Atticus Run along, now. I'll see you there for dinner.

(*The three children exit down the steps.*)

(**Robert E. Lee Ewell**, *a short, bantam cock of a man, approaches* **Atticus** *and blocks his way.*)

Mr Ewell.

Ewell Cap'n, I . . . I'm real sorry they picked you to defend that nigger that raped my Mayella. I don't know why I didn't kill him myself instead of goin' for the sheriff. That would have saved you and the sheriff and the taxpayers a lot of trouble.

Atticus Excuse me, Mr Ewell, I'm very busy.

Ewell Hey, Cap'n, somebody told me just now that they thought you believed Tom Robinson's story agin ours. Do you know what I said? I said you're wrong, man . . . you're clear wrong. Mr Finch ain't takin' his story agin ours.

(**Atticus** *eyes him impassively.*)

Well, they was wrong, wasn't they?

Atticus I've been appointed to defend Tom Robinson and now that he's been charged that's what I intend to do.

Ewell You're takin' his . . .

Atticus If you'll excuse me, Mr Ewell . . .

(**Atticus** *exits as* **Ewell** *turns, watching him, astounded.*)

Ewell What kind of a man are you? You got chillun of your own.

EXTERIOR: FINCH PORCH. NIGHT.

Scout *and* **Jem** *are sitting there.* **Dill** *comes running into the yard and over to them.*

Dill Hey, Jem . . . Jem.

(**Jem** *goes running toward him.* **Scout** *follows. The two boys run toward Miss Stephanie's yard.* **Scout**, **Dill**, *and* **Jem** *leap over the wall separating Miss Stephanie's and Atticus' yards.*)

Scout (*Cautiously*) I think we ought to stay right here in Miss Stephanie's yard.

Jem You don't have to come along, Angel May.

(*The boys start to go out of Miss Stephanie's yard.* **Scout** *follows.*)

(*Moving shot: They walk down the sidewalk silently. They can hear the porch swings creaking with the weight of the neighbourhood and the night murmurs of the grown people on the street. They come to the sidewalk in front of the Radley house, and* **Jem** *looks at the house.* **Dill** *and* **Scout** *stand beside him, looking too.*)

Scout   What are you going to do?

Jem   We're going to look in the window of the Radley house and see if we can get a look at Boo Radley. Come on, Dill.

Scout   Jem, please, I'm scared.

Jem   (*Angrily*)   Then go home if you're scared. I swear, Scout, you act more like a girl all the time. Dill, come on.

(**Jem** *and* **Dill** *start on.* **Scout** *watches for a moment, then runs after them.*)

Scout   Wait for me. I'm coming.

Jem   (*Whispering*)   Ssh! We'll go around the back and crawl under the high wire fence at the rear of the Radley lot. I don't believe we can be seen from there.

(*The children go on quietly to the back of the Radley property.*)

Come on!

EXTERIOR: THE BACK OF THE RADLEY PROPERTY.

The fence encloses a large garden. **Jem**, **Scout**, *and* **Dill** *come in.* **Jem** *holds the bottom wire up and motions* **Dill** *to crawl under. He does so.* **Scout** *follows. Then* **Scout** *holds up the wire for* **Jem**. *It is a very tight squeeze for him, but he manages to make it.*

Jem   (*Whispering*)   Come on. Now help me. Don't make a sound.

(*The children cautiously approach the house.* **Scout** *is so intimidated by Jem's warning that she moves barely a step a minute; then, when she looks up and sees* **Jem** *quite a distance ahead, she begins to move faster. They reach the gate which divides the garden from the backyard.* **Jem** *touches it. The gate squeaks.*)

Dill   (*Whispering*)   Spit on it!

(*The three spit on the gate hinges until they have no spit left.*)

Jem   All right.

(*The gate squeaks again.*)

Scout   Jem.

Jem   Ssh! Spit some more.

(*They try to muster up more spit, and then* **Jem** *opens the gate slowly, lifting it aside and resting it on the fence.*)

All right.

(*The backyard is even less inviting than the front. A ramshackle porch runs the width of the house. There are two doors and two dark windows between the doors. Instead of a column, a rough two-by-four supports one end of the porch. Above it a hat rack catches the moon and shines eerily.*)

Come on.

(*They cross the yard and go to the back porch.* **Jem** *puts his foot on the bottom step; the step squeaks. He stands still, then tries his weight by degrees. The step is silent.* **Jem** *skips two steps, puts his foot on the porch, heaves himself to it, and teeters a long moment. He regains his balance and drops onto his knees. He crawls to a window, raises his head, and looks in.* **Scout** *suddenly looks up and sees a shadow. It is the shadow of a man. The back porch is bathed in moonlight, and the shadow moves across the porch toward* **Jem**. **Dill** *sees it next. He puts his hands to his face. The shadow crosses* **Jem**. **Jem** *sees it. He puts his arms over his head and goes rigid. The shadow stops about a foot beyond* **Jem**. *Its arms come out from its sides, drop, and are still. Then it turns and moves back across* **Jem**, *walks along the porch and off the side of the house, returning as it had come.* **Jem** *leaps off the porch and gallops toward* **Scout** *and* **Dill**. *He pushes* **Dill** *and* **Scout** *through the gate and the collards.*)

Move, move!

(**Jem** *holds the bottom of the fence, and* **Scout** *and* **Dill** *roll through.* **Jem** *starts under the fence and is caught. He struggles as the wire holds his pants.* **Jem** *looks up, terrified, as he tries to pull free.*)

Scout!

(**Scout** *and* **Dill** *run to him.*)

Scout!

(**Jem** *is on his hands and knees under the fence.* **Scout** *kneels down and tries to free Jem's pants.* **Scout** *and* **Dill** *remove Jem's pants as he kicks and struggles. Then he rises.*)

(*Moving shot: They run.*)

Scout. Quick – over here.

(**Jem**, **Scout**, *and* **Dill** *continue running through the bushes behind their garage. They are frightened and breathing hard. They all fall to their knees and huddle against the garage wall. They look at one another but are unable to speak.* **Dill** *cannot get his breath and starts to cough.*)

Ssh! Ssh!

(**Dill** *buries his head in his knees.* **Jem** *finally gets up and peers around the corner of the garage.* **Scout** *watches him.*)

Scout (*Whispering*) What are you going to do for pants, Jem?

Jem I don't know.

Stephanie (*Calling off camera*) Dill! Dill! You come on in now.

(*They all jump.* **Dill** *turns to the others, very frightened.*)

Dill I'd better go.

Stephanie (*Shouting off camera*) Dill!

Dill (*Calling*) Coming, Aunt Stephanie. (*Whispering to* **Jem** *and* **Scout**) So long. I'll see you next summer.

Jem So long.

Scout So long.

(**Dill** *runs across the driveway and climbs the fence into Miss Stephanie's yard.*)

Stephanie (*Calling*) Dill!

Dill I'm coming.

Jem I'm going back after my pants.

Scout Oh, please, Jem, come on in the house.

Jem I can't go in without my pants. (*He starts to go.*)

Scout Well, I'm going to call Atticus.

Jem (*Grabbing her collar and wrenching it tight*) No, you're not. Now listen. Atticus ain't never whipped me since I can remember, and I plan to keep it that way.

Scout Then I'm going with you.

Jem No, you ain't. You stay right here. I'll be back before you can count to ten.

(**Scout** *watches* **Jem** *vault over the low fence and disappear in the high bushes. She starts counting.*)

Scout One . . . two . . . three . . . four . . .

Atticus (*Calling*) Jem. Scout. Come on in.

Scout (*Counting*) . . . five . . . six . . . seven . . . eight . . . nine . . . ten . . . eleven . . . twelve . . . thirteen . . . fourteen . . .

(*There is a sound of a shotgun blast.* **Scout** *stands there stunned. Suddenly she shuts her eyes and presses her hands over her ears. She looks as if she's about to scream. At that moment,* **Jem** *bursts through the bushes and jumps the fence, crashing into* **Scout**.)

Jem!

Jem (*Clapping his hand over her mouth*) Ssh! (*He begins frantically to pull on his pants.*)

(*There is the sound of dogs barking.*)

EXTERIOR: STREET IN FRONT OF THE RADLEY HOUSE.

Atticus and **Miss Maudie** *are there talking to* **Mr Radley,** *who is holding a shotgun. They both start up the street toward Miss Stephanie's house.* **Miss Stephanie** *comes running off her front porch, pulling on a robe over her nightgown.*

Stephanie What's going on? What happened? What's going on? What is it? Atticus, what is it? Will somebody please tell me what's going on?

Atticus Mr Radley shot at a prowler out in his collard patch.

Stephanie A prowler. Oh, Maudie . . . (*Moves to* **Maudie,** *who comforts her.*)

Maudie Well, whoever it was won't be back any time soon. Mr Radley must have scared them out of their wits.

Atticus Well, good night.

Stephanie Good night.

Maudie Good night, Atticus.

    (**Atticus** *goes toward his house, and* **Maudie** *and* **Stephanie** *go toward Stephanie's house.*)

Stephanie Oh, it scared the living daylights out of me.

    (**Atticus** *sees* **Scout** *and* **Jem** *in the yard.*)

Atticus Come on in the house. The excitement is over. Time for bed. Scout. Jem.

    (**Scout** *and* **Jem** *look at each other. Then they start for the house. As they climb the steps,* **Jem** *looks back over his shoulder toward the Radley house.*)

INTERIOR: FINCH KITCHEN. THE NEXT MORNING.

Atticus *and* **Jem** *are eating breakfast.* **Calpurnia** *is serving them.* **Miss Maudie** *comes into the kitchen.*

Maudie Good morning.

Calpurnia Good morning, Miss Maudie.

Atticus Good morning, Maudie.

Calpurnia (*Going to the hall door and calling*) Scout!

Maudie I came to see Jean Louise ready for her first day of school.

    (**Calpurnia** *gets the coffeepot from the stove.*)

    Hey, Jem.

Calpurnia (*Calling*) Scout! (*Pours the coffee.*)

Atticus What are you going to do with yourself all morning, Cal, with both the children in school?

Calpurnia I don't know, and that's the truth. I was thinking about that just now. (*Goes back to the hall door and calls.*) Scout! Scout! Did you hear me, Scout? Now hurry!

    (**Calpurnia** *comes back in, and* **Scout** *follows. She has on a dress and feels very awkward in it.* **Jem** *sees her.*)

Jem Hey, everybody . . . look at Scout!

(*He is about to make a comment and laugh, but* **Miss Maudie** *gives him a poke.*)

Maudie Ssh!

Atticus Come on in, Scout.

(**Jem** *giggles.*)

Have your breakfast.

Maudie I think your dress is mighty becoming, honey.

(**Scout** *is not reassured; she begins to tug at it.* **Miss Maudie** *nods her head to* **Atticus** *to let him know she approves of the dress.*)

Calpurnia Now, don't go tugging at that dress, Scout. You want to have it all wrinkled before you even get to school?

Scout I still don't see why I have to wear a darn old dress.

Maudie You'll get used to it.

(**Scout** *sits at the table and starts to eat.* **Jem** *has eaten his breakfast – all he's going to – and gets up.*)

Jem I'm ready.

Atticus Jem! It's half an hour before school starts. Sit right down and wait for your sister.

Jem (*Returning to the table and sitting*) Well, hurry up, Scout.

Scout I'm trying to. (*Takes a few halfhearted bites, then gets up.*)

Jem Well, come on . . . it's your first day. Do you want to be late?

Scout I'm ready.

Jem Come on, let's go.

(**Jem** *exits as* **Scout** *drops her books in the doorway. She picks them up and then runs to* **Atticus** *and kisses his cheek. She runs out the door as* **Jem** *runs in, grabbing his books.*)

Scout Bye.

Jem Goodbye, everyone!

(**Miss Maudie**, **Atticus**, *and* **Calpurnia** *go as far as the screen door with them.* **Scout** *and* **Jem** *go out of the screen door.*)

EXTERIOR: SCHOOL GROUNDS.

Scout *sees* **Walter Cunningham, Jr**, *seven, standing in the school yard. She grabs him, throws him down, and begins to rub his nose in the dirt.*

Scout Darn you, Walter Cunningham.

(*The other children gather around, watching the fight.* **Walter** *and* **Scout** *are on the ground. She pounds him on the back with her fists.* **Jem** *comes running up and pulls her off.*)

Jem   Cut that out! What do you think you're doing?

Scout   He made me start off on the wrong foot. I was trying to explain to that darn lady teacher why he didn't have no money for his lunch, and she got sore at me.

Jem   (*Continuing to hold her as they struggle*)   Stop it! Stop it!

(*A group of children have gathered around* **Jem** *holding* **Scout**. *He releases her.* **Jem** *walks to* **Walter** *as the others start to disperse.* **Walter** *has picked himself up and stands with his fists half-cocked.* **Jem** *looks him over.*)

Your daddy Mr Walter Cunningham from Old Sarum?

(**Walter** *nods his head 'yes'.*)

Well, come home and have dinner with us, Walter. We'd be glad to have you.

(*Walter's face brightens, then darkens.*)

Well, our daddy's a friend of your daddy's. Scout here is crazy. She won't fight you no more.

(**Walter** *stands biting his lip, thinking but not answering.*)

INTERIOR: FINCH LIVING ROOM – DINING ROOM.

The living room is comfortable but unpretentiously furnished. There are a sofa, two overstuffed chairs, and a rocker in the room. Through an alcove the dining room can be seen. The table is set for dinner and **Jem**, **Scout**, *and* **Walter** *are there with* **Atticus**. **Calpurnia** *is serving the food.*

Atticus   That's a dinner that you'll enjoy.

(**Walter** *looks down at his plate. There are string beans, roast, corn bread, turnips, and rice.* **Walter** *looks at* **Atticus**.)

Walter   Yes Sir. I don't know when I've had a roast. We've been having squirrels and rabbits lately. My pa and I go hunting in our spare time.

Jem   You got a gun of your own?

Walter   Uh huh.

Jem   How long have you had a gun?

Walter   Oh, a year or so.

(**Jem** *looks at* **Atticus**.)

Can I have the syrup, please?

Atticus Certainly, Son. (*Calls to* **Calpurnia**) Cal, will you please bring in the syrup dish?

Calpurnia (*Calling back*) Yes Sir.

Jem How old were you when you got your first gun. Atticus?

Atticus Thirteen or fourteen. I remember when my daddy gave me that gun. He told me that I should never point it at anything in the house. And that he'd rather I'd just shoot tin cans in the backyard, but he said that sooner or later he supposed the temptation to go after birds would be too much, and that I could shoot all the blue jays I wanted, if I could hit them, but to remember it is a sin to kill a mockingbird.

Jem Why?

Atticus Well, I reckon because mockingbirds don't do anything but make music for us to enjoy. They don't eat people's gardens, don't nest in the corncribs, they don't do one thing but just sing their hearts out for us. (*Looks at* **Scout**.) How did you like school, Scout?

Scout All right.

(**Calpurnia** *enters with the syrup dish.*)

Atticus Oh, thank you, Cal. That's for Walter.

(*She takes the dish to* **Walter**. *He begins to pour it liberally all over his food.* **Scout** *is watching this process. She makes a face of disgust.*)

Scout What in the Sam Hill are you doing, Walter?

(*Atticus' hand thumps the table beside her.*)

But, Atticus . . . he has gone and drowned his dinner in syrup.

(*The silver saucer clatters.* **Walter** *places the pitcher on it and quickly puts his hands in his lap and ducks his head.* **Atticus** *shakes his head at* **Scout** *to keep quiet.*)

Calpurnia Scout!

Scout What?

Calpurnia Come out here. I want to talk to you.

(**Scout** *eyes her suspiciously, sees she is in no mood to be trifled with, and goes out to the kitchen.* **Calpurnia** *stalks after her.*)

INTERIOR: KITCHEN.

Scout *and* **Calpurnia** *enter.*

Calpurnia   That boy is your company. And if he wants to eat up that tablecloth, you let him, you hear? And if you can't act fit to eat like folks, you can just set here and eat in the kitchen.   (*Sends her back into the dining room with a smack.*)

INTERIOR: LIVING ROOM – DINING ROOM.

Atticus, **Jem**, *and* **Walter** *continue eating as* **Scout** *runs through the dining room and living room to the front porch.*

EXTERIOR: FRONT PORCH.

Scout *sits on the swing.*

Atticus   (*Calling*)   Scout!   (*Comes out on the porch.*)   Scout. Scout, what in the world's got into you? Now, now . . .   (*Sits on the swing next to her.*)

Scout   Atticus, I'm not going back to school anymore.

Atticus   Now, Scout, it's just the first day.

Scout   I don't care. Everything went wrong. My teacher got mad as the devil at me and said you were teaching me to read all wrong and to stop it. And then she acted like a fool and tried to give Walter Cunningham a quarter when everybody knows Cunninghams won't take nothin' from nobody. Any fool could have told her that.

Atticus   Well, maybe she's just nervous. After all, it's her first day, too, teachin' school and bein' new here.

Scout   Oh, Atticus.

Atticus   Now, wait a minute. If you can learn a single trick, Scout, you'll get along a lot better with all kinds of folks. You never really understand a person until you consider things from his point of view.

Scout   Sir?

Atticus   Until you climb inside of his skin and walk around in it.

Scout   But if I keep goin' to school, we can't ever read anymore.

Atticus   Scout, do you know what a compromise is?

Scout   Bending the law?

Atticus   No. It's an agreement reached by mutual consent. Now, here's the way it works. You concede the necessity of goin' to school, we'll keep right on readin' every night, the same as we always have. Is that a bargain?

(**Scout** *and* **Atticus** *continue talking as* **Jean Louise's** *voice is heard.*)

Jean Louise   (*Voice over*)   There just didn't seem to be anyone or thing Atticus couldn't explain. Though it wasn't a talent that would arouse the admiration of any of our friends. Jem and I had to admit he was very good at that, but that was all he was good at, we thought.

EXTERIOR: FINCH HOUSE. DAY.

Scout *and* **Jem** *are playing, using sticks as guns.* **Scout** *stops and watches* **Jem** *for a beat.*

Scout   What are you looking at?

Jem   That old dog down yonder.

Scout   That's old Tim Johnson, ain't it? What's he doing?

Jem   I don't know, Scout. We better get inside.

(*They run into the house.*)

EXTERIOR: FRONT PORCH OF FINCH HOUSE. DAY.

Scout, **Jem**, *and* **Calpurnia** *come out of the house onto the front porch and look down the road.*

Jem   See, there he is.

(*They see the dog, not much more than a speck in the distance, walking erratically as if his right legs were shorter than his left legs. He snarls and jumps.* **Calpurnia** *turns to* **Jem** *and* **Scout** *and makes them go inside.*)

Calpurnia   Scout, Jem, come on inside. Come on, come on, get in!

INTERIOR: KITCHEN. DAY.

Calpurnia *and the children run into the kitchen. She goes to the telephone, shouting in her excitement.*

Calpurnia   Mr Finch? This is Cal. I swear to God there's a mad dog comin' down the street a piece. He's comin' this way.

EXTERIOR: FINCH HOUSE. DAY.

It is quiet and deserted. A black Ford swings into the driveway. **Atticus** *and the sheriff,* **Heck Tate**, *get out.* **Tate** *carries a heavy rifle.* **Calpurnia** *comes out on the porch. She points down the street. The children stare out of the screen door. There is a total stillness.* **Heck Tate** *sniffs and then blows his nose. He shifts the gun to the crook of his arm.*

Atticus   (*Softly*)   There he is.

(*The dog comes into sight, walking dazedly in the inner rim of a curve parallel to the Radley place.*)

Tate   He's got it all right, Mr Finch.

(*The dog is still advancing at a snail's pace. He seems dedicated to one course and motivated by an invisible force that inches him toward the Finches'. He reaches the street which runs in front of the Radley place. He pauses as if with what is left of his poor mind he is trying to consider what road to take. He makes a few hesitant steps, reaches the Radley gate, tries to turn around, but is having difficulty.*)

Atticus   He's within range, Heck.

Tate   Take him, Mr Finch.

(*He hands the rifle to* **Atticus**.)

Scout   (*Calling out*)   Oh, no, Mr Tate. He don't shoot.

Atticus   Don't waste time, Heck.

Tate   For God's sake, Mr Finch, he's got to be killed right away before he starts runnin'. Look where he is. I can't shoot that well. You know it.

Atticus   I haven't shot a gun in twenty years.

Tate   (*Almost throwing the gun at* **Atticus**)   I'd feel mighty comfortable if you did now.

(**Atticus** *accepts the gun. He walks out of the yard and to the middle of the street. He raises his glasses, pushes them to his forehead. They slip down, and he drops them in the street. In the silence, we can hear them crack.* **Atticus**, *blinking hard, rubs his eyes and his chin. The dog has made up his mind. He takes two steps forward, stops, raises his head. The dog's body goes rigid.* **Atticus** *brings the gun to his shoulder. The rifle cracks. The dog leaps, flops over, and crumples on the sidewalk.* **Heck Tate** *runs toward the Radleys'.* **Atticus** *stoops, picks up his glasses and grinds the broken lens to powder, and walks toward the dog.*)

(**Jem** *and* **Scout** *are dumbfounded.* **Scout** *regains her senses first and pinches* **Jem** *to get him moving. They run out of the door.* **Heck Tate** *and* **Atticus** *are walking toward the house. They meet the still awestruck* **Scout** *and* **Jem**. *The children approach* **Atticus** *reverently.*)

Atticus   Don't go near that dog, you understand? He's just as dangerous dead as alive.

Jem   Yes Sir, Atticus. Atticus?

Atticus   Yes, Son.

Jem   Nothin'.

Tate   What's the matter, boy? Can't you talk? Didn't you know your daddy's the best shot in this county?

Atticus   Oh, hush, Heck. Let's get back to town. Remember now, don't go near that dog.

Jem   Yes Sir.

Tate   I'll send Zeebo out right away to pick him up.

(*He and* **Atticus** *get into the car and drive off.* **Jem** *and* **Scout**, *still stunned, watch them go.*)

EXTERIOR: FINCH GARAGE. NIGHT.

Atticus *backs the car out. It is an old car, not very well kept.* **Scout** *and* **Jem** *come running toward him.*

Jem   Atticus, can we go with you, please?

Scout   Can we?

(**Atticus** *keeps the motor running and calls out of the window.*)

Atticus   No, I have to go to the country on business, and you'll just get tired.

Scout   No. Not me, I won't get tired.

Atticus   Well, will you promise to stay in the car while I go in and talk to Helen Robinson?

Scout   Uh huh.

Atticus   And not nag about leavin' if you do get tired?

Jem   No.

Atticus   All right. Climb in.

>   (**Scout** and **Jem** *run for the car.* **Jem** *gets in the back seat,* **Scout** *gets in beside her father.*)

Scout   Who's Helen Robinson?

Atticus   The wife of the man I'm defending.

>   (*The car moves on.* **Scout** *is asleep in the front seat in a few minutes.* **Atticus** *looks down and sees she is and pulls her closer to him.*)

EXTERIOR: TOM ROBINSON'S HOUSE AND YARD. NIGHT.

It is a small, neat house and yard. Tom's son, Jem's age, is playing in the yard. Atticus' car drives up. The boy stops playing and watches the car. **Helen Robinson**, *twenty-nine, comes to the door of the house. She has a baby in her arms, and three small children hang on her dress.* **Atticus** *gets out of the car and goes to the porch. He calls to the boy.*

Atticus   Evening, David.

David   Evening.

Atticus   Evening, Helen.

Helen   Evening, Mr Finch.

Atticus   I came over to tell you about my visit with Tom.

Helen   Yes.

Atticus   And to let you know that I got a postponement.

>   (**Helen** *holds the door open for* **Atticus**, *and they go in. The boy,* **David**, *stares at* **Jem** *for a beat. They wave at each other. He then looks off toward the dirt road.* **Jem** *turns and looks in the same direction. Down the dirt road, drunk, toward the car, comes* **Bob Ewell**. **Jem** *is frightened and starts to leave the car, and then remembers the sleeping* **Scout**. *He climbs into the front seat beside his sister, all the while watching the approach of* **Ewell**.)

Jem   (*Calling to* **David**)   Tell my daddy to come out here, please.

>   (**David** *runs into the house.*)

>   (**Jem** *gets close to* **Scout** *and watches* **Ewell** *get closer and closer.* **Ewell** *comes right up to the car and stares in the window at* **Scout** *and* **Jem**. *He is unshaven and looks as if he'd been on a long drunk. He is unsteady and holds on to the side of the car, staring at the two children.* **Atticus**

comes to the car. **Ewell** *stares drunkenly at him.* **Atticus** *gets in the car beside* **Scout**.)

Atticus No need to be afraid of him, Son. He's all bluff.

(**Ewell** *takes a swig of whiskey from a bottle he has taken from his back pocket and goes reeling off down the road.* **Jem** *climbs in the back seat.* **Atticus** *starts the car.* **Atticus** *turns the car around and goes slowly back down the dirt road. The lights of the car pick up* **Ewell** *standing drunkenly in the middle of the road looking like some terrible figure of wrath.* **Atticus** *has to slow the car down to almost a crawl in order to pass* **Ewell** *without hitting him. As he passes,* **Ewell** *yells.*)

Ewell Nigger lover!

(**Jem** *leans across the front seat and puts his hand on his father's shoulder.* **Atticus** *senses the boy's fright and pats his hand.* **Scout** *sleeps through it all. They drive on, leaving the drunken fury of a man shouting in the darkness.*)

EXTERIOR: FINCH HOUSE. NIGHT.

Atticus *drives the car up. He glances back at* **Jem**.

Atticus There's a lot of ugly things in this world, Son. I wish I could keep 'em all away from you. That's never possible.

(**Atticus** *leans down and lifts the sleeping* **Scout** *off the seat. He carries* **Scout** *toward the house as* **Calpurnia** *comes out from the kitchen.*)

If you wait until I get Scout in bed, I'll drive you home.

Calpurnia Yes Sir.

(**Atticus** *starts for the house.* **Jem** *sits on the porch in the rocking chair.*)

Atticus (*Coming out*) Jem, would you mind staying here with Scout until I get Cal home?

Jem No Sir.

Calpurnia Night, Jem.

Jem Night, Cal.

(**Jem** *sees his father and* **Calpurnia** *get into the car and start off. A tree rustles, a shadow passes over the porch where* **Jem** *sits, a night bird calls. He is struck with sudden terror.*)

(*Moving shot: He starts to run toward the Radley place in the direction of his father's car.* **Jem** *runs awhile longer, past the Radley oak, calling 'Atticus, Atticus.' He realises it is futile and stops. He freezes. He sees something gleaming and reflecting the moonlight in the knothole of the oak tree, where it is hollow. He stops, looks around, sticks his hand in the* *knothole, and takes out a shiny medal. He quickly puts it in his pocket. He runs past the Radley house, into his yard, and into the house.)*

EXTERIOR: SCHOOL GROUNDS. DAY.

Scout *and two other girls are jumping rope. A boy,* **Cecil Jacobs**, *who is Scout's age, pulls the rope away, ending the jumping. He and* **Scout** *face each other in anger. Other kids group around as they argue.* **Scout** *jumps on* **Cecil** *and throws him to the ground as they fight. The other children gather around and begin yelling, egging them on.* **Jem** *rushes in and pulls* **Scout** *off* **Cecil**, *as she struggles.* **Cecil** *runs off. The other children move away.*

Jean Louise (*Voice over*)   Atticus had promised me he would wear me out if he ever heard of me fightin' any more. I was far too old and too big for such childish things, and the sooner I learned to hold in, the better off everybody would be. I soon forgot . . . Cecil Jacobs made me forget.

EXTERIOR: FINCH FRONT PORCH. AFTERNOON.

Scout *sits on the front steps, her head buried in her arms.* **Atticus** *comes into the yard.* **Scout** *looks up.*

Atticus   Well, what is it, Scout?

Scout   Atticus, do you defend niggers?

Atticus   Don't say 'nigger', Scout.

Scout   I didn't say it . . . Cecil Jacobs did. That's why I had to fight him.

Atticus   (*Sternly*)   Scout, I don't want you fightin'!

Scout   I had to, Atticus . . . He . . .

Atticus   (*Interrupting*)   I don't care what the reasons are. I forbid you to fight.

Scout   Yes Sir.

(**Atticus** *sits down beside* **Scout**, *putting his hat and briefcase down on the porch.*)

Atticus   Anyway, I'm simply defending a Negro, Tom Robinson. Scout . . . there are some things you're not old enough to understand just yet. There's been some high talk around town to the effect that I shouldn't do much about defending this man.

Scout   (*Looking up*)   If you shouldn't be defending him, then why are you doing it?

Atticus   (*Putting his arm around* **Scout**, *hugging her close to him*)   For a number of reasons. The main one is if I didn't, I couldn't hold my head up in this town. I couldn't even tell you and Jem not to do somethin' again. Scout, you're gonna hear some ugly talk about this in school. But I want you to promise me one thing . . . that you won't get into fights over it, no matter what they say to you.

Scout (*Breaking loose*) Yes Sir.

(**Atticus** *gets up and goes inside the house.* **Scout** *sees* **Jem** *on the sidewalk and goes toward him. He is walking most peculiarly, with his feet out and his arms held to his sides. He is doing an imitation of ancient Egyptians.* **Scout** *runs to meet him. When she gets five feet from him, she becomes aware of his peculiar walk and stops and looks more closely.*)

What are you doing?

Jem Walking like an Egyptian. We were studyin' about them in school. Teacher says we wouldn't be no place without them.

Scout Is that so?

(*She begins to try to imitate his walk. They go toward the Radleys'.*)

Jem Cradle of civilisation. They invented embalming and toilet paper . . . (*He sees her imitation. He stops and goes to her, kneels and takes her feet.*) That's wrong, Scout. You do your feet this way. (*He takes her feet and tries to fix them. He is kneeling in front of the Radley oak tree with the knothole. While he is kneeling,* **Scout** *glances around at the oak and sees two figures carved out of soap in the knothole.*)

Scout Look, Jem.

(*She points to the figures and gets close beside him and peers at them. He tenderly takes the two soap figures out of the knothole. One is the figure of a boy. The other wears a crude dress.*)

Look . . . the boy has hair in front of his eyebrows like you do.

Jem And the girl wears bangs like you . . . these are us!

(**Mr Radley** *enters from behind the tree and looks at* **Jem**. **Jem** *jumps back, frightened.* **Mr Radley** *starts filling the knothole with cement from a trowel.* **Jem** *and* **Scout** *stand watching him. They start to back away, and then go running down the street, as* **Mr Radley** *continues filling the hole with cement.*)

INTERIOR: JEM'S ROOM. NIGHT.

Jem *is seated on the bed with an open cigar box in front of him. He picks up both dolls and puts them inside the box and closes it quickly as* **Scout** *enters the room.*

Scout Jem . . . are you awake?

Jem Go back to bed!

(*She moves to the bed and sits down at the foot of it.*)

Scout I can't go to sleep.

Jem Go back to bed!

(*She notices the cigar box.*)

Scout What you got in the box?

Jem Nothin'. Go back to bed!

Scout Come on.

Jem If I show you, will you swear never to tell anybody?

Scout I swear . . .

Jem Cross your heart . . .

(*She crosses her heart with her left hand and raises it in a swearing gesture, then lowers it and waits as* **Jem** *takes the box and opens the top. They look in the box. There is a spelling medal, a pocket watch, some pennies, a broken pocketknife. He takes the medal out and holds it up for* **Scout** *to see. She is wide-eyed.*)

I found all these in the knothole of that ole tree . . . at different times. This is a spelling medal. You know, they used to award these in school to spelling winners before we were born. And another time I found this . . . (*He picks up the pocket watch.*) And this . . . (*He holds up the pocketknife.*) And Scout, you know something else I never told you about that night I went back to the Radleys'?

Scout Something else? You never told me anything about that night.

Jem Well . . . you know the first time when I was gittin' outta my britches?

Scout Uh huh.

Jem Well, they was all in a tangle, and I couldn't get 'em loose. Well, when I went back, though, they were folded across the fence . . . sorta like they was expectin' me.

(**Scout** *is looking at the watch. She is goggle-eyed.* **Jem** *holds the soap figures of the boy and the girl he found in the knothole.*)

Jean Louise (*Voice over*) It was to be a long time before Jem and I talked about Boo again.

INTERIOR: FINCH KITCHEN. DAY.

Calpurnia *is at the sink.* **Scout** *and* **Jem** *are eating.* **Dill** *comes in.*

Jean Louise (*Voice over*)   School finally ended and summer came . . . and so did Dill.

Dill   Good mornin'.

Calpurnia   Good mornin'. My, you're up mighty bright and early.

Dill   Oh, I've been up since four.

Calpurnia   Four?

Dill   Oh, yes, I always get up at four. It's in my blood. You see, my daddy was a railroad man till he got rich. Now he flies airplanes. One of these days, he's just goin' to swoop down here to Maycomb, pick me up, and take me for a ride.

EXTERIOR: FINCH HOUSE. LATE AFTERNOON.

Atticus *sits on the porch reading as* **Jem** *comes out with a pitcher of juice. He moves back to* **Atticus** *and puts the pitcher on the chair beside him, then he takes a cookie from a plate on the chair.* **Atticus** *lifts his briefcase and starts putting his papers inside. The Sheriff's car comes by.*

Jem   Who's that in the car with Sheriff Tate?

Atticus   (*Looking up*)   Tom Robinson, Son.

Jem   Where's he been?

Atticus   In the Abbottsville jail.

Jem   Why?

Atticus   The sheriff thought he'd be safer there. They're bringin' him back here tonight because his trial is tomorrow.   (*He gets up and goes into the house.*)

INTERIOR: JEM'S ROOM. NIGHT.

In his room, **Jem** *is lying in bed beside the sleeping* **Dill**. *He hears a knock at the screen door.*

INTERIOR: LIVING ROOM. NIGHT.

Atticus *goes to the door and opens it.* **Heck Tate** *is standing there.*

Atticus   Well, good evenin', Heck.

Tate   Evenin', Mr Finch.

Atticus   Come in.

Tate   (*Coming in*)   The news has gotten 'round the county about my bringin' Tom Robinson back to the jail. I heard there might be trouble from that bunch out at Old Sarum.

INTERIOR: KITCHEN. NIGHT.

Atticus *goes into the kitchen to* **Calpurnia**.

Atticus   Cal, if I need you to stay here tonight, can you do it?

Calpurnia   Yes Sir . . . I can.

Atticus   Thank you. I think you better count on stayin'.

Calpurnia   Yes Sir.

   (**Atticus** *goes out.* **Calpurnia** *goes back to work.*)

INTERIOR: JEM'S ROOM. NIGHT.

Jem *is lying in bed, still awake.* **Dill** *is asleep.* **Atticus** *comes in and gets something from the shelf and goes out again.* **Jem** *gets out of bed and listens by the door. He gets his clothes from the closet and starts to get dressed.* **Dill** *awakens and sits up in bed.* **Scout** *comes into the room.*

Dill   What's going on?

Jem   Sssh. Go back to sleep!

Scout What's going on?

Jem Sssshhh!

(*The three of them go out of the room.*)

EXTERIOR: FINCH HOUSE. NIGHT.

They come outside and walk down the sidewalk towards town.

EXTERIOR: TOWN SQUARE. NIGHT.

It is deserted and dark. The stores around the square are dark except for night lights burning back by the safes and cash registers.

Moving shot: The three children walk down the street by Atticus' office. They see his car parked in front of the building. They look in the doorway of the building. It is dark. **Jem** *tries the knob of the door. It is locked.*

Jem Hey, there's his car.

(*They walk up the sidewalk. They see a solitary light burning in the distance. It is from the jail. As they approach the jail, they can see the long extension cord* **Atticus** *brought from the house running between the bars of the second-floor window and down the side of the building. In the light from its bare bulb they see* **Atticus** *propped against the front door. He is sitting on one of the office chairs, and he is reading a newspaper, oblivious of the night bugs hovering above his head.*)

See, there he is . . . over there!

(**Scout** *starts to run toward him.*)

No, Scout . . . don't go to him. He might not like it. I just wanted to see where he was and what he was up to. He's all right. Let's go back home. Come on.

(*The children start back across the square, taking a shortcut, when they hear a noise and pause. They see four dusty cars come in from the Meridian Highway, moving slowly, in a line. They go around the square, pass the bank building, and stop in front of the jail. Nobody gets out.* **Atticus** *looks up from his newspaper, closes it, deliberately folds it, drops it in his lap, and pushes his hat to the back of his head. He seems to be expecting the men.* **Scout**, **Jem**, *and* **Dill** *run to the cover of some bushes and hide behind them, watching.*)

(*In ones and twos, the men get out of the cars. They are country men.* **Walter Cunningham, Sr**, *is among them. They surround* **Atticus**.)

Man He in there, Mr Finch?

Atticus He is. He's asleep. Don't wake him.

Cunningham You know what we want. Get aside from that door, Mr Finch.

Atticus Walter, I think you ought to turn right around and go back home. Heck Tate's around here somewhere.

Kelley No, he ain't. Heck's bunch is out chasin' around Ole Sarum lookin' for us.

Tex We knowed he was, so we came around the other way.

Kelley And you hadn't never thought about that, had you, Mr Finch?

Atticus I thought about it.

(*The children run over to the car.*)

Scout I can't see Atticus.

(**Scout** *darts out toward the men,* **Dill** *behind her, before* **Jem** *can reach out and grab them.*)

Atticus Well, that changes things, doesn't it?

(**Scout** *and* **Dill** *run,* **Jem** *behind them. They run to the men and push themselves through until they reach* **Atticus**.)

Scout Atticus!

(*She smiles up at him, but when she catches the look of fear on his face, she becomes insecure.* **Scout** *looks around at the men surrounding her. Most are strangers to her.*)

Hey, Atticus . . .

(**Atticus** *gets up from his chair and begins to move slowly, like an old man, toward them.*)

Atticus Jem, go home. And take Scout and Dill home with you.

(**Scout** *looks up at* **Jem**. *She sees he is not thinking of leaving.* **Jem** *shakes his head 'no'. Atticus' fists go to his hips and so do Jem's, and they face each other in defiance.*)

Son, I said, 'Go home!'

Jem No Sir!

(**Jem** *shakes his head. A burly man grabs* **Jem** *roughly by the collar.*)

Man I'll send him home!

(*The man almost yanks* **Jem** *off his feet.* **Atticus** *flushes. His fists clench; he reaches for* **Jem**. *But before he gets to him,* **Scout** *kicks the man swiftly.*)

Scout Don't you touch him! Let 'im go! Let 'im go!

(*The man falls back in pain.* **Atticus** *puts his hand on her shoulder.*)

Atticus That'll do, Scout.

Scout Ain't nobody gonna do Jem that-a-way.

Man (*Growling in the back*) Now, you get 'em outta here, Mr Finch.

Atticus Jem, I want you to please leave.

Jem No Sir.

Atticus Jem!

Jem I tell ya, I ain't goin'!

(**Scout** *becomes bored by this exchange; she looks back at the men. She sees a man she recognises. She moves toward him.*)

Scout Hey, Mr Cunningham . . .

(**Walter Cunningham, Sr**, *does not seem to hear her.*)

I said, 'Hey', Mr Cunningham. How's your entailment getting along?

(*The man blinks and hooks his thumbs into his overall straps. He seems uncomfortable. He clears his throat and looks away.* **Scout** *walks a little closer to him.*)

Don't you remember me, Mr Cunningham? I'm Jean Louise Finch. You brought us some hickory nuts early one morning, remember? We had a talk. I went and got my daddy to come out and thank you. I go to school with your boy. I go to school with Walter. He's a nice boy. Tell him 'hey' for me, won't you? You know something, Mr Cunningham, entailments are bad. Entailments . . .

(*Suddenly,* **Scout** *realises she is the centre of everyone's attention: the men, her brother,* **Dill**, **Atticus**. *She becomes self-conscious. She turns to* **Atticus**.)

Atticus, I was just sayin' to Mr Cunningham that entailments were bad but not to worry. Takes a long time sometimes . . .

(*She begins to dry up. She looks up at the country men staring at her. They are quite still.*)

What's the matter?

(*She looks at* **Atticus**. *He says nothing. She looks back at* **Mr Cunningham**.)

I sure meant no harm, Mr Cunningham.

Cunningham No harm taken, young lady. (*He moves forward and takes* **Scout** *by the shoulders.*) I'll tell Walter you said 'hey', little lady. (*He straightens up and waves a big hand.*) Let's clear outta here. Let's go, boys.

(*As they had come, in ones and twos, the men struggle back into their cars. We hear doors slam, engines cough, and the cars drive off.* **Scout**, **Jem**, *and* **Dill** *watch them leave.*)

Atticus Now you go home, all of you. I'll be there later.

Jem Come on . . . come on.

(*The three children go on down the street.* **Atticus** *sits again in the chair, waiting.* **Tom Robinson** *calls out from the darkness of the jail.*)

Tom (*Off camera*) Mr Finch . . . they gone?

Atticus They've gone. They won't bother you any more.

(*He sits back in his chair and continues watching.*)

EXTERIOR: STREET IN FRONT OF FINCH HOUSE. EARLY MORNING. DAY.

People are coming from all parts of the county for the trial. It is like Saturday. Wagons carrying country people on the way to the trial stream past the house. Some men ride horseback. **Scout**, **Jem**, *and* **Dill** *sit on the curb of the sidewalk watching the wagons and the horses go by.*

Jem Morning, Mr Stevens. How do you do?

(*A man rides by on a mule and waves to the children, and they wave back. A wagonload of ladies rides past. They wear cotton sunbonnets and dresses with long sleeves. A bearded man in a wool hat drives them. A wagonload of stern-faced citizens comes by next.*)

Scout Did you ever see so many people? Just like on Saturday . . .

(**Jem** *suddenly gets up.*)

Where you goin'?

Jem I can't stand it any longer. I'm goin' downtown to the courthouse to watch.

Scout You better not! You know what Atticus said.

Jem I don't care if he did. I'm not gonna miss the most excitin' thing that ever happened in this town!

(*They all look at each other and start toward town.*)

EXTERIOR: COURTHOUSE SQUARE. DAY.

It is deserted, as everyone is inside watching the trial. **Scout**, **Jem**, *and* **Dill** *come into the square. They stand looking up at the courthouse. They all start toward the entrance.* **Scout**, **Jem**, *and* **Dill** *go up the stairs toward the entrance.*

INTERIOR: ENTRANCE HALL OF COURTHOUSE. DAY.

When they get to the entrance, **Jem** *peeks through the hole of the door. He looks back at the other two.* **Reverend Sykes**, *the black Baptist preacher, comes up the stairs. The children go over to him.*

Jem It's packed solid. They're standin' all along the back . . . Reverend!

Sykes Yes?

Jem Reverend Sykes, are you goin' upstairs?

Sykes Yes, I am.

(*He starts up the stairs and they follow him.*)

INTERIOR: COLOURED BALCONY OF COURTHOUSE.

Reverend Sykes *enters the coloured balcony with* **Jem**, **Dill**, *and* **Scout**. *He leads them among the black people in the gallery. Four blacks in the front row get up and give them their seats when they see them come in.*

Sykes Brother John, thanks for holding my seat.

   (*They sit down and peer over the balcony. The coloured balcony runs along three walls of the courtroom like a second-story veranda, and from it the children see everything.*)

   (*The jury sits to the left under long windows. Sunburned, lanky, they are nearly all farmers, but this is only natural. Townfolk rarely sit on juries. They are either struck or excused. The circuit solicitor and another man,* **Atticus**, *and* **Tom Robinson** *sit at tables with their backs to the children. Just inside the railing, which divides the spectators from the court, the witnesses sit in cowhide-bottomed chairs.* **Judge Taylor** *is on the bench, looking like a sleepy old shark.*)

   (**Jem**, **Scout**, **Dill**, *and* **Reverend Sykes** *are listening intently.*)

Bailiff This court is now in session. Everybody rise.

   (*The* **Judge** *bangs his gavel.*)

INTERIOR: COURTROOM. LATER.

The solicitor **Mr Gilmer** *is questioning the sheriff* **Heck Tate**.

Tate On the night of August twenty-first I was just leavin' my office to go home when Bob . . . Mr Ewell . . . come in, very excited, he was. And he said, get to his house quick as I could . . . that his girl had been raped. I got in my car and went out there as fast as I could. She was pretty well beat up. I asked her if Tom Robinson beat her like that. She said, 'Yes, he did.' I asked if he'd taken advantage of her and she said, 'Yes, he did.' That's all there was to it.

Gilmer Thank you.

   (**Atticus** *is sitting behind his table, his chair skewed to one side, his legs crossed, and one arm is resting on the back of the chair.*)

Judge Any questions, Atticus?

Atticus Yes Sir. Did anybody call a doctor, Sheriff?

Tate No Sir.

Atticus Why not?

Tate Well, I didn't think it was necessary. She was pretty well beat up. Something sho' happened. It was obvious.

Atticus Now, Sheriff, you say that she was mighty beat up. In what way?

Tate Well, she was beaten around the head. There were bruises already comin' on her arms. She had a black eye startin' an' . . .

Atticus Which eye?

Tate Let's see . . . (*Blinks and runs his hand through his hair. He points to an invisible person five inches in front of him.*) It was her left.

Atticus Well, now, was that, was her left facing you . . . or lookin' the way that you were?

Tate Oh yes . . . that . . . would make it her right eye. It was her right eye, Mr Finch. Now I remember. She was beaten up on that side of her face.

(**Heck Tate** *blinks again and then turns and looks at* **Tom Robinson** *as if something had been made clear to him at the same time.* **Tom Robinson** *raises his head. Something has been made clear to* **Atticus**, *too, and he gets to his feet. He walks toward* **Heck Tate**.)

Atticus Which side, again, Heck?

Tate The right side. She had bruises on her arms and she showed me her neck. There were definite finger marks on her gullet.

Atticus All around her neck? At the back of her throat?

Tate I'd say they were all around.

(**Atticus** *nods to* **Mr Gilmer** *as he sits down.* **Mr Gilmer** *shakes his head at the* **Judge**. *The* **Judge** *nodes to* **Tate**, *who rises stiffly and steps down from the witness stand.*)

Judge Witness may be excused.

Bailiff (*Booming out*) Robert E. Lee Ewell . . .

(**Bob Ewell** *rises and struts to the stand. He raises his right hand, puts his left on the Bible, and is sworn in as a witness.*)

Place your hand on the Bible, please. Do you promise to tell the truth, the whole truth, and nothin' but the truth, so help you God?

Ewell I do.

Bailiff Sit down.

(**Mr Gilmer** *addresses* **Ewell**.)

Gilmer Now, Mr Ewell . . . will you tell us, just in your own words, what happened on August twenty-first.

Ewell Well, that night I was comin' in from the woods with a load of kindlin', and I heard Mayella screamin' as I got to the fence. So

I dropped my kindlin', and I run into the fence. But when I got loose, I run up to the window and I seen him with my Mayella!

(*The rest of the testimony is drowned out by the people in the courtroom, who begin to murmur with excitement.* **Judge Taylor** *begins to bang his desk with his gavel.* **Heck Tate** *goes to the aisle, trying to quiet the crowd.* **Atticus** *is on his feet, whispering to the* **Judge**. *The spectators finally quiet down, and* **Mr Gilmer** *continues.*)

Gilmer   What did you do after you saw the defendant?

Ewell   I ran around the house tryin' to get in, but he done run through the front door just ahead o' me. But I seen who it was, all right. I seen him. And I run in the house and po' Mayella was layin' on the floor squallin'. Then I run for Mr Tate just as quick as I could.

Gilmer   Uh huh. Thank you, Mr Ewell.

(**Mr Gilmer** *sits down.* **Atticus** *rises and goes to the stand and faces* **Ewell**.)

Atticus   Would you mind if I just ask you a few questions, Mr Ewell?

Ewell   No Sir, Mr Finch, I sho' wouldn't.

Atticus   Folks were doin' a lot of runnin' that night. Let's see, now, you say that you ran to the window, you ran inside, you ran to Mayella, and you ran to the sheriff. Now, did you, during all the runnin', run for a doctor?

Ewell   There weren't no need to. I seen who done it.

Atticus   Now, Mr Ewell . . . you've heard the sheriff's testimony. Do you agree with his description of Mayella's injuries?

Ewell   I agree with everything Mr Tate said. Her eye was blacked. She was mighty beat up . . . mighty.

Atticus   Now, Mr Ewell, can you . . . er . . . can you read and write?

Ewell   Yes Mr Finch. I can read and I can write.

Atticus   Good . . . then will you write your name, please. Write there, and show us?

(**Atticus** *takes paper and pen out of his coat. He hands them to* **Ewell**. **Ewell** *looks up and sees* **Atticus** *and* **Judge Taylor** *looking at him intently.*)

Ewell   Well, what's so interestin'?

Judge   You're left-handed, Mr Ewell.

(**Ewell** *turns angrily to the* **Judge**.)

Ewell Well, what's that got to do with it, Judge? I'm a God-fearin' man. That Atticus Finch is tryin' to take advantage of me. You got to watch lawyers like Atticus Finch.

Judge (*Banging his gavel*) Quiet! Quiet, Sir! Now the witness may take his seat.

(**Ewell** *sullenly leaves the witness stand*.)

Bailiff Mayella Violet Ewell . . .

(*A silence comes over the court as* **Mayella Ewell** *walks to the witness stand. She is a thick-bodied girl, accustomed to strenuous labour*.)

Put your hand on the Bible, please. Do you swear to tell the truth, the whole truth, and nothing but the truth, so help you God?

(**Mayella** *nods.* **Mr Gilmer** *rises and begins to question her*.)

Gilmer Now, Mayella, suppose you tell us just what happened, huh?

Mayella (*Clearing her throat*) Well, Sir . . . I was sittin' on the porch, and . . . and he comes along. Uh, there's this old chifforobe in the yard . . . and I . . . I said, 'You come up here, boy, and bust up this chifforobe, and I'll give you a nickel.' So he . . . he come on in the yard and I go into the house to get him the nickel and I turn around, and 'fore I know it, he's on me . . . and I fought and hollered . . . but he had me around the neck, and he hit me again and again, and the next thing I knew, Papa was in the room a-standin' over me, hollerin', 'Who done it, who done it?'

Gilmer Thank you, Mayella. Your witness, Atticus.

(**Gilmer** *walks away.* **Atticus** *gets up smiling. He opens his coat, hooks his thumbs in his vest, walks slowly across the room to the windows*.)

Atticus Miss Mayella, is your father good to you? I mean, is he easy to get along with?

Mayella He does tol'able . . .

Atticus Except when he's drinking?

(*A pause. She glares at* **Atticus**.)

When he's riled, has he ever beaten you?

(**Mayella** *looks in Ewell's direction*.)

Mayella My pa's never touched a hair o' my head in my life.

(**Atticus'** *glasses slip a little and he pushes them back on his head*.)

Atticus Now, you say that you asked Tom to come in and chop up a . . . what was it?

Mayella A chifforobe.

Atticus Was this the first time that you ever asked him to come inside the fence?

Mayella (*Acting confused and shrugging*) Yes.

Atticus Didn't you ever ask him to come inside the fence before?

Mayella (*Evasively*) I mighta.

Atticus But can you remember any other occasion?

Mayella (*Shaking her head*) No!

Atticus You say, 'He caught me and he choked me and he took advantage of me,' is that right?

(**Mayella** *nods her head.*)

Do you remember his beating you about the face?

Mayella (*Hesitating*) No, I don't recollect if he hit me. I . . . mean . . . yes! He hit me . . . he hit me!

Atticus (*Turning*) Thank you! Now, will you identify the man who beat you?

Mayella (*Pointing to* **Tom**) I most certainly will . . . sittin' right yonder.

Atticus Tom, will you stand up, please? Let's let Mayella have a good look at you.

(**Tom Robinson** *rises to his feet. It is our first good look at him. He is thirty.* **Atticus** *goes to the table and picks up a water glass.*)

Tom, will you please catch this?

(**Atticus** *throws the glass.* **Tom** *is standing at the defense table. He catches the glass with his right hand.*)

Thank you.

(**Atticus** *walks to* **Tom** *and takes the glass.*)

Now then, this time will you please catch it with your left hand?

Tom I can't, Sir.

Atticus Why can't you?

Tom I can't use my left hand at all. I got it caught in a cotton gin when I was twelve years old. All my muscles were torn loose.

(*There are murmurs from the crowd in the courtroom. The* **Judge** *pounds his gavel.*)

Atticus Is this the man who raped you?

Mayella He most certainly is.

Atticus How?

Mayella I don't know how. He done . . . it . . . (*She starts to sob.*) He just done it.

Atticus You have testified that he choked you and he beat you. You didn't say that he sneaked up behind you and knocked you out cold, but that you turned and there he was. Do you want to tell us what really happened?

Mayella I got somethin' to say. And then I ain't gonna say no more. (*She looks in Tom's direction.*) He took advantage of me.

(**Atticus** *glances in Mayella's direction with a grim expression. She shouts and gestures with her hands as she speaks.*)

An' if you fine, fancy gentlemen ain't gonna do nothin' about it, then you're just a bunch of lousy, yellow, stinkin' cowards, the . . . the whole bunch of you, and your fancy airs don't come to nothin'. Your Ma'am'in' and your Miss Mayellarin' — it don't come to nothin', Mr Finch. Not . . . no . . .

(*She bursts into real tears. Her shoulders shake with angry heaving sobs.* **Atticus** *has hit her in a way that is not clear to him, but he has had no pleasure in doing it. He sits with his head down.* **Mayella** *runs as* **Ewell** *and a man grab her.*)

Ewell You sit down there!

Man Come on, girl.

(**Ewell** *holds Mayella's arms and starts for his seat.* **Ewell** *helps* **Mayella** *to her seat. She hides her head as* **Ewell** *sits down.*)

(*The* **Judge** *looks in* **Atticus**' *direction.*)

Judge Atticus? Mr Gilmer?

Gilmer (*Rising*) The State rests, Judge.

Bailiff Tom Robinson, take the stand.

(**Tom** *stands up and goes to the witness chair.*)

Put your hand on the Bible.

(**Tom** *puts his hand on the Bible.*)

Do you solemnly swear to tell the truth, the whole truth, and nothing but the truth, so help you God?

Tom I do.

Bailiff Sit down!

(*The* **Bailiff** *turns away as* **Tom** *starts to sit.* **Atticus** *starts toward the* **Judge** *and* **Tom**.)

Atticus Tom, were you acquainted with Mayella Violet Ewell?

Tom Yes Sir. I had to pass her place goin' to and from the field every day.

Atticus Is there any other way to go?

Tom (*Shaking his head*) No Sir. None's I know of.

Atticus Did she ever speak to you?

Tom Why, yes Sir. I'd tip m'hat when I'd go by, and one day she ask me to come inside the fence and bust up a chifforobe for her. She give me the hatchet and I broke it up and then she said, 'I reckon I'll hafta give you a nickel, won't I?' And I said, 'No Ma'am, there ain't no charge.' Then I went home. Mr Finch, that was way last spring, way over a year ago.

Atticus And did you ever go on the place again?

Tom Yes Sir.

Atticus When?

Tom Well, I went lots of times. Seemed like every time I passed by yonder, she'd have some little somethin' for me to do . . . choppin' kindlin', totin' water for her.

Atticus What happened to you on the evening of August twenty-first of last year?

Tom Mr Finch, I was goin' home as usual that evenin' and I passed the Ewell place. Miss Mayella were on the porch like she said she were.

(*The spectators, white and coloured, all lean forward. It is very quiet in the room.*)

An' she said for me to come there and help her a minute. Well, I went inside the fence and I looked aroun' for some kindlin' to work on, but I didn't see none. An' then she said to come in the house, she . . . she has a door needs fixin' . . . so I follow her inside an' looked at the door an' it looked all right, an' she shut the door. All the time I was wonderin' why it was so quiet like . . . an' it come to me, there was not a child on the place, an' I said to Miss Mayella, where are the chil'ren? An' she said, they all gone to get ice cream. She said it took her a slap year to save seb'm nickels, but she done it, an' they all gone to town.

(**Tom** *runs his hands over his face. He is obviously very uncomfortable.*)

Atticus What did you say then?

Tom Oh, I . . . I said somethin' like, 'Why Miss Mayella, that's right nice o' you to treat 'em.' An' she said, 'You think so?' Well, I said I best be goin', I couldn't do nothin' for her, an' she said, oh, yes I could. An' I ask her what, and she said to jus' step on the chair yonder an' git that box down from on top of the chifforobe. So I done what she told me, and I was reachin' when the next thing I knew she . . . grabbed me aroun' the legs. She scared me so bad I hopped down an' turned the chair over. That was the only thing, only furniture 'sturbed in that room, Mr Finch, I swear, when I left it.

Atticus And what happened after you turned the chair over?

(**Tom** *comes to a dead stop. He glances at* **Atticus**, *then at the jury.*)

Tom? You've sworn to tell the whole truth. Will you do it? What happened after that?

Tom (*Running his hand nervously over his mouth*)   Mr Finch, I got down off the chair, and I turned around an' she sorta jumped on me. She hugged me aroun' the waist. She reached up an' kissed me on the face. She said she never kissed a grown man before an' she might as well kiss me. She says for me to kiss her back.

(**Tom** *shakes his head with his eyes closed, as he reacts to this ordeal.*)

And I said, Miss Mayella, let me outta here, an' I tried to run, when Mr Ewell cussed at me from the window an' says he's gonna kill her.

Atticus   And what happened after that?

Tom   I was runnin' so fast, I don't know what happened.

Atticus   Tom, did you rape Mayella Ewell?

Tom   I did not, Sir.

Atticus   Did you harm her in any way?

Tom   I . . . I did not, Sir.

(**Atticus** *turns and walks to his desk.* **Gilmer** *rises and goes to the witness chair.*)

Gilmer   Robinson, you're pretty good at bustin' up chifforobes and kindlin' with one hand, aren't you? Strong enough to choke the breath out of a woman and sling her to the floor?

Tom   (*Meekly*)   I never done that, Sir.

Gilmer   But you're strong enough to.

Tom   I reckon so, Sir.

Gilmer   Uh huh. How come you're so all-fired anxious to do that woman's chores?

(**Tom** *hesitates. He searches for an answer.*)

Tom   Looks like she didn't have nobody to help her. Like I said . . .

Gilmer   With Mr Ewell and seven children on the place? You did all this choppin' and work out of sheer goodness, boy? You're a mighty good fella, it seems. Did all that for not one penny.

Tom   Yes, Sir. I felt right sorry for her. She seemed . . .

Gilmer   You felt sorry for her? A white woman? You felt sorry for her?

(**Tom** *realises his mistake. He shifts uncomfortably in his chair.*)

INTERIOR: COURTROOM. LATER — SAME DAY.

Atticus *rises and walks toward the jury. They watch with no show of emotion. As* **Atticus** *talks, he looks into the eyes of the men of the jury as if to find one to encourage him.*

Atticus   To begin with, this case should never have come to trial. The State has not produced one iota of medical evidence that the crime Tom Robinson is charged with ever took place. It has relied instead on the testimony of two witnesses . . . whose evidence has not only been called into serious question on cross-examination, but has been flatly contradicted by the defendant. There is circumstantial evidence to indicate that Mayella Ewell was beaten savagely by someone who led almost exclusively with his left. And Tom Robinson now sits before you having taken the oath with his right hand, the only good hand he possesses. I have nothing but pity in my heart for the chief witness for the State. She is a victim of cruel poverty and ignorance. But my pity does not extend so far as to her putting a man's life at stake, which she has done in an effort to get rid of her own guilt. Now, I say guilt, gentlemen, because it was guilt that motivated her. She has committed no crime, she has merely broken a rigid and time-honored code of our society. A code so severe that whoever breaks it is hounded from our midst as unfit to live with. She must destroy the evidence of her offense. But what was the evidence of her offense? Tom Robinson, a human being. She must put Tom Robinson away from her. Tom Robinson was for her a daily reminder of what she did. And what did she do? She tempted a Negro. She was white, and she tempted a Negro. She did something that in our society is unspeakable. She kissed a black man. Not an old uncle, but a strong, young Negro man. No code mattered to her before she broke it, but it came crashing down on her afterwards. The witnesses for the State, with the exception of the Sheriff of Maycomb County, have presented themselves to you gentlemen, to this court, in the cynical confidence that their testimony would not be doubted. Confident that you gentlemen would go along with them on the assumption, the evil assumption, that all Negroes lie, that all Negroes are basically immoral beings, all Negro men are not to be trusted around our women. An assumption one associates with minds of their calibre, and which is in itself, gentlemen, a lie, which I do not need to point out to you. And so, a quiet, humble, respectable Negro, who has had the unmitigated temerity to feel sorry for a white woman, has had to put his word against two white people. The defendant is not guilty, but somebody in this courtroom is. Now, gentlemen, in this country our courts are the great levellers, and in our courts all men are created equal.

(*The faces of the men of the jury haven't changed expression. Atticus' face begins to perspire. He wipes it with a handkerchief.*)

I'm no idealist to believe firmly in the integrity of our courts and in the jury system. That is no ideal to me. It is a living, working reality. Now I am confident that you gentlemen will review without passion the evidence that you have heard, come to a decision, and restore this man to his family. In the name of God, do your duty. In the name of God, believe Tom Robinson.

(**Atticus** *turns away from the jury. He walks and sits down next to* **Tom** *at the table.*)

INTERIOR: BALCONY OF COURTROOM – SEVERAL HOURS LATER. NIGHT.

Jem *is leaning on the rail of the balcony.* **Reverend Sykes** *is behind him, with* **Dill** *sleeping next to him. The* **Reverend** *fans himself with his hat.*

Jem How long has the jury been out now, Reverend?

Sykes Let's see... (*He pulls out his pocket watch and looks at it.*) Almost two hours now.

Jem I think that's an awful good sign, don't you?

(**Reverend Sykes** *doesn't answer him.*)

INTERIOR: COURTROOM. NIGHT.

The jury comes back into the courtroom. **Tom** *is brought in and walks toward* **Atticus**. *The jailer unlocks the handcuffs from* **Tom**. **Tom** *sits next to* **Atticus**. *The* **Bailiff** *enters the courtroom, followed by the* **Judge**.

Bailiff Court's now in session. Everybody rise.

(*The group in the courtroom rises. The* **Judge** *climbs to his chair and sits down. The spectators are then seated.*)

Judge Gentlemen of the jury, have you reached a verdict?

Foreman We have, your honor.

Judge Will the defendant please rise and face the jury.

(**Tom Robinson** *rises and faces the jury.*)

What is your verdict?

Foreman We find the defendant guilty as charged.

(**Tom** *sits down beside* **Atticus**.)

Judge Gentlemen, this jury is dismissed.

Bailiff Court's adjourned.

(*The* **Judge** *rises and exits through the door. The crowd murmurs and begins to disperse. The jailer moves to* **Tom** *and puts handcuffs on him.* **Atticus** *walks with* **Tom**.)

Atticus I'll go to see Helen first thing in the morning. I told her not to be disappointed, we'd probably lose this time.

(**Tom** *looks at him but doesn't answer.*)

Tom . . .

(**Atticus** *turns from the door and walks to his table. He starts to gather up the papers on his desk. He puts them in his briefcase. He starts to leave the courtroom. He walks down the middle aisle.* **Scout** *is leaning over the rail watching her father and the people below. As* **Atticus** *walks down the aisle, the Negroes in the balcony start to rise until all are standing.* **Scout** *is so busy watching* **Atticus** *that she isn't aware of this.* **Reverend Sykes** *taps her on the shoulder.*)

Sykes Miss Jean Louise . . . Miss Jean Louise.

(**Scout** *looks around.*)

Miss Jean Louise, stand up, your father's passin'.

(**Scout** *rises. The* **Reverend** *puts his arm around her. Everyone in the coloured balcony remains standing until* **Atticus** *exits out the courtroom door.*)

EXTERIOR: MISS MAUDIE'S PORCH. NIGHT.

Miss Maudie *is alone on her porch. She sees* **Atticus** *and the children coming down the sidewalk. She goes out to her yard.* **Atticus** *and the children come up to her.*

Maudie   Atticus... (*The children go to the porch and sit down.*)   I...I'm sorry, Atticus.

Atticus   Well, thank you, Maudie.

(*A car comes down the road and stops in front of Miss Maudie's house.* **Heck Tate** *is at the wheel.*)

Tate   Atticus, can I see you for a minute?

Atticus   Would you excuse me?

(**Maudie** *nods, and* **Atticus** *moves to the car and talks to* **Tate**. **Maudie** *sits next to* **Jem** *on the steps.*)

Maudie   Jem.

Jem   Yes'm.

Maudie   I don't know if it'll help, but I want to say this to you. There are some men in this world who were born to do our unpleasant jobs for us. Your father's one of them.

(**Heck Tate** *drives off.* **Atticus** *stands quietly for a moment and then walks back to the steps.*)

What's the matter, Atticus?

Atticus   Tom Robinson's dead. They were taking him to Abbottsville for safekeeping. Tom broke loose and ran. The deputy called out to him to stop. Tom didn't stop. He shot at him to wound him and missed his aim. Killed him. The deputy says Tom just ran like a crazy man. The last thing I told him was not to lose heart, that we'd ask for an appeal. We had such a good chance. We had more than a good chance. I have to go out and tell his family. Would you look after the children, Maudie?

Jem   (*Starting after him*)   Atticus, you want me to go with you?

Atticus   No Son, I think I'd better go there alone.

Jem   (*Still going after him.*)   Atticus, Atticus, I'm goin' with you.

Atticus   All right, Son.

(*He waits for* **Jem** *to catch up to him.* **Maudie**, **Dill**, *and* **Scout** *stay huddled together on the steps watching them go.* **Atticus** *drives the car out of the garage and they go off.*)

EXTERIOR: TOM ROBINSON'S HOUSE. NIGHT.

The house is dark and quiet, as are all the little houses near it. **Atticus** *drives the car in and shines the headlights on the porch of the house where the* **Robinson** *family is seated and standing, talking.* **Spence**, *Tom's father, sits on the steps of the house.* **Atticus** *and* **Jem** *drive up to the house.* **Atticus** *stops the car and gets out.* **Spence** *sees who it is and comes to him.*

Spence Hello, Mr Finch. I'm Spence, Tom's father.

   (*They shake hands.*)

Atticus Hello, Spence. Is Helen here?

Spence Yes Sir. She's inside, lyin' down, tryin' to get a little sleep. We been talkin' about the appeal, Mr Finch. How long do you think it'll take?

Atticus Spence, there isn't going to be any appeal now. Tom is dead.

   (**Helen Robinson** *comes out of the front door. They all move toward her.* **Atticus** *takes off his hat.*)

Helen . . .

(**Helen** *gives a little moan and falls over into the dirt of the yard.* **Spence** *and* **Atticus** *go to her. They lift her. She is crying. They half-carry her into the house as the others watch.*)

(**Bob Ewell** *comes up the road and stands near Atticus' car. He calls to one of the Negro children in the yard.* **Jem** *watches from inside the car.*)

Ewell Boy, go inside and tell Atticus Finch I said to come out here. Go on, boy.

(*The boy goes inside the house.* **Ewell** *stands in front of the car. He turns and looks at* **Jem**. **Atticus** *comes out of the house and stands on the porch. He walks down the steps, past the Negroes, and goes to* **Ewell** *and stands in front of him.* **Ewell** *spits in Atticus' face.* **Atticus** *stares at him, wipes off his face, and starts to get into the car. He and* **Jem** *drive off as* **Ewell** *watches them angrily.*)

EXTERIOR: FINCH HOUSE. NIGHT. AUTUMN.

Jean Louise (*Voice over*)   By October, things had settled down again. I still looked for Boo every time I went by the Radley place.

   (**Scout** *is walking on the sidewalk by the picket fence. She turns and runs to the house.*)

INTERIOR: SCOUT'S BEDROOM.

She comes in and takes her Halloween costume.

Jean Louise (*Voice over*)   This night my mind was filled with Halloween. There was to be a pageant representing our county's agricultural products.

EXTERIOR: HOUSE. NIGHT.

Scout, *in her Halloween costume, comes out followed by* **Jem**.

Moving shot: They walk to the school building, past carriages and cars parked on the street. They exit into the building.

Jean Louise (*Voice over*)   I was to be a ham. Jem said he would escort me to the school auditorium. Thus began our longest journey together.

EXTERIOR: SCHOOLHOUSE. NIGHT.

The carriages and cars are now gone. **Jem** *is seated on the steps of the schoolhouse. He gets up, walks up the steps to open the door, and looks inside.*

Jem   Scout.

Scout (*Off camera*)   Yeah.

Jem   Will you come on. Everybody's gone.

Scout (*Off camera*)   I can't go home like this.

Jem   Well, I'm goin'. It's almost ten o'clock and Atticus will be waitin' for us.

(*He turns and comes down the steps.*)

Scout (*Off camera*)   All right. I'm comin'.

(*He turns and looks as* **Scout** *comes out of the door with her ham costume on.*)

But I feel like a fool walkin' home like this.

Jem   Well, it's not my fault that you lost your dress.

Scout   I didn't lose it. Just can't find it.

(*She comes down the steps to* **Jem**.)

Jem   Where are your shoes?

Scout   Can't find them either.

Jem   You can get 'em tomorrow.

Scout   But tomorrow is Sunday.

Jem   You can get the janitor to let you in. Come on.

(*They start out.*)

(*Moving shot: They walk into the wooded area.* **Jem** *stoops down and picks up sticks and hits trees with them as they walk along. It is black dark out there.*)

Here, Scout, let me hold onto you before you break your neck. (*Takes her hand as they walk.*)

Scout Jem, you don't have to hold me.

Jem Sshhhh.

Scout What's the matter?

Jem Hush a minute, Scout. (*Moves and looks to his right.*) Thought I heard somethin'. Ah, come on. (*They go about five paces when he makes her stop again.*) Wait.

Scout Jem, are you tryin' to scare me?

Jem Sshhh.

(*There is stillness except for the breathing of the children. Far away a dog howls.*)

Scout You know I'm too old.

Jem Be quiet.

Scout I heard an old dog then.

Jem It's not that. I hear it when we're walking along. When we stop, I don't hear it any more.

Scout You hear my costume rustlin'. Halloween's got you. (*Moves and then stops.*) I hear it now.

(*The two of them stand still and listen.*)

I'll bet it's just old Cecil Jacobs tryin' to scare us. (*She yells.*) Cecil Jacobs is a big wet hen.

(*There is not a sound except the word 'hen' reverberating.*)

Jem Come on.

(**Scout** *and* **Jem** *start walking.* **Jem** *looks frightened. He holds his hand on* **Scout**'s *head, covered by the ham costume. More than a rustle is heard now. Footsteps are heard, as if someone were walking behind them in heavy shoes.* **Jem** *presses* **Scout**'s *head. They stop to listen. They can hear someone running toward them.*)

Run, Scout!

(*She takes a big step and she reels; she can't keep her balance in the dark. A form descends on her and grabs her, and she falls to the ground and*

To Kill a Mockingbird 59

rolls. From nearby, she can hear scuffling, kicking sounds, sounds of shoes and flesh scraping dirt and root. **Jem** *rolls against her and is up like lightning, pulling* **Scout** *with him, but she is so entangled by the costume they can't get very far.*)

Run, Scout!

(*They are nearly to the road when Jem's hand leaves her. There is more scuffling and a dull crunching sound, and* **Scout** *screams. The scuffling slowing dies away and then there is silence. She can see a man now. He groans and is pulling something heavy along the ground. The man walks away from her, heavily and unsteadily, toward the road.*)

(*She makes her way to where she thinks the road is.*)

(*Scout's point of view: She looks down the road to the street light. A man passes under it. He is carrying the limp body of* **Jem**. *The man continues on, crosses the Finch yard. The front door opens and* **Atticus** *runs down the steps.*)

(*Back to* **Scout** *as she runs to him, and he picks her up.*)

Atticus   What happened? What happened?

Scout   I swear, I don't know. I just don't know.

> (**Calpurnia** *comes out of the door.* **Atticus** *turns and carries* **Scout** *up the steps.*)

Atticus   You go and tell Dr Reynolds to come over.

Calpurnia   Yes Sir.

INTERIOR: JEM'S ROOM. NIGHT.

Atticus *enters with* **Scout**. *He puts* **Scout** *down in the front of Jem's room.* **Jem** *is lying on the bed.*

Atticus   You all right?

Scout   Yes Sir.

Atticus   Are you sure?

Scout   Yes Sir.

> (**Atticus** *rises and leaves the room.* **Scout** *turns and looks at* **Jem** *lying on the bed.*)

INTERIOR: HALL. NIGHT.

Atticus *goes to the phone.* **Scout** *runs to* **Atticus**.

Atticus   Sheriff Tate, please.

Scout   Atticus, is Jem dead?

Atticus No, he's unconscious. We won't know how bad he's hurt until the doctor gets here. (*Talking on the phone.*) Heck? Atticus Finch. Someone's been after my children.

INTERIOR: JEM'S ROOM. NIGHT.

Jem's door is slightly open. **Calpurnia** *opens the door all the way for* **Dr Reynolds**. **Atticus** *and* **Scout** *are there.* **Dr Reynolds** *enters and examines* **Jem**.

Dr Reynolds He's got a bad break, so far as I can tell, like somebody tried to wring his arm off. I'll be right back, Atticus.

EXTERIOR: PORCH. NIGHT.

Dr Reynolds *goes out of the front door.* **Tate** *comes on the porch with the ham costume.*

Tate How's the boy, Doc?

Dr Reynolds He'll be all right.

INTERIOR: JEM'S ROOM. NIGHT.

Tate *is at the door of Jem's room. The room is dim. Jem's reading light is shaded with a towel.* **Jem** *lies on his back, asleep. There is an ugly mark on the side of his face. His left arm is out from the side of his body. The man who brought* **Jem** *stands in a corner, leaning against the wall.* **Atticus** *is by Jem's bed.* **Scout** *and* **Heck Tate** *come in.*

Atticus What is it, Heck?

(**Tate** *runs his hands down his thighs. He looks around the room.*)

Tate Bob Ewell's lyin' on the ground under that tree down yonder with a kitchen knife stuck up under his ribs. He's dead, Mr Finch.

(**Atticus** *gets up from the bed. He looks shocked.*)

Atticus Are you sure?

Tate Yes Sir. He ain't gonna bother these children no more. Miss Scout, you think you could tell us what happened?

(**Scout** *goes to* **Atticus**. *He puts his arms around her.*)

Scout I don't know. All of a sudden somebody grabbed me. Knocked me down on the ground. Jem found me there and then Mr Ewell, I reckon, grabbed him again, and Jem hollered. Then somebody grabbed me. Mr Ewell, I guess. Somebody grabbed him, and then I heard someone pantin' and coughin'. Then I saw someone carrying Jem.

Tate Well, who was it?

Scout Why, there he is, Mr Tate. He can tell you his name . . .

(*She points to the man in the corner who brought* **Jem** *home. He leans against the wall. He has a pale face and his hair is thin and dead white, and as she points to him, a strange spasm shakes him. At this moment, it comes to* **Scout** *who he is, and she gazes at him in wonder as a timid smile comes to his face.*)

Hey, Boo.

Atticus Miss Jean Louise, Mr Arthur Radley, I believe he already knows you.

(**Scout** *is embarrassed and tries to hide her embarrassment. She goes to cover* **Jem** *up.*)

Heck, let's go out on the front porch.

(**Atticus** *and* **Tate** *start out the door.* **Scout** *walks to* **Boo**, *standing in the corner behind the door.*)

Scout Would you like to say good night to Jem, Mr Arthur?

(*She holds out her hand and he takes it.* **Jem** *is lying in bed asleep as* **Boo** *and* **Scout** *walk to the bed.*)

You can pet him, Mr Arthur. He's asleep. Couldn't if he was awake, though. He wouldn't let you.

(**Boo** *looks down at* **Jem**.)

Go ahead.

(*He bends down, and his hand reaches out and pats* **Jem**, *asleep in bed. Then he withdraws his hand from Jem's head. He straightens up, still looking down at* **Jem**. **Scout** *takes* **Boo** *by the hand.*)

EXTERIOR: FINCH PORCH. NIGHT.

Scout, *holding Boo's hand, opens the door and they both come out on the porch.* **Atticus** *and* **Tate** *are there.*

Scout Let's sit in the swing, Mr Arthur.

(**Scout** *and* **Boo** *walk to the swing and they sit down in it.*)

Atticus Heck, I guess that the thing to do is . . . good Lord, I must be losing my memory. I can't remember whether Jem is twelve or thirteen. Anyway, it'll have to come before the County Court. Of course, it's a clear case of self-defence. I'll . . . well . . . I'll run down to the office . . .

Tate Mr Finch, you think Jem killed Bob Ewell? Is that what you think? Your boy never stabbed him.

(**Atticus** *looks up.* **Boo** *and* **Scout** *are seated in the swing.* **Scout** *looks up at* **Boo**.)

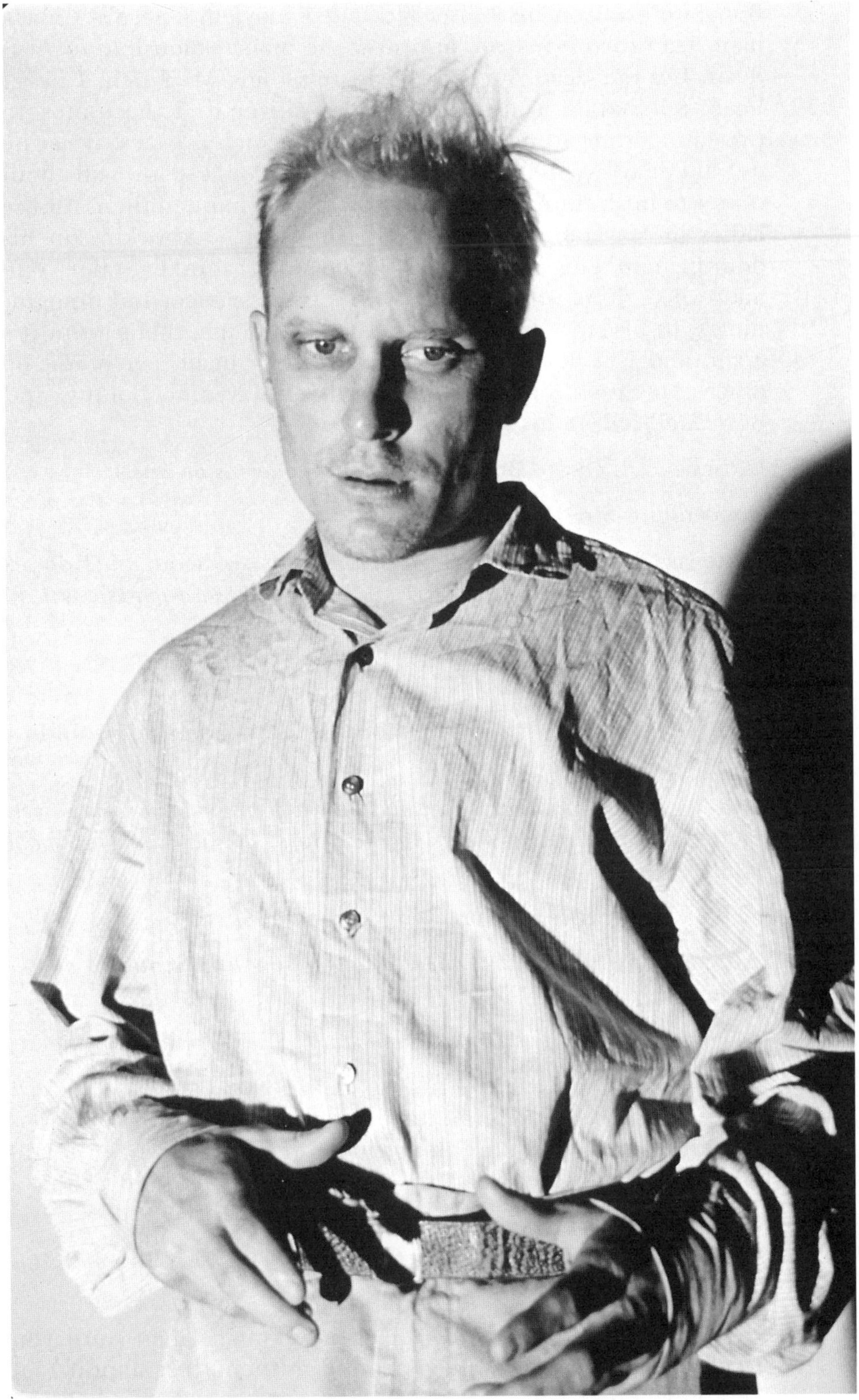

Bob Ewell fell on his knife. He killed himself. There's a black man dead for no reason, and now the man responsible for it is dead. Let the dead bury the dead this time, Mr Finch. I never heard tell that it's against the law for a citizen to do his utmost to prevent a crime from being committed, which is exactly what he did. But maybe you'll tell me it's my duty to tell the town all about it, not to hush it up. Well, you know what'll happen then. All the ladies in Maycomb, includin' my wife, will be knockin' on his door bringin' angel food cakes. To my way of thinkin', takin' one man who's done you and this town a great service, and draggin' him, with his shy ways, into the limelight, to me, that's a sin. It's a sin, and I'm not about to have it on my head. I may not be much, Mr Finch, but I'm still Sheriff of Maycomb County, and Bob Ewell fell on his knife.

(**Atticus** *looks over at* **Boo**. *Tate's meaning dawns on him.*)

Good night, Sir.

(**Tate** *goes down the steps of the porch and to his car.* **Scout** *and* **Boo** *are still seated in the swing.* **Scout** *gets up and walks over to* **Atticus**.)

Scout Mr Tate was right.

Atticus What do you mean?

Scout Well, it would be sort of like shooting a mockingbird, wouldn't it?

(**Atticus** *hugs her to him.* **Boo** *walks over to Jem's window, bends over, and looks inside.* **Atticus** *walks over to* **Boo** *at the window. They shake hands.*)

Atticus Thank you, Arthur. Thank you for my children.

(**Atticus** *turns and walks into the house.* **Boo** *and* **Scout** *go off the porch.*)

(*Moving shot: They walk along the sidewalk. They turn in at the Radley gate and go up the front walk.*)

Jean Louise (*Voice over*) Neighbours bring food with death, and flowers with sickness, and little things in between. Boo was our neighbour. He gave us two soap dolls, a broken watch and chain, a knife, and our lives.

(*They go up the steps and onto the porch to the front door.* **Boo** *opens the door and goes inside.*)

One time Atticus said you never really knew a man until you stood in his shoes and walked around in them. Just standin' on the Radley porch was enough.

(*Moving shot:* **Scout** *turns and walks down the steps of the porch.*)

The summer that had begun so long ago had ended, another summer had taken its place, and a fall, and Boo Radley had come out.

(**Scout** *turns at the gate and looks back at the house. She turns and goes down the walk.*)

I was to think of these days many times; of Jem, and Dill, and Boo Radley, and Tom Robinson . . .

INTERIOR: JEM'S ROOM. NIGHT.

Atticus *and* **Scout** *are inside Jem's room on Jem's bed.*

. . . and Atticus. He would be in Jem's room all night. And he would be there when Jem waked up in the morning.

FADE OUT.

• Drama Activities •

APPRECIATING THE PLAY

PAGES 3–8

1. The voice of young Jean Louise Finch is heard at the beginning of the script. What does she tell the audience about Maycomb?
2. What do you learn about the character of Atticus from his meeting with Walter Cunningham at the beginning of the script?
3. 'Every time I want him to do something . . . he's too old . . . He's too old for anything.' What causes Jem to say this about his father?
4. What aspect of Dill's physical appearance does the script writer emphasise when Dill and Jem first meet?

PAGES 8–17

5. Why do you think Scout and Jem become subdued when Mr Radley first appears?
6. '*The house is low and was once white with a deep front porch and green shutters . . .*' What impression are you given of the Radley house?

7   What does Miss Stephanie's description of Boo Radley stabbing his father with the scissors suggest about the character of Boo Radley?

8   When Atticus first approaches Mrs Dubose's house, she is angry and aggressive. How does Atticus change her mood?

9   When Judge Taylor asks Atticus to take the case of defending Tom Robinson, what is Atticus' response? What do you think this reveals about Atticus?

10 When Scout is inside the tyre and then rolls up to the steps of the Radley porch, how does the script writer show that Jem and Scout are afraid?

PAGES 17–27

11 When Atticus is leaving the courthouse he is confronted by Robert E. Lee Ewell. How is the tension created in this scene?

12 When Jem goes up onto the Radley porch and looks in, how is the suspense suddenly increased?

13 After Jem goes back for his pants '*There is a sound of a shotgun blast.*' How does this increase the suspense?

14 'I could shoot all the blue jays I wanted, if I could hit them, but to remember it is a sin to kill a mockingbird.' Why does Atticus say, 'it is a sin to kill a mockingbird'? How does this statement relate to the overall message of the film?

15 'But, Atticus . . . he has gone and drowned his dinner in syrup.' Why does Calpurnia take Scout outside and smack her for saying this?

PAGES 27–34

16 'You never really understand a person until you consider things from his point of view.' What does Atticus hope to achieve by telling Scout this? How does this statement relate to the overall message of the film?

17 What actions of the dog suggest that it is a 'mad dog'?

18 After Atticus has shot the 'mad dog', the screen directions state, '*JEM and SCOUT are dumbfounded.*' Why are they 'dumbfounded'?

19 When Atticus is visiting Helen Robinson's house to inform her that he has gained a postponement for Tom, Bob Ewell appears near Atticus' car. 'He is unshaven and looks as if he'd been on a long drunk.' How does Bob Ewell's presence build up the tension in this scene?

20 Atticus says to Scout, 'Anyway, I'm simply defending a Negro, Tom Robinson.' How does this statement of Atticus' relate to the main issues of the film?

PAGES 34-44

21 Jem says, 'I found all these in the knothole of that ole tree . . . at different times. This is a spelling medal . . . ' Why are the presents in the knothole important in the film?

22 When Scout pushes through the men at the jail to reach Atticus, why is there a 'look of fear on his face'?

23 'Son, I said, "Go home!"' What conflict is there between Jem and Atticus? Why do you think Jem is so determined not to go home?

24 'Let's clear outta here. Let's go boys.' What has Scout done to bring about the departure of the lynch mob?

25 Heck Tate, the Sheriff says, 'It was her right eye, Mr Finch. Now I remember. She was beaten up on the right side of her face.' Why is this evidence important?

PAGES 44-49

26 When Mr Gilmer questions Bob Ewell, what does Bob Ewell tell the court?

27 What do you think Atticus is trying to show the court by asking Bob Ewell the question, 'Now, did you, during all the runnin', run for a doctor?'

28 'You're left-handed, Mr Ewell.' Why is this evidence important?

29 'You come up here, boy, and bust up this chifforobe.' What does Mayella's use of the word 'boy' reveal about her attitude to Tom Robinson?

30 'Except when he's drinking?' What is Atticus trying to show the court about Bob Ewell's character?

PAGES 49-51

31 'I can't use my left hand at all. I got it caught in a cotton gin when I was twelve years old. All my muscles were torn.' Why is this evidence very important?

32 How does the script writer show the audience that Atticus does not enjoy making Miss Mayella cry?

33 '. . . an it come to me, there was not a child on the place.' Why was this so? Why do you think Mayella had arranged this?

34 'She said she had never kissed a grown man before an' she might as well kiss me.' What does this reveal about Mayella's attitude to Tom?

35 'You felt sorry for her? A white woman? You felt sorry for her?' What 'mistake' has Tom made in saying he felt sorry for Mayella? How does this relate to the main issue of the script?

PAGES 52–56

36 Atticus' final speech to the jury is very important. What important evidence does he present to prove that Tom couldn't have raped Mayella?

37 In his speech, what reasons does Atticus give for Mayella's accusing Tom of raping her?

38 What is the meaning of Atticus' words, '. . . in our courts all men are created equal'?

39 'Miss Jean Louise, stand up, your father's passin'.' Why do all the Negroes stand as Atticus passes? What feelings do you experience here?

40 'Ewell spits in Atticus' face. Atticus stares at him, wipes off his face, and starts to get into the car.' This is a very dramatic moment in the script. How would you have expected Atticus to react? Why did Ewell spit in Atticus' face?

PAGES 57–63

41 'Hush a minute, Scout. Thought I heard somethin'.' How is the suspense built up in this scene where Scout and Jem are returning home from the school auditorium?

42 'Run, Scout!' Why isn't Scout able to run?

43 'Bob Ewell fell on his knife. He killed himself.' Why is Heck Tate so determined that Boo Radley should not be brought to trial for the death of Bob Ewell?

44 'Well, it would be sort of like shooting a mockingbird, wouldn't it?' Why does Scout liken Boo Radley's being brought to trial to the shooting of a mockingbird?

45 What does Scout mean at the end when she says, 'He gave us two soap dolls, a broken watch and chain, a knife, and our lives.'?

46 What do you consider to be the major themes of *To Kill a Mockingbird*?

47 Why is Jean Louise Finch important?

48 Do you think *To Kill a Mockingbird* is a good title? Why or why not?

49 Imagine you have been chosen to play the part of Atticus Finch. What aspects of his character would you want to emphasise?

50 Did you enjoy reading this script? Why or why not?

ATTICUS FINCH — THE CENTRAL CHARACTER

Each character plays a vital part in the script: Scout narrates the story and comments on the central issues; Boo Radley is the mysterious figure who saves the lives of Scout and Jem; Tom Robinson, the epitome of goodness, pays with his life because he has been born a Negro. Yet it is the kind, soft-spoken Atticus Finch who dominates the film. It is he, above all others, who determinedly struggles against the evils of racial prejudice. The script centres on him. It is also true, however, there are times in the script when his children, Jem and Scout, with their childish innocence and sincerity, steal some of Atticus' importance.

We learn much about Atticus by his words and actions in the script. But it is also important for us to consider what other characters in the script say about Atticus. To what extent are we to trust their judgements of him?

Below are some of the judgements made about Atticus in the script. Write them down and explain why you believe they are accurate or not.

Ewell: Nigger lover!

Tate: What's the matter, boy? Can't you talk. Didn't you know your Daddy's the best shot in this county?

Jem: He's too old . . . He's too old for anything.

Scout: Atticus said you never really knew a man until you stood in his shoes and walked around in them.

Mayella: Your Ma'am'in' and your Miss Mayellarin' – it don't come to nothin' Mr Finch.

Maudie: He can make somebody's will so airtight you can't break it.

NOVEL TO SCREEN

These days film companies are energetically buying up the film rights to best-selling novels. Some best-selling novelists are now able to demand and receive more than a million dollars for the film rights to their books. Sometimes it takes years for a novel to be transferred to the screen. Of course, once a film is made there is great resurgence in the sales of the novel because of the intensive publicity campaign associated with a film.

Once the film rights have been purchased, the producer then seeks out a script writer or a team of script writers to translate the novel to a screenplay. The screenplay can be rewritten many times before the producer and director are satisfied with it.

Horton Foote, the writer of the Academy Award-winning script for *To Kill a Mockingbird*, makes these comments about adapting a novel for the screen: 'After I decide to adapt a work, I read it over and over making notes. The essential story is given to you; the characters have been named and defined. Your creativity has to work within a given framework – but not in a straitjacket that reduces you to uninspired literalness. I try to absorb the author's world and to find a creative way to enter it.'

Often you will find that a scene spanning many pages of a novel is reduced by the script writer to a few minutes on the screen. If this were not done, the impact of the scene would be lost and the film would be too long.

Let's now look at a short scene from Harper Lee's novel, *To Kill a Mockingbird*, and then see how the script writer, Horton Foote, has translated it to a scene in the screenplay. You will see there has been a reduction in the novelist's description and dialogue to enable the scene to have greater dramatic impact on the screen. Horton Foote has made every word and action count.

Atticus summoned Calpurnia, who returned bearing the syrup pitcher. She stood waiting for Walter to help himself. Walter poured syrup on his vegetables and meat with a generous hand. He would probably have poured it into his milk glass had I not asked what the sam hill he was doing.

The silver saucer clattered when he replaced the pitcher, and he quickly put his hands in his lap. Then he ducked his head.

Atticus shook his head at me again. 'But he's gone and drowned his dinner in syrup,' I protested. 'He's poured it all over — '

It was then that Calpurnia requested my presence in the kitchen.

She was furious, and when she was furious Calpurnia's grammar became erratic. When in tranquillity, her grammar was as good as anybody's in Maycomb. Atticus said Calpurnia had more education than most coloured folks.

When she squinted down at me the tiny lines around her eyes deepened. 'There's some folks who don't eat like us,' she whispered fiercely, 'but you ain't called on to contradict 'em at the table when they don't. That boy's yo' comp'ny and if he wants to eat up the table-cloth you let him, you hear?'

'He ain't company, Cal, he's just a Cunningham — '

'Hush your mouth. Don't matter who they are, anybody sets foot in this house's yo' comp'ny, and don't you let me catch you remarkin' on their ways like you was so high and mighty! Yo' folks might be better'n the Cunninghams but it don't count for nothin' the way you're disgracin' 'em — if you can't act fit to eat at the table you can just set here and eat in the kitchen!'

Calpurnia sent me through the swinging door to the dining room with a stinging smack. I retrieved my plate and finished dinner in the kitchen, thankful, though, that I was spared the humiliation of facing them again.

from **To Kill a Mockingbird** *by Harper Lee*

(**Calpurnia** *enters with the syrup dish.*)

Atticus Oh, thank you, Cal. That's for Walter.

(*She takes the dish to* **Walter**. *He begins to pour it liberally all over his food.* **Scout** *is watching this process. She makes a face of disgust.*)

Scout What in the Sam Hill are you doing, Walter?

(*Atticus' hand thumps the table beside her.*)

But, Atticus . . . he has gone and drowned his dinner in syrup.

(*The silver saucer clatters.* **Walter** *places the pitcher on it and quickly puts his hands in his lap and ducks his head.* **Atticus** *shakes his head at* **Scout** *to keep quiet.*)

Calpurnia Scout!

Scout What?

Calpurnia Come out here. I want to talk to you.

> (**Scout** *eyes her suspiciously, sees she is in no mood to be trifled with, and goes out to the kitchen.* **Calpurnia** *stalks after her.*)
>
> INTERIOR: KITCHEN.
>
> > **Scout** *and* **Calpurnia** *enter.*
>
> **Calpurnia**   That boy is your company. And if he wants to eat up that tablecloth, you let him, you hear? And if you can't act fit to eat like folks, you can just set here and eat in the kitchen.   (*Sends her back into the dining room with a smack.*)
>
> INTERIOR: LIVING ROOM — DINING ROOM.
>
> > **Atticus**, **Jem**, *and* **Walter** *continue eating as* **Scout** *runs through the dining room and living room to the front porch.*
>
> from **To Kill a Mockingbird** by Horton Foote

WRITING A SCENE

Here is a courtroom scene from Harper Lee's novel, *To Kill a Mockingbird*. Try your hand at converting it into a scene of a screenplay. When you have finished, find the actual scene in Horton Foote's screenplay and compare your attempt with it.

> # MAYELLA v. ATTICUS
>
> Atticus's glasses had slipped a little, and he pushed them up on his nose. 'We've had a good visit, Miss Mayella, and now I guess we'd better get to the case. You say you asked Tom Robinson to come chop up a – what was it?'
> 'A chifforobe, a old dresser full of drawers on one side.'
> 'Was Tom Robinson well known to you?'
> 'Whaddya mean?'
> 'I mean did you know who he was, where he lived?'
> Mayella nodded. 'I knowed who he was, he passed the house every day.'
> 'Was this the first time you asked him to come inside the fence?'
> Mayella jumped slightly at the question. Atticus was making his slow pilgrimage to the windows, as he had been doing: he would ask

a question, then look out, waiting for an answer. He did not see her involuntary jump, but it seemed to me that he knew she had moved. He turned around and raised his eyebrows. 'Was – ' he began again.

'Yes it was.'

'Didn't you ever ask him to come inside the fence before?'

She was prepared now, 'I did not, I certainly did not.'

'One did not's enough,' said Atticus serenely. 'You never asked him to do odd jobs for your before?'

'I mighta,' conceded Mayella. 'There was several niggers around.'

'Can you remember any other occasions?'

'No.'

'All right, now to what happened. You said Tom Robinson was behind you in the room when you turned around, that right?'

'Yes.'

'You said he "got you around the neck cussing and saying dirt!" – is that right?'

''t's right.'

Atticus's memory had suddenly become accurate. 'You say "he caught me and choked me and took advantage of me!" – is that right?'

'That's what I said.'

'Do you remember him beating you about the face?'

The witness hesitated.

'You seem sure enough that he choked you. All this time you were fighting back, remember? You "kicked and hollered as loud as you could!" Do you remember him beating you about the face?'

Mayella was silent. She seemed to be trying to get something clear to herself. I thought for a moment she was doing Mr Heck Tate's and my trick of pretending there was a person in front of us. She glanced at Mr Gilmer.

'It's an easy question, Miss Mayella, so I'll try again. Do you remember him beating you about the face?' Atticus's voice had lost its comfortableness; he was speaking in his arid, detached professional voice. 'Do you remember him beating you about the face?'

'No, I don't recollect if he hit me. I mean yes I do, he hit me.'

'Was your last sentence your answer?'

'Huh? Yes, he hit – I just don't remember, I just don't remember . . . it all happened so quick.'

from **To Kill a Mockingbird** *by Harper Lee*

2

Adam's Ark

by Harold Hodgson

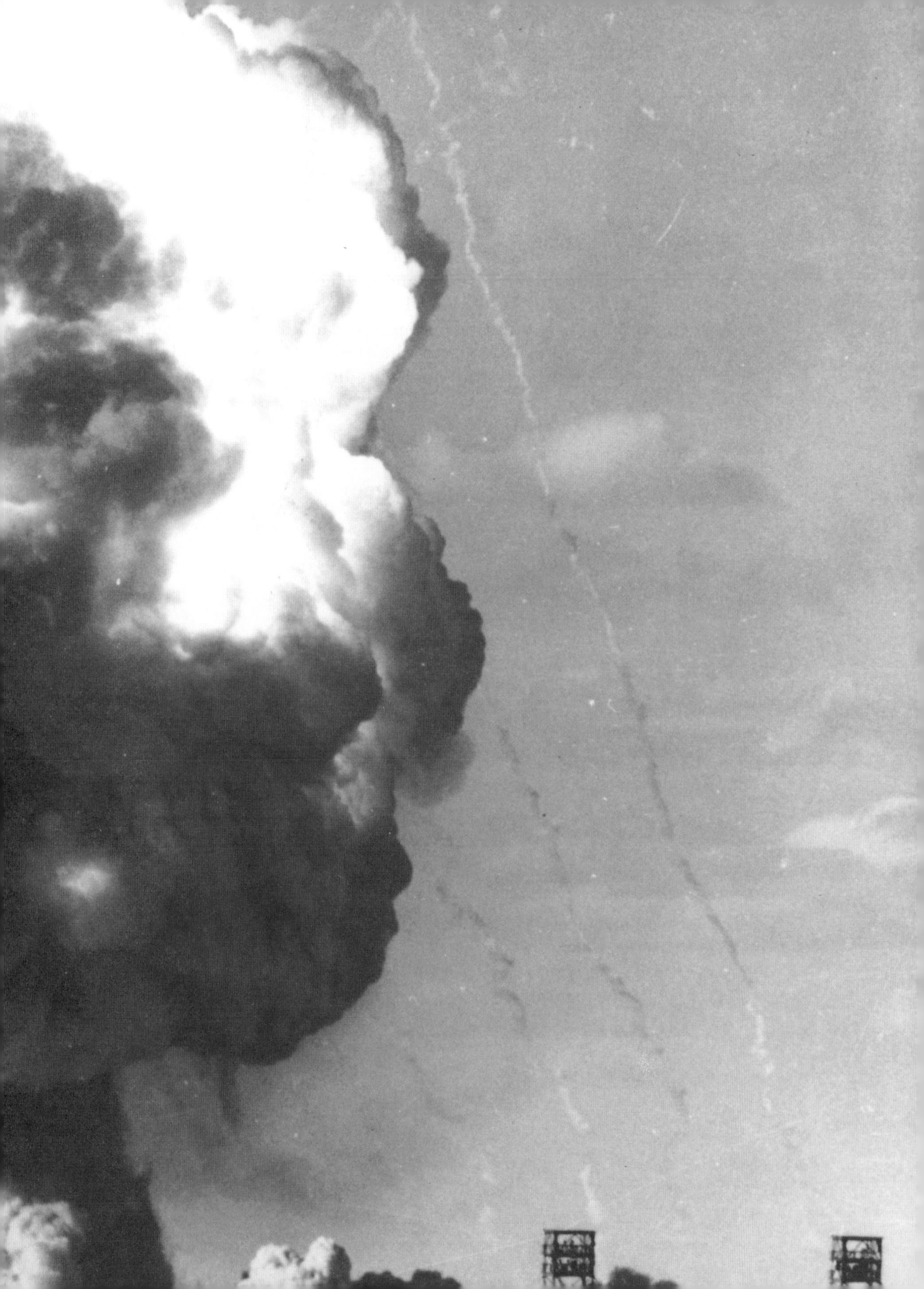

Adam's Ark

by Harold Hodgson

The play *Adam's Ark* by Harold Hodgson portrays a group of young teenagers in a horrifying predicament. They have taken refuge in a specially built nuclear shelter and they survive a nuclear explosion that destroys almost every other living being for hundreds of miles around. What are they to do? The playwright Harold Hodgson confronts the audience with important issues including how human nature confronts and survives disaster.

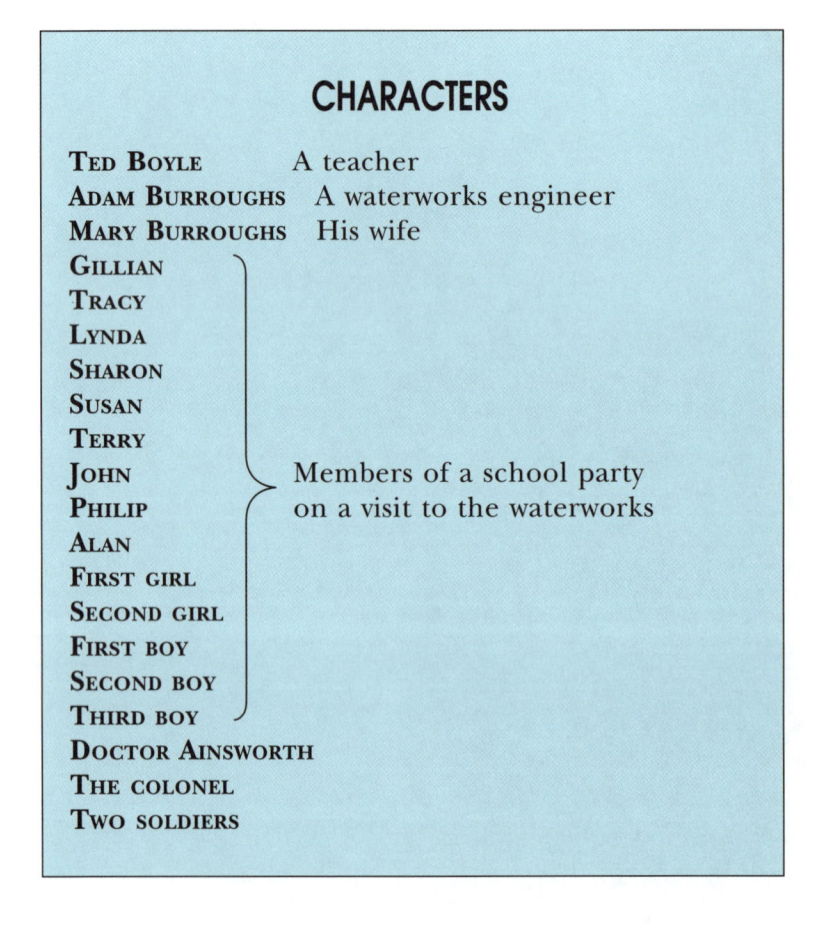

CHARACTERS

Ted Boyle	A teacher
Adam Burroughs	A waterworks engineer
Mary Burroughs	His wife
Gillian	
Tracy	
Lynda	
Sharon	
Susan	
Terry	
John	Members of a school party on a visit to the waterworks
Philip	
Alan	
First girl	
Second girl	
First boy	
Second boy	
Third boy	
Doctor Ainsworth	
The colonel	
Two soldiers	

> **THE SCENES**
>
> | | | |
> |---|---|---|
> | **Act 1** | **Scene 1** | The Shelter, one day in summer |
> | | **Scene 2** | The Shelter, two days later |
> | **Act 2** | **Scene 1** | The Shelter, eight months later |
> | | **Scene 2** | The Shelter, half-an-hour later |
> | **Act 3** | **Scene 1** | An isolated roadside bungalow, an hour later |
> | | **Scene 2** | An isolated roadside bungalow, four days later |

ACT 1
SCENE 1

The interior of R.S.G. 21, situated underground, somewhere in the northern counties. It is the main communal room, which is entered from outside through a heavy door, down a short flight of steps. At one side, two doors lead off to a dormitory and kitchen. On the opposite side are doors to toilets and a second dormitory. Ventilation trunking, with louvres, runs the length of the wall. The room is sparsely furnished with two formica tables and 'utility' chairs. A telephone, a radio set and a panel of dials are located on a metal desk. The letters R.S.G. 21 are painted in white over the central door. The walls are a drab olive-green.

(At the rise of the curtain the room is empty and in darkness. Angry voices are heard off-stage. The door is flung open and from the off-stage lighting in the outer corridor we see a man being bundled forcibly into the room by other figures crowding him in.)

A Voice Where are the lights?

Another Voice Try the wall.

(The lights go up to reveal **Adam Burroughs** *getting up off the floor. He is a burly man in his fifties. A windcheater covers his slacks and sweater. Coming down the steps is* **Ted Boyle**, *a teacher in his late twenties. He is followed by a number of teenagers, the boys first. The boys and girls are,*

in the main, in school uniform. There is a buzz of comment in the room. 'It's a shelter.' 'Like a prison.' 'Just like school.' Some laughter.)

Burroughs (*Authoritatively*) You'll suffer for this. This is government property and you're trespassing.

Boyle It's an R.S.G., isn't it?

Philip What's an R.S.G., sir?

(*A few of the boys and girls are wandering into the room but others stay on the steps with most of the girls.*)

Burroughs You're in charge of this lot. The visit's over. Get 'em into their bus and off back to school. Or their homes.

Boyle There may be no homes to go back to.

Burroughs I can't help that. I've got my job to do. And there's no room in here for a load of kids.

Philip Hey, sir! What is an R.S.G.? It's got it up there. (*Pointing to lettering.*)

Boyle It's a shelter against atom bombs. (*To* **Burroughs**) Look, I can't take them back till I know what I'm taking them back to. Have the bombs been dropped?

Burroughs They're on their way. That's my information.

Terry Are they bombing us, sir?

Boyle Maybe. We'll know soon.

Gillian Does that mean our homes'll go?

Boyle That depends. It's not going to be healthy anywhere, no matter where they drop.

Burroughs (*Moving to steps*) Is that outer door closed?

Tracy No.

Burroughs Let me up.

(*He pushes through and goes out briefly.* **Boyle** *is besieged by questions.*)

Susan What are we going to do, sir?

Lynda Will our mums and dads be O.K.?

First Boy Are we going back now, sir?

Boyle Look. Look. We don't even know it's happened yet. It may be a false alarm.

John It'll be a false alarm. You'll see. They wouldn't start anything.

Boyle   We'll wait here for as long as we can. Till we get some news.

Burroughs   (*Returning and speaking from steps*)   That's just as long as you can wait. Till there's some news. Then you go. Out of my way.

(*He pushes down the steps towards the telephone.*)

Philip   Listen to the tough guy.

(**Second** *and* **Third Boys** *mime shooting one another and speak in mock-American accents.*)

Third Boy   Are you going quietly.

Second Boy   Go for your gun, cop.   (*He clutches his stomach*)   Ya got me in de guts, ya doity rat.

Burroughs   You can laugh, sonny. That's just what I'm supposed to do.

(*He rattles the telephone impatiently.*)

Boyle   Stop fooling, you lot.   (*To* **Burroughs**)   What do you mean by that?

Burroughs   I mean just what I said. I'm authorised to shoot anyone illegally entering this bunker in times of emergency. Anyone –

whether he's the enemy or a schoolkid being shown round the reservoir or the schoolmaster in charge of him. (*Rattling the phone*) Damn! Why doesn't she hear?

Boyle   You mean you'll turn us out at gunpoint if the bombs drop.

Burroughs   Just that.

Terry   Who's it for, then?

Burroughs   It's for the V.I.P.s, laddie. The emergency controllers. The ones whose job is to clean up the mess, direct the emergency services.

Boyle   You think there'll be anything left to clean up?

Burroughs   There may be. I wouldn't . . . Hello, hello, Mary? Adam here. Listen. Drop everything right now and get over to the bunker. Now. The balloon's gone up. Of course I'm not joking. Get over here right away.

(*He puts the phone down and begins operating the short-wave radio.*)

Boyle   The four-minute warning, eh?

Burroughs   (*Working the set*)   Yes. And not much of the four minutes left either.

Third Boy   What's that mean, sir?

Boyle   It means we should know in less than four minutes whether the bomb has dropped.

Gillian   You mean it's actually happening, sir?

John   It'll be a rehearsal. They wouldn't start a megatonic war.

(*The radio begins to crackle and a distorted voice is heard.*)

Burroughs   Shut up. We'll know soon enough.

Radio   R.S.G. control. This is R.S.G. control. R.S.G. control calling all R.S.G. stations. Keep your channels open for an important announcement. I repeat. This is R.S.G. control calling all R.S.G. stations. Keep your channels open for an important announcement.

(*There is an expectant pause.*)

Tracy   They can't be sending the bombs.

Susan   What'll we do, sir?

Burroughs   Just keep quiet and listen.

Radio   R.S.G. control calling all R.S.G. stations. Stand by for an important announcement from the Deputy Controller. Stand by. (*Voice changes*) This is your Deputy Controller. Code word Doomsday. Code word Doomsday. Reports from Fylingdales state that enemy rockets were launched at 14.30 hours. Their course is being monitored but everything indicates a major attack on this country. Our own forces are retaliating. Alert all personnel to join their stations, wherever possible. Individual stations to report details of enemy attack on their areas using their own channels in accordance with Emergency Code Two. This channel to be kept open at all times except when transmitting. I repeat. This is your Deputy Controller. Code word Doomsday, code word Doomsday. Reports from Fylingdales . . .

(**Burroughs** *turns down the radio to a murmur, picks up the phone, dials and waits.*)

Burroughs Well, you heard it. Now, will you get out?

Boyle Now?

Sharon Sir, he's not going to send us out to be bombed, is he?

Boyle He's going to try.

Burroughs (*Still at the telephone*) Look, I don't want to seem hard on you kids, but I have my orders.

Terry (*Moving to him*) You mean you'd turn us out in the open to be bombed?

Burroughs They're not going to drop their bombs on a reservoir way out in the hills. The cities'll get it.

Terry Our homes you mean.

Gillian Oh, no!

Boyle We're not going. We're staying here.

Burroughs Look, I've told you my orders. I shoot anyone invading this bunker illegally.

Philip He hasn't got a gun.

Burroughs (*Putting down phone and opening drawer in desk*) No, but I can soon get one. (*Takes out revolver*) Now, you're all going out through that door and into the tunnel. You can stay there for a little while if you like. You'll have some protection from the shock waves, from the initial blast and the heat. Then I advise you to get in that school bus of yours and head north. Don't try going back home, it won't be a pretty sight. Get to hell out of the area and good luck to you.

Boyle We're not going.

Alan That's it, sir. Stand up to him.

Burroughs He won't stand up to a bullet. Now, take your party and go – quietly.

(*He moves threateningly towards* **Boyle**. **Terry** *is on his left.* **Mary Burroughs** *enters: she stands at the door, distraught.*)

Mrs Burroughs Adam. Adam. I've seen it – the cloud. Over the hill, Manchester way. They've . . . Adam, look out! Adam!

(**Terry** *launches himself at* **Burroughs** *and grabs the arm holding the gun.* **Boyle** *closes in and also grapples with him. The gun goes off harmlessly into the air and falls from* **Burroughs**' *grasp. Alan picks it up and gives it to* **Boyle** *as the scuffle subsides.*)

Boyle Is anybody hurt?

Alan The gun went off in the air, sir.

Mrs Burroughs (*Approaching* **Burroughs**) Are you all right, love?

Burroughs Yes, I'm all right.

Boyle You might have killed someone.

Burroughs But I didn't. And I don't think I would. The gun went off because you jumped me. I wouldn't have fired. I don't think so anyway. I was just trying to get you out.

Third Boy Chuck him out, sir.

Second Boy Yeah, let's chuck him out, and his missus.

Boyle There's no need for that. We may need him.

Burroughs You're right there, teacher. You can't run this place without me. What do you lot know about survival in an atomic attack?

Boyle Nothing, that's true. But then nobody ever told us what to do. We weren't expected to survive, were we?

Burroughs Some will survive. It's my job, along with others, to help them. When the others arrive they'll maybe make you see sense.

Boyle We'll see about that when they arrive – if they arrive – and if we let them in.

Terry Why let them in, sir? First come, first served.

John Yes, why should we be chucked out for a bunch of old men?

Burroughs What you call the old men will include doctors to help the wounded. And some of those wounded may include your schoolmates – and your parents.

First Girl I don't want to stay here anyway. I want to go home.

Second Girl So do I.

Boyle We can't go back till we know what the damage is. (*To* **Burroughs**) When will you know?

Burroughs I'll try to contact the other R.S.G.s. (*Crosses to radio, speaking to his wife*) You said that cloud was Manchester way, love?

Mrs Burroughs Near enough.

Burroughs (*Throwing switches to transmit, and operating dials*) We'll try them first. R.S.G. 24? This is R.S.G. 21. Are you receiving me? Over.

(*There is no reply. He tries again.*)

R.S.G. 24? This is R.S.G. 21. Are you receiving me? Over.

Radio R.S.G. 21? This is R.S.G. 24. I am receiving you. How is it in your area? Report please. Over.

Burroughs No enemy action yet but I haven't yet checked the scanner, or radiation levels. Post is not effective yet as I am the only operative. I have to report intruders in the post. Over.

Radio You know the drill, 21. Carry it out. Over.

Burroughs I'm afraid that is not possible at the moment. How are things your area? Over.

Radio Things are hotting up here. Attack on the area estimated at fifty megatons. We are assuming our post will be ineffective owing to radiation levels. Over.

Burroughs Thank you, 24. Over and out.

Mrs Burroughs It's a bad attack, Adam, isn't it?

Burroughs Bad enough. There won't be much of Manchester left standing. (*To* **Boyle**) Where are you from? Little Hulton was it?

Boyle Yes.

Burroughs That's too near Manchester for comfort. I don't want to sound too pessimistic but the heat will have started fires and the radiation levels are likely to be near-lethal.

Third Boy What does that mean?

Boyle It means we'd be most unwise to go back home, Tom.

Third Boy But I can't just stay here when my mum may be lying there badly burnt.

First Girl I've got to go back too. I can't just stay here and do nothing.

Burroughs Look, I've been trying to get you lot out of here ever since you burst in on me, but I don't advise you to head for Manchester. You'd just be walking into danger. Maybe certain death. Get into your bus and head north. It's going to be too hot for comfort up top even here.

(*The boys and girls have all crept into the room by now and are sitting on chairs, tables and steps.* **Boyle** *moves to stand on the steps.*)

Boyle Now listen carefully, everyone. If we leave this shelter we put ourselves in danger of death from radiation. And it'll be a slow death. If we go back home, we're merely going to bring that death nearer. And, I'm sorry to have to say this, but it's extremely unlikely that we can save anyone at home who has been subject to intense radiation. You may think it's easy for me to say this because I'm not married and I've no one to go back to. But if you go back you're probably making a useless journey and putting yourselves in real danger. I strongly advise you to stay here. I'm sure your parents would wish it. They wouldn't want you to sacrifice yourselves out of a mistaken sense of duty. For God's sake stay here where you're safe – for the moment, anyway.

First Girl I still want to go back, sir.

Third Boy My mind's made up, sir. I'm going back. I can drive the old bus. Who's coming? We'll collect our mums and dads and be back here inside a couple of hours.

Burroughs Now look. This is just foolish. You can't go bringing loads of sick and wounded people back here. Don't you understand that you'll only be bringing them here to die? They can't possibly survive. This place is built to support about a dozen people, not an army.

Terry There's nothing I can do about my mum and dad. They both work in Salford and I suppose . . . well . . . I suppose they've had it . . . and I . . . But that's no reason why those who feel they can do something about it shouldn't try, and good luck to them. And if they get back I vote we take them in and do our best for them.

Boyle I can't stop anyone going back who feels he must but I strongly advise you not to, because I honestly don't think we shall see you again. I mean that.

Third Boy Well, I think there'll be plenty of survivors.

Second Boy Yeah, and another thing, the longer we leave it, the worse it'll get for anybody at home. The sooner we get away and back again the better. I vote we go now. Tom'll drive us, won't you, Tom?

Third Boy Sure I will. You can trust me. Never had an accident yet.

Boyle You've never been on the road yet, Tom. And don't forget the roads may be swarming with people getting out as fast as they can.

Third Boy I'll risk it, sir.

(*He heads for the door and turns on the steps*)

Well, who's coming with me? Anybody?

Second Boy (*Moving*) Me for one.

First Boy And me.

First Girl Me too. I've got to find out what's happened.

Second Girl I'm going as well.

Alan I think you should take Mr Boyle's advice and stay – for the time being, anyway.

Third Boy If we wait they'll all be dead. Anybody else coming?

Susan I don't know what to do for the best.

Boyle Stay here, Susan. I don't think there's anything they'll be able to do.

Third Boy We'll have a damn' good try. Let's not waste any more time arguing. Off we go.

(*He goes out followed by* **First** *and* **Second Boys**, *and* **First** *and* **Second Girls**)

Boyle Good luck to you.

Burroughs They'll need it.

Boyle (*Calling after them*) Get back as soon as you can. You can't afford to hang around.

Susan (*Crying*) It doesn't seem right. They're trying to do something and we just sit here safe as houses. It's selfish.

Gillian Come and sit down, love. (*Leads her to a chair*) I don't think we could do much if we went. We're not doctors. We wouldn't know what to do.

Susan I could bring them back. My mum, at least.

Gillian We still wouldn't be able to treat them.

Lynda Well, I wouldn't go back for my dad. He hates me.

Boyle Now come on, Lynda.

Lynda No, I wouldn't. He's been rotten to me ever since my mum died.

Boyle Well, maybe he had his reasons. (*Joking*) Can't have been easy bringing *you* up Lynda.

Lynda I wasn't that bad. Not really. You know, I think Mr Boyle is right. When he says our parents wouldn't want us to risk our lives, bringing them back. I know my dad wouldn't. 'Go on,' he'd say. 'Look after Number One, lass.'

Burroughs (*Who has been listening to the muted radio*) Shut up a minute, will you. I want to listen.

(*Turns up radio.*)

Radio . . . on centres of dense population. Reports from all the major conurbations indicate heavy attacks. The Manchester/Liverpool area, the Birmingham complex, and especially the London area confirm this. Casualties are expected to be severe and it is likely that telephone services will be completely disrupted. All R.S.G.s should rely on police wavelengths for local communications. End of message. Out.

Boyle It sounds bad, doesn't it?

Burroughs Bad enough.

Mrs Burroughs What'll happen, Adam?

Burroughs I don't know yet, love. Without the telephone we're stymied. The only thing I can think of is to contact the police and check they're directing people to safe areas, wherever they are. Find out the general situation. What I can't understand is why nobody else has checked in. Doc Ainsworth should be here with his ambulances. And the Superintendent, and the Colonel.

Mrs Burroughs Maybe they've just . . . you know . . .

Terry Goners, you mean, don't you?

Burroughs It's too early to say. After all, they weren't on the spot like us.

John What do we know then?

Burroughs We sit and wait, laddie.

(*General movement to seats*)

Tracy I'm getting hungry.

Philip And I could do with a fag.

Burroughs There'll be no smoking in here, young fellow. The good air's too precious.

Mrs Burroughs Shall I organise a cup of tea and a snack, Adam?

Burroughs Good idea, love. Take a couple of girls to help you.

Mrs Burroughs (*Crossing to the kitchen*) Anybody like to help?

Gillian (*To* **Susan**) Come on, let's give a hand, hey?

Susan (*Moving off with her and* **Mrs Burroughs**) O.K.

Boyle (*To* **Burroughs**) You mentioned good air. How do you make it good?

Burroughs Air is blown through that trunking and out of the louvres. (*He points to the ventilation trunking*) There's a pretty sophisticated filtration system. Same with the water, only that shouldn't need filtering yet — it comes from an underground spring.

Boyle And the power?

Burroughs Hydroelectric. Works from the dam. Powers my own house as a matter of fact. Should last for years with just a minimum of maintenance.

Boyle And food?

Burroughs Plenty for the proper staff, but not enough to feed the five thousand. Dried and canned stuff mainly.

Philip Are there any toilets here? I could use one.

Burroughs That door there. (*Indicating the door.* **Philip** *crosses.*) Serves as a decontamination room as well. The other two rooms are for sleeping. (*To* **Philip**) Remember, laddie, no smoking in these toilets.

(**Philip** *makes a face behind his back and goes out.*)

Boyle I don't see what purpose all this serves, except to provide a convenient private air-raid shelter for a lot of V.I.P.s. What do you hope to do?

Burroughs We're supposed to direct rescue and relief operations in our area. Organise evacuation. Direct hospital services. Bring in food where necessary. Bury the dead, I suppose.

Boyle Do you honestly think there's much you can do?

Burroughs Privately, I don't mind telling you now, I think it's a lot of wishful thinking. But I was the logical man to put in charge of this bunker and I'd have been a fool to turn down a comfortable private air-raid shelter. Now, excuse me, I must try the police wavelengths.

(*He moves to the radio and begins operating.* **Philip** *enters.*)

Philip Not a single word on the toilet walls. We'll have to alter that, won't we? 'Philip loves Lynda.' How's that for a start?

Lynda Bighead.

Burroughs This is R.S.G. 21 calling Police. Are you receiving me? Over.

(*There is a silence*)

Hello, Police. This is R.S.G. 21 calling. Are you receiving me? Over.

(*Another silence*)

I'll try later.

Sharon Why not try your transistor, Tracy?

Tracy Why don't you try your own?

Sharon I didn't bring it, silly. That was my cassette recorder I was playing on the bus.

Tracy All right. I'll have a go.

(*She takes a small transistor from her bag and tries to find a station. There is an expectant silence but nothing is heard except static.*)

Sharon Try another station.

Tracy I've tried them all. There's nothing.

John Keep trying. Somebody must be alive somewhere.

(**Mrs Burroughs** *enters, followed by the girls, carrying trays of cups of tea and biscuits which are handed round.*)

Mrs Burroughs Tea's up. There's nothing to eat except biscuits, I'm afraid. Not till we open up the tins. It's powdered milk too, but we can't expect it straight from the cow, can we? Help yourselves to the biscuits. There are plenty more where those came from. Very British and all that, aren't we, Adam? In the middle of Armageddon, we have a cup of tea.

(*Before she finishes speaking, the door opens and* **Dr Ainsworth**, *a man in his late fifties, enters, looking grim and distraught.*)

Burroughs Doc! Good to see you. Is there anybody with you?

Dr Ainsworth No.

Mrs Burroughs You're just in time for a cup of tea, Jim.

Dr Ainsworth I need more than tea, Mary. Adam, get me some of the radiation pills from the cabinet, will you? Bring them into the showers. I must get through the decontamination routine as soon as I can.

(*Crosses to the toilet door*)

Burroughs Is it bad up top, Jim?

Dr Ainsworth It's lethal, Adam. If I survive I'll start saying my prayers again.

SCENE 2

Two days later. It is the end of the evening meal. All are seated at the tables apart from **Adam Burroughs** *and* **Dr Ainsworth**.

Boyle That was very good, Susan. My compliments to the chef.

Philip Yeah, very 'more-ish' that was. Very good, but I could have done with more.

Lynda Gutsy!

Philip In case you should ever marry me, Lynda, I should tell you, I'm very fond of my stomach.

Lynda You'd have to be the last man on earth for me to marry you.

Philip The way things are going, that could well happen.

Alan Oh, stop rowing, you two. It was very nice, Susan.

Tracy She was always teacher's pet in Cookery.

Sharon That's more than I was. I used to burn everything.

Alan That I can believe.

Sharon Pig! No, but it's true. Some people are born to be domestic slaves. I was born for higher things.

Terry Like what?

Sharon I was born to inspire some genius. Like Alan. You're the school genius, aren't you, Alan? Everybody says you are.

Alan Who am I to deny it? If I'm ever in need of inspiration, I'll let you know, Sharon.

Boyle Who's supposed to clear and who's doing the washing-up?

Terry I'm on washing-up with Gillian. John and Tracy are clearing.

Gillian (*Rising and moving to kitchen,* **Terry** *following*) Come on, Terry. Get your pinny on.

Philip Hey, they sound just like an old married couple, don't they? Darby and Joan. My mum used to say that to my dad and he . . . well he . . .

Boyle Yes. Well, let's clear away, shall we? John, Tracy? (*They begin clearing*) You know, I feel just like Philip when I've had a meal. I'm dying for a fag.

Mrs Burroughs I'm quite sure it wouldn't make any difference if you had one, in spite of what Adam says. We've got a most efficient Expelair system.

Boyle Trouble is I've run out. I was very naughty last night, smoked my last one in the toilets.

John Write out a hundred times 'I must not smoke in the toilets'.

Boyle I won't do it again, so I'll let myself off this time.

Lynda Why don't you go out and get some, sir? Put on a white suit like the doctor and Mr Burroughs and walk out and go in the first shop and help yourself. Just think, everything's for free! You can walk into any shop and you'll know the shopkeeper can't stop you picking up anything you like, 'cos he's dead or dying. Like my dad, like everybody except us, burrowing under the earth like rabbits.

Mrs Burroughs Susan, I put two dinners in the oven for Adam and the doctor. Would you like to see if they're all right?

Susan (*Leaving*) Yes.

Mrs Burroughs I'm worried about them, Ted. They should have been back ages ago.

Boyle Now come on Mrs B., they're only half an hour late. And they do have protection.

Mrs Burroughs I'm not sure those white suits and air bottles are any protection against this horrible thing that's hit us. I don't even feel very safe underground.

Boyle We're the lucky ones, Mrs B. From what the doctor says there aren't going to be many survivors up top.

Mrs Burroughs That's what worries me. Do you suppose it's like this all over the world?

Boyle I shouldn't think it'll be as bad as that. There must be lots of places untouched.

Mrs Burroughs America. It'll be bad there, I suppose.

Boyle Probably. But it's a big place. Why do you ask?

Mrs Burroughs My son David's out there. Texas. They wanted doctors and they paid well, so he went. Married out there. We went over for the wedding, Adam and I. They have two children now, but I haven't seen them. I don't suppose . . .

Boyle Well, as I said, it's a big place.

   (*Voices are heard, off.*)

Lynda That sounds like the Doc.

Sharon Shall I get their dinner?

Mrs Burroughs Not yet, love. They'll have to go through all that decontamination routine.

   (*The door opens and* **Burroughs** *and* **Dr Ainsworth** *enter, wearing white overall suits, with oxygen bottles strapped to their backs.* **Burroughs** *has his helmet off;* **Dr Ainsworth** *is removing his, although hampered by his medical bag.*)

Burroughs Hello, Mary. Sorry we're late. I hope you haven't been worrying. No, don't come near us. We're pretty hot. The radiation's worse than ever. We'll get under the showers.

   (**Burroughs** *and* **Dr Ainsworth** *go out hurriedly.*)

John (*Who has been clearing the tables with* **Tracy**) Move off you lot and let the workers wipe the tables.

Philip What's the hurry? You're not going any place. Nor is anybody.

(*They make a general move from the tables, taking chairs with them.*)

Lynda If you're bored, why don't you take a walk outside?

Philip What! And get myself . . . Oh, very funny!

Sharon No, you're right, Phil. It is boring. I was on washing-up yesterday and today I miss it. I never thought I'd miss washing-up.

Lynda It's not exactly the swinging scene, is it? No radio, no telly. Not even a book to read.

Philip (*Taking out a pack of cards*) We could have another game of pontoon.

Alan Oh, no! We played pontoon all last night.

Sharon And I lost all my money.

Philip What use is money now? Let's play for love.

Lynda Who wants your love?

Philip Just say the word and it's all yours, darling. (*Sings*) 'If you were the only girl in the world, And I were the only boy . . .'

(*There is some half-hearted laughter.*)

Alan It's nearly come to that, hasn't it though? I mean, just assume that nobody survives except us, then . . . Well, we'd have to start the English race all over again.

Sharon Hey, that's a thought, Alan. What do we do, draw names out of a hat?

Boyle Look, if you're so bored, and it is boring I know, we'll have to draw up some programme. Sharon's got her cassette. We could have a dance.

Sharon That won't last us long.

Boyle If you like, I could organise some lessons. (*There is a chorus of groans*) Well, discussion groups . . . or something.

John What do we discuss, world affairs?

Tracy 'Should there be universal world disarmament?' Bit late, isn't it?

Boyle You suggest something, then.

Lynda Let's settle for a game of cards. What about rummy?

Philip Come on, folks. Better than sitting around biting your fingernails.

(*There is a movement to the tables.*)

Mrs Burroughs   Sit at that one, will you? The doctor and Adam have to eat yet.

(*She indicates one of the tables and arranges cutlery on the other.*)

Philip   Eyes down for the big game.

John   Are you playing, Mr Boyle?

Boyle   I'll have a game later, maybe. You'll have to teach me again. It's a long time since I played.

Philip   (*In his 'posh' voice*)   He only plays bridge, you know.

Boyle   As a matter of fact I can play bridge. Our first lesson tomorrow will be 'Bridge for Beginners'.

(**Burroughs** *and* **Dr Ainsworth** *come in, having discarded their white suits.* **The doctor** *still carries his bag, which he leaves on the radio table.*)

Burroughs   Right. Bring on the food. I'm ravenous.

Mrs Burroughs   I'll go and get it, love. Sit down.

(*She goes out.* **Dr Ainsworth** *and* **Burroughs** *sit at the places set.*)

Boyle   How are things up top? You said the radiation was worse.

Burroughs   So it was. Much worse. Has to do with the wind direction, I think. We didn't get far.

Boyle   What kept you then?

Dr Ainsworth   My fault, Ted.

Burroughs   The Doc felt he had to carry his duties to the letter and check on the hospitals.

Boyle   And?

Dr Ainsworth   It's over. Finished. Those that aren't dead already are too sick to work. Everything is grinding rapidly to a halt. I suppose those who could get out have gone north. There were still a few people moving out in cars. Otherwise the road is clear.

(*The card game is halted as the players listen.*)

Boyle   Will any of them escape?

Burroughs   As long as the wind stays in the south there's not much hope for people round here. As fast as they move north the radiation is following in the wind.

(**Mrs Burroughs** *and* **Susan** *enter, each with a plate of food. They are followed by* **Terry** *and* **Gillian**. *All stand by the door and listen.*)

Dr Ainsworth If the wind changed, or it rained, there might be some hope in the short term. Not in the long run, though. Anyone subjected to massive radiation is going to die eventually.

Alan Then all our folks at home . . .

Dr Ainsworth I'm afraid you're all going to have to face the fact that you're not going to see your parents again. Nor any of your friends. Nor anything of the world you knew.

Tracy It doesn't seem possible.

John Not for everything to be finished.

Sharon (*Crying*) Everybody dying.

Philip And we're alive and kicking.

Lynda It doesn't seem fair.

Dr Ainsworth There's no need to feel guilty about it. You're the lucky ones. With more luck and patience you may survive. But it's going to be a long wait.

Alan What do you mean, a long wait?

Dr Ainsworth I mean you're going to have to live, or exist if you prefer in, in this shelter until it's safe to emerge.

Boyle And how long is that likely to be?

Dr Ainsworth I can't tell. But it'll be months rather than days. We have to wait for the winds to change, for the rains to come, for the earth and sky to be washed clean. And I don't know how long that will take.

Terry You mean we're going to have to spend months in this rabbit warren?

Dr Ainsworth That's the only way you'll survive.

Mrs Burroughs Now come on. You two won't survive unless you eat.

(*She and* **Susan** *bring the plates.* **Burroughs** *and* **Dr Ainsworth** *eat.*)

Terry How will we know when it's safe to leave?

Dr Ainsworth (*Between mouthfuls*) The geiger counter up top (*Gestures with his fork*) will tell us when it's safe here . . . For the rest we'll have to rely on other R.S.G.s . . . They'll report on their areas . . . assuming they're in operation.

Gillian And we go on living here for months.

Dr Ainsworth For as long as it takes, or the food lasts.

Boyle We're like those shipwrecked sailors, aren't we? So much food divided by x number of days. Only what is the value of x? How many days before that liner picks us up?

Dr Ainsworth There'll be no liner, Ted. We've got to make a landfall ourselves. We've got to assume we're on our own. Nobody to pick us up.

Susan (*Hesitantly*) Isn't there plenty of food . . . ?

Dr Ainsworth Where?

Susan Up there.

Dr Ainsworth No food up there is worth eating once it's been subjected to radiation.

Burroughs There's supposed to be food in there for twelve people for one year. That's what my inventory says. How many are we?

Mrs Burroughs There are thirteen of us.

Burroughs I hope nobody's superstitious. If you don't like eating thirteen to the table you'll have to get out.

Lynda I'm superstitious – but I'm staying all the same.

Boyle We've enough food for a year then – more or less.

Burroughs Unless anyone else turns up, and that's not likely now.

Dr Ainsworth If anyone else should turn up now, Adam, we'd have to turn him out.

Burroughs Why, Jim?

Dr Ainsworth Because we'd be harbouring a little package of radiation. A human body giving off lethal radiation until it died, and even after.

Alan So it's just us.

Dr Ainsworth That's it. Thirteen lucky people.

Sharon And we stay here for a year?

Dr Ainsworth Maybe.

Sharon What shall we do for a year?

Boyle We're going to have to exercise a lot of patience, Sharon.

Lynda It'll take all my patience to live with that one for a year.

(*She indicates* **Philip**.)

Philip You'll learn to love me, darling.

Lynda Huh!

Terry Hey, listen. There's somebody outside.

Burroughs In the passage?

Terry Yes.

(*All eyes focus on the door which opens to reveal the* **Third Boy**, **Tom**. *He can barely stand and is obviously very sick.*)

Boyle Tom! You made it.

Third Boy Just about.

Boyle (*Moving to him*) Are you all right?

Dr Ainsworth (*Savagely*) Don't touch him. Any of you.

Boyle We can't just . . .

Dr Ainsworth He's lethal! A leper! Get to your quarters. All of you. I'll deal with him.

(*They reluctantly move off to their respective dormitories.* **Terry** *and* **Gillian** *go back to the kitchen.*)

Go on. Quickly. You too, Mary. Adam, you can stay and give me a hand.

Boyle   I'll stay as well.

Dr Ainsworth   All right, if you must. It's your own risk.

Burroughs   What shall we do with him?

Dr Ainsworth   Decontamination first. Under the showers with him. Follow me . . . Tom, is it?

Third Boy   Yes. What's . . .

Dr Ainsworth   (*To* **Boyle** *who is moving to help*)   Leave him alone. Let him walk on his own. Come on, son.

(**Dr Ainsworth** *leads him off to the showers.* **Tom** *follows weakly.*)

Boyle   Can the Doc do anything?

Burroughs   I doubt it. Make it easier for him, no doubt.

Boyle   Sedate him you mean?

Burroughs   Put him out of his misery, more likely.

Boyle   You don't mean . . . kill him?

Burroughs   Let's call it euthanasia . . . it sounds better.

Boyle   But it's still murder.

Burroughs   See the Doc's little black bag there? That's just about all he's got in it. Mercy drugs, they're called. One pill is supposed to make you as drunk as a lord and then you gradually slip into a stupor . . . and you don't waken up. That's what's supposed to happen, but I don't expect anybody reported back on the effects.

Boyle Is there nothing else we can do?

Burroughs The lad's had two days of intense radiation. You heard what the Doc said earlier. We can't afford to harbour anyone like that.

(**Dr Ainsworth** *enters and picks up his bag.*)

Dr Ainsworth He's under the shower now. I've put his clothes in the disposal chute. Get something to cover him with, Adam.

Boyle (*Bitterly*) A winding sheet?

Dr Ainsworth (*Sadly*) It would be appropriate, Ted. There's nothing I can do for him. He should have stayed here with the rest of you.

Burroughs Did he find his parents?

Dr Ainsworth His mother, anyway. I gather he watched her die. He's not very coherent and he's vomiting most of the time.

Boyle What will you do?

Burroughs I've been telling him about your little pills, Jim.

Dr Ainsworth Oh, I see. There's nothing else to do, Ted, believe me. We have to think of all the others. It's not pleasant, but you don't have to watch. Adam and I will attend to it. We've had a little more time to think this thing through.

Boyle How bad is he?

Dr Ainsworth Very bad. It's a wonder he got back here. He'll be dead anyway inside twenty-four hours. We can't afford to wait that long.

Boyle How will you . . . bury him?

Dr Ainsworth Leave that to us, Ted.

(*He moves to the door.*)

Boyle No, I'll give you a hand.

Burroughs No need to, Ted. Doc and I can manage.

Boyle I think I'd better. He was my responsibility. Maybe I should have forced them all to stay. (*He follows* **Dr Ainsworth** *out.*)

Burroughs You tried to persuade him, Ted. You couldn't do any more.

(*He follows. The stage is empty for a moment, then* **Gillian** *and* **Terry** *come in, from the kitchen.*)

Gillian Nobody here.

Terry They'll be in the showers.

Gillian I suppose we ought to join the others, like the Doc ordered.

Terry (*Taking her hand*) Let's have a minute to ourselves. We don't get much opportunity. (*He pulls her to him*)

Gillian (*Resisting*) Not now, Terry. Somebody might come in. And it doesn't seem right with Tom . . . Do you think he'll be all right, Terry?

Terry No. He's dying. Didn't you see his face?

Gillian Sort of glazed look he had.

Terry He's bound to be dying if what the Doc said is true.

Gillian I wonder if he found his mum and dad.

Terry Can't have done or he'd have brought them back.

Gillian That means that our . . . Oh, Terry, I don't like to say it.

Terry (*Comforting her*) We've got to face it, love. We're not going to see them again, ever. It's just you and me now. They'd have been pleased about that, I'm sure.

Gillian My mum would. She always liked you, Terry.

Terry You know what Alan was talking about earlier, about starting the English race all over again.

Gillian Yes.

Terry Well, I know he was partly joking but . . . I'd like to think that we . . . well that we were two of the first . . .

Gillian Are you proposing to me, Terry Heslop?

Terry Sort of.

Gillian The answer's 'Yes'. (*She gives him a quick kiss*) Right, now you ought to join the other boys and I'd better get back to the girls. Heaven knows what they'll be saying behind my back.

(*She pushes him away and then goes to dormitory door, where she turns to blow him a kiss.*)

Bye, love. And thanks. I think you'll make a marvellous husband.

(*They both go out.*)

ACT 2

SCENE 1

Eight months later. The R.S.G. is much the same as in the previous scenes, apart from some rearrangement of furniture. There is a large map of the British Isles on the wall near the radio. It is marked with red flags to indicate highly radioactive areas. It is early morning. **Adam Burroughs** *sits at the radio-table writing in a log book and studying a large map. He is wearing a white overall-suit but not the helmet and gloves.*

> (**Mrs Burroughs** *comes in, wearing a dressing gown, and carrying a cup of tea.*)

Mrs Burroughs   I thought you'd like a cup of tea, Adam.

> (*She takes it to him.*)

Burroughs   Thanks, Mary. Have you got one for Ted? He's coming with me to do the labouring.

Mrs Burroughs   (*Concerned*)   You won't be long, will you, Adam?

Burroughs   Don't worry, love. It shouldn't take more than twenty minutes if everything goes O.K. Don't forget I'll be switching over to the batteries while we fix the generator so don't go using the cooker or any heaters. I don't want the batteries draining.

Mrs Burroughs   Right-o, love. I'll get Ted's tea.

> (*She goes out. There is a pause during which* **Burroughs** *continues writing.* **Ted** *comes in, wearing a white overall-suit, carrying the helmet.*)

Boyle   Ready, Adam.

Burroughs   (*Finishing writing*)   Good. We'll have a cup of tea and then go. Mary's just bringing yours. Anyone else stirring?

Boyle   Doc opened one eye and then went back to sleep. The others are all snoring. Except Terry. He wasn't in his bunk. Have you seen him?

Burroughs   No.

> (**Mrs Burroughs** *enters with* **Ted's** *cup of tea.*)

Mrs Burroughs   There you are, Ted. Here's your cup of tea. (*Giving it to him*)   Now take care of my husband, won't you. I'd be lost without him.

Boyle Wouldn't we all? I'm sure I wouldn't know how to fix hydro-electric generators when they grow temperamental.

Mrs Burroughs He works too hard. He's been up since the crack of dawn. Not that we ever see the dawn, but you know what I mean.

Burroughs She calls eight o'clock the crack of dawn. (*To* **Ted**) I had to get up a bit earlier. I'd arranged to contact the Welsh group at seven-thirty. Their survey figures are through. I've been plotting them on the map. Quite encouraging really. They're thinking of leaving the bunker when they've got themselves organised. The radiation seems to be down to an acceptable level over a wide area round Aberystwyth even with an east wind.

Boyle So we could join them.

Burroughs If we can find that way through. There's still a band of heavy radiation stretching from Liverpool to Sheffield and no way through that I can see, not without radiation suits for everyone, which we haven't got.

Boyle By sea?

Burroughs My navigational know-how wouldn't get me round a duck pond. How's yours?

Boyle About the same.

Mrs Burroughs I don't know why we don't settle for the Lake District. Join those two fellows at Lancaster.

Burroughs Simply because we've no radiation figures for the whole area. They both strike me as being too scared to venture out yet. After all, the radiation levels in Lancaster are every bit as encouraging as the Welsh. There doesn't seem any reason to expect anything but a further improvement up in the Lakes.

Boyle Why don't we survey it ourselves? We could be there in a couple of hours.

Mrs Burroughs Why don't we, Adam?

Burroughs The Welsh group is bigger – more of a community when we do settle down on top. Anyway, there's no immediate hurry. Nothing pushing us until the food gets short. If you've finished your tea, Ted, we'll be on our way.

(*They begin to put on their helmets.*)

Boyle Do we really need these? I feel like a kid playing at spacemen.

Burroughs We're probably safe enough. I do it to please Mary who thinks I'll drop down dead if I take a breath of fresh air.

Mrs Burroughs Fresh air, he says! I wonder if there's any left anywhere.

Boyle Oh, have you seen Terry, Mrs B.? He's not in his bunk.

Mrs Burroughs I haven't, love. Probably sneaked off to be alone with Gillian, though where they find to hide themselves in this hole I don't know.

Boyle I suspect he may have gone up top. They're all getting restless, Terry in particular.

Mrs Burroughs Well he has his reasons, hasn't he? Now off you go and look after Adam.

Boyle I will. See you soon.

(*Fastens his helmet and goes. As he goes out,* **Gillian** *enters. She walks heavily and is obviously very pregnant.*)

Gillian Good morning, Mrs B. Was that Terry?

Mrs Burroughs No, love. It was Ted. He's gone off to give Adam a hand with the generators. What made you think it might be Terry? Ted's just been enquiring after him – says he's not in his bunk.

Gillian (*Sitting*) I'm worried about him, Mrs B. I think he may have gone out again.

Mrs Burroughs Again?

Gillian He was out last week. I happened to say I fancied some tinned peaches and he sneaked off down to the village and brought me four tins.

Mrs Burroughs Did you eat them?

Gillian No. I think I was fancying bananas by the time he brought them. Anyway, I thought they might damage the baby. You know . . . if they were still – what do they say? – hot.

Mrs Burroughs (*Sitting*) And why do you suspect that Terry's out again?

Gillian I happened to say I could do with some proper smocks now that I'm getting so big. So Terry said he'd see to it. Well, I knew what he meant so I begged him not to go out again.

Mrs Burroughs And what did he say?

Gillian He said Mr Burroughs and the doctor were being far too cautious and it was safe enough for anybody to go out now and . . .

Mrs Burroughs And what?

Gillian Well, he said nobody had the right to keep us in if we wanted to leave. And he wasn't going to be treated like a kid in a schoolroom.

Mrs Burroughs He's not all that long out of the schoolroom, is he?

Gillian It's not like Terry to talk like that, Mrs B. He usually has plenty of common sense and he's usually very polite. It's just . . . well being a father . . . or nearly . . . he feels he ought to have me out of here. In some place where we'd have a proper home of our own. It's not easy being sort of married and living with a lot of other people.

Mrs Burroughs Well, my dear, Adam and I are 'sort of married' and we manage to live with all the rest of you.

Gillian It's different for you, you've . . . you've had all your young life together. You know what I mean.

Mrs Burroughs I know, love. All young couples should have a place of their own.

Gillian (*Tearful*) And Terry gets furious when some of the others make jokes about the baby. It's not our fault we can't get married, is it?

Mrs Burroughs Of course it isn't, love. Stop fretting about it.

(**Susan** *comes in with a towel.*)

Susan Morning, Mrs B. Where is everybody?

Mrs Burroughs Adam and Ted are doing something to the generator.

Susan Oh, yes. No breakfast till they've finished.

(*She goes into the bathroom. As she disappears,* **Philip** *enters heading in the same direction.*)

Mrs Burroughs You can't go in there, young man. Susan's getting washed.

Philip (*Sitting*) And I thought I was the early bird.

Lynda (*Coming in*) You're the worm.

(*She also goes into the bathroom.*)

Philip Why is everybody up and about so early? Mr Burroughs and Mr Boyle are up and so is Terry.

Mrs Burroughs Adam and Ted are working on the generator. And what's all this about Terry? Gillian thinks he may have gone outside.

Philip (*To* **Gillian**) Does Mrs B. know?

Gillian Yes. I told her. I was worried about Terry.

Mrs Burroughs Has he gone outside?

Philip I wouldn't be surprised. He was talking about it last night. Said he might sneak off to the village if he could wake up early. Something for Gill, I think.

Gillian I knew it. (*To* **Mrs Burroughs**) You don't have to tell the doctor and Mr Burroughs, do you? He might get into trouble. I mean, they wouldn't try to throw him out, would they?

Mrs Burroughs Of course they wouldn't. Not now. Adam's always telling me it's safe enough to go out without any protection. Only I make him put a suit on, to be on the safe side. I don't see any sense in taking risks until we have to. That's why Terry's being silly.

Philip Hey, Gill, do you remember Terry describing what it was like outside? Like a ghost town the village was, he said. Not a sound except some bits of paper blowing round in a corner and a door banging in the wind. And not a person in sight and not an animal. Just a few birds floating around. The silence, he said. You never heard anything like the silence.

(*There is a thoughtful pause and then a burst of pop music comes from the girls' dormitory. The volume increases as* **Sharon** *comes in with her cassette recorder and a towel.*)

Mrs Burroughs (*Shouting*) Turn it down, Sharon. (**Sharon** *obliges*) You'll wake everybody up. We don't want them all swarming out hungry for breakfast. It won't be ready for a while.

Sharon I'll turn if off then. (*She does*) Save the batteries.

Mrs Burroughs I thought the batteries were finished long ago.

Sharon Well they were, but Terry . . . Oh, I forgot.

Gillian Mrs B. knows about Terry going out.

Mrs Burroughs So he got batteries as well as tinned peaches. Quite the little forager, isn't he? Well, he's out foraging again by all accounts. I hope he doesn't bring back more batteries. I'd got used to the silence after the last lot gave out.

Sharon Don't you like pop, Mrs B.?

Mrs Burroughs I can live without it, love.

Philip There won't be any more pop now, will there?

Sharon 'Course there will. There are plenty of tapes and records around, just waiting to be picked up.

Philip Yes, but there won't be anything new, will there? It'll all be old. We'll have heard it all before.

Sharon We'll have to make our own. How are you on the guitar, Philip?

Philip Rotten. But I can swing my hips. (*He does so*) Hey, I can play the mouth-organ.

Gillian You'll have to practise, Phil.

Mrs Burroughs Wait till we get outside, Philip.

(**Alan** and **John** *come in.*)

Alan Did I hear pop?

Sharon Oh, here's the professor. He's like you, Mrs B., he prefers classical music.

Mrs Burroughs Oh, I don't like classical music, love. I like the oldies.

Philip Join the queue, you two. The bathroom's occupied by the ladies.

Sharon Is it? Oh, good. I'll go in. (*She goes out.*)

Gillian (*Rising*) I may as well use the bathroom now. Then I'm not holding up the queue.

John Is Tracy up yet?

Gillian Not yet. Shall I call her?

John I'll get her out. (*He crosses the room as* **Gillian** *goes out.*)

John (*Shouting through the partly-open door*) Come on, Tracy. Wakey, wakey. Rise and shine, the morning's fine. The sun's scorching your eyes out.

(**Dr Ainsworth** *enters.*)

Dr Ainsworth Where on earth did you learn that, John?

John That's the way my dad used to get me up for school. I used to bury my head under the bedclothes and curse him. Still . . . I wouldn't mind . . . you know, hearing it again.

(**Tracy** *comes in with a towel and crosses towards the bathroom.*)

Tracy (*To* **John**) What's all the rush? I've been up for hours. How could anybody sleep through all this racket?

(**Tracy** *goes into the bathroom.* **Susan** *and* **Lynda** *come in.*)

Lynda (*Sweetly*) Still waiting, Philip, dear?

Philip For you, darling, I'll wait for ever.

Lynda You may have to.

(*She crosses to the dormitory.*)

Susan Have they finished with the generators yet, Mrs B.?

Mrs Burroughs Not yet, love, but they shouldn't be long. Let's go and make a start.

(**Mrs Burroughs** *and* **Susan** *go into the kitchen.*)

Alan Who won't be long?

Philip Mr Burroughs and Mr Boyle. They've gone outside to fix the generator.

Dr Ainsworth We're all present or accounted for, except Terry. Where is he? I heard him stirring ages ago.

(*There is a pause.*)

Alan Don't you ever sleep, Doctor?

Dr Ainsworth At my age, Alan, I sleep lightly. And I notice things . . . like changes in the atmosphere. What's the mystery?

John I haven't seen him.

Dr Ainsworth Has he gone up top?

Alan We don't really know.

Philip You may as well tell the doctor. Mrs B.'s found out and she didn't throw a fit.

Alan He did speak of going down to the village.

Philip And it's pretty certain he has.

Dr Ainsworth Well, I don't suppose it's the end of the world at this stage. He's not going to come to much harm, providing he doesn't stay too long.

Alan He doesn't spend too long. Last time he was only . . .

Dr Ainsworth Last time? You mean he's been out before?

Alan Yes.

Dr Ainsworth How often?

John Just once. About a week ago.

(**Gillian**, **Sharon** and **Tracy** *enter, and cross to the dormitory.*)

Tracy All right, Philip, it's your turn now.

Dr Ainsworth You boys go in. I can wait.

(**Alan**, **John** and **Philip** *go into the bathroom. There is a pause while* **Dr Ainsworth** *studies the map.* **Mrs Burroughs** *comes in and begins to lay the tables for breakfast.*)

Mrs Burroughs Good morning, Jim. You must have slept well. You're last up.

Dr Ainsworth I never sleep well, Mary. I simply sleep enough for a man of my age. I've been aware of people creeping out of that dormitory ever since young Terry sneaked off and that must have been six o'clock.

Mrs Burroughs You've heard then?

Dr Ainsworth I gather he's off down the village again. Here, let me help you.

(*He begins to set cutlery on the tables.*)

Mrs Burroughs You don't think it's important?

Dr Ainsworth I'm surprised it hasn't happened before.

Mrs Burroughs And you don't think it will have harmed Terry?

Dr Ainsworth We've all got to go up top sometime, Mary. And soon. We shall have to live with the danger of radiation blowing in on adverse winds. God knows what physical effect it will have on us in the long run. All that depends on luck, where we settle, where the winds blow, how much it rains, how quickly the radiation dies.

Mrs Burroughs You're not very optimistic, Jim.

Dr Ainsworth I've no reason to be, Mary. It's touch and go for the human race. You and I, Mary, we're not going to live as long as we hoped. And these youngsters, I doubt if they'll reach their three-score years and ten. But the next generation, Gillian's baby, they may attain something like normality, unless . . .

Mrs Burroughs Well?

Dr Ainsworth I was just going to say, unless there's some imponderable, something that hasn't been observed or considered about radiation. Something that alters the genes, causes mutation, kills us off maybe. We don't know, Mary.

Mrs Burroughs Oh, Jim! Change the subject. Try to think of something cheerful.

Dr Ainsworth You asked for my considered opinion, Mary.

(**Adam** and **Ted** *come in, removing their helmets.*)

Mrs Burroughs Adam, you're back.

Burroughs You weren't expecting anyone else were you, Mary?

Mrs Burroughs Of course not, except . . .

Burroughs Except who?

Dr Ainsworth She probably means young Terry. He's apparently taken a trip to the village.

Mrs Burroughs But he's not going to come to any harm. Jim admits as much. So we're not going to have a scene, are we Adam?

Burroughs Haven't I been telling you for weeks, Mary, that it's safe to go out for short periods without a suit? Now she tells me. And here we've been sweating over that generator in these heavy suits! Women!

Mrs Burroughs Can we start breakfast?

Boyle Any time you like, Mrs B.

(**Mrs Burroughs** *goes into the kitchen.*)

Burroughs It seems a pointless exercise, Ted, but we may as well get under the showers. (*To* **Dr Ainsworth**) Is there anyone in there?

Dr Ainsworth Some of the boys. They shouldn't be long.

Burroughs As a matter of interest, Jim, just pass the geiger counter over us.

Dr Ainsworth I'll get it. It's in my bag.

(*He goes into the dormitory.*)

Boyle Do you think we're clean, Adam?

Burroughs The readings on the surface geiger counter suggest we ought to be. I'd just like to make sure. We need to be as near 100 per cent sure as possible, before we make a dash for Wales or the Lakes.

(**Dr Ainsworth** *returns with his medical bag which he places on the radio table. He takes from it a small geiger counter which he passes over* **Burroughs** *and* **Boyle**.)

Dr Ainsworth Are you thinking of making a dash for it, Adam?

Burroughs I was on to the Welsh group this morning, Jim. Their surveys show that the area's habitable. Question is, how do we get there? It would have to be by sea because of the intense radiation belt. Mary's pressing for the Lake District. Taking a chance on it's being clear.

Dr Ainsworth Well, you two seem to be clear. (*He replaces the geiger counter in his bag*) I don't see any sense in showering off. Dump your gear and we'll have some breakfast.

(**John** *and* **Alan** *enter.*)

John Did I hear breakfast?

Dr Ainsworth Shouldn't be long. Especially if you two give a hand in the kitchen.

John (*Crossing*) I don't see why we have to do the housework with all these girls around.

Alan (*Also crossing*)   It's the new world, John. Get used to it.

Boyle   Let's get out of these suits. They're too hot.

   (*He goes out.*)

Burroughs   I'm with you there, Ted. I lose pounds in one of these.

   (*He follows.*)

Dr Ainsworth   I may as well join you. I haven't washed yet.

   (*He also follows.* **Alan** *and* **John** *return with cups, bread and butter, etc. and complete laying the table.*)

John   Time Terry was back. He said he'd be back before anyone was stirring.

Alan   I hope nothing's happened to him.

John   What could?

Alan   Nothing I suppose, except an accident and that's not likely.

John   Do you think he'll have had it when Adam sees him?

Alan   No. Doc Ainsworth took it calmly enough.

   (**Lynda** *comes in and goes to sit at the table.*)

Lynda   Breakfast?

Alan   Workers first.

Lynda   I worked yesterday. Who do you think baked that bread?

Alan   You didn't!

John   She did. I saw her.

   (**Sharon** *and* **Tracy** *come in and move to sit at the tables.*)

Lynda   I thought I'd better learn how it's done.

Sharon   I'm going to start.

   (*She takes a piece of bread and begins to eat it.*)

Lynda   What's it like?

Sharon   Fine. Susan couldn't have done better.

Tracy   (*Taking a piece*)   I'll join you.

   (**Burroughs**, **Boyle** *and* **Dr Ainsworth** *stroll in.* **Boyle** *goes to the table.* **Dr Ainsworth** *and* **Burroughs** *linger by the map.*)

Boyle   Have we started?

Alan Some of the pigs couldn't wait to get to the trough.

Sharon Charming!

Boyle (*Taking bread*) I'll join the pigs. I'm hungry.

(*The door bursts open and* **Terry** *is precipitated into the room at gunpoint by the* **Colonel. Two soldiers** *deploy to right and left. There is an 'alien' look about the intruders and their menace is immediate and overpowering. Their features are European in cast, but Mongoloid in colouring. The combat uniforms and 'crash' helmets might indicate spacemen, or air-crew, or perhaps riot police. Their guns have a technologically advanced appearance. There are exclamations of surprise and screams from the assembled group.* **Mrs Burroughs** *and* **Susan** *appear at the kitchen door.*)

Colonel (*In accented but correct English*) This bunker is under military law. I formally take possession of it in the name of the Federation.

SCENE 2

Half-an-hour later. The **Colonel** *is finishing his meal at the head of one of the tables. Most of the company have finished breakfast and are sitting away from the tables. One* **soldier** *still eats, the other* **soldier** *stands guard at the door.*

Colonel That was very good. Now, all I need is a cigarette and a good long sleep. (*He stretches and yawns*)

Philip It's only half-past nine.

Colonel We have been on duty for several days, boy, and will sleep when we can. (*To the company at large*) Cigarettes? No?

Burroughs (*Shortly*) No. We don't smoke because of the air supply. And anyway the cigarettes up top will be contaminated.

Colonel I think not, Mr . . . er . . .

Burroughs Burroughs.

Colonel Mr Burroughs. I cannot believe that our bombs would contaminate your supplies to that extent. That young man (*Pointing to* **Terry**) was wandering around in the open air, yet large areas of my homeland are a radioactive desert.

Burroughs And so are large areas of Britain. We happen to be lucky, as I presume you were.

Colonel We were lucky, but not, I think, as lucky as you.

(**Burroughs** *has risen and wandered over to the radio.*)

Colonel Mr Burroughs, you would not, I hope, be so foolish as to try to use that radio.

Burroughs No.

Colonel I was going to explain to you, Mr Burroughs, to all of you, why you are to be considered lucky.

Terry (*Sitting apart with* **Gillian**) Our luck's just turned. If I hadn't been down the village, you might not have caught us.

Colonel You are mistaken, young man. We knew exactly where you were. Also the location of other groups. We have monitored your radio transmissions for many months. So you must not blame yourself. You forgot that we are still at war, a war of unprovoked aggression against the Federation.

Boyle We don't know who started it. We're unimportant civilians who happened to survive. For all we know, you may have started it. It –

Colonel That is impossible.

Dr Ainsworth It's history anyway. Let's get back to the present. Mr Boyle has just said that we're unimportant civilians, and so we are. Why should you people be interested in us?

Colonel A good question, sir. And one that I was coming to when I spoke of your luck.

Burroughs And why are we so lucky, apart from surviving?

Colonel Because, Mr Burroughs, (*He spreads his hands*) you have women.

Mrs Burroughs Women!

Colonel Exactly, Madame. You have five young women, all capable of bearing children.

Mrs Burroughs But they're only girls. Schoolchildren.

Colonel (*Indicating* **Gillian**) I observe that English schoolchildren are capable of bearing children.

Burroughs Good God, man! You mean you've come all this way for the girls?

Colonel Precisely.

(*Consternation in the company.*)

Dr Ainsworth And you mean to take them?

Colonel Exactly.

Boyle But you can't. It's . . . it's inhuman. It's against international law. As civilians we have rights.

Colonel It is the fortune of war, my friend. If you wish to protest, you can take your case to the International Court . . . if you can find it.

Burroughs Have you no women of your own?

Colonel Unfortunately not, Mr Burroughs. Not of a suitable age. No doubt there are some areas where women survive, but we are not in contact with them. And you will understand that it would be impossible for us to search a large country. We prefer to take from our enemies.

Terry You're not taking them. We won't let you.

Colonel (*Patting his gun*) You have no option, young man. As I said, it is the fortune of war. We have the guns. We give the orders.

Terry (*Starting up*) I won't let you take Gillian. She's mine.

Colonel Ah! The anxious father, hey? You do not need to fear for her safety or her comfort. Your five girls here will be the future mothers of our citizens and as such will be honoured.

Lynda But we're English. We're not like you at all.

Colonel Your children will be like us. That is enough.

Terry (*Advancing*) Gillian's baby is English and that's the way it stays.

Colonel (*Drawing his gun*) Do not advance any further, or I may be obliged to shoot you.

Gillian (*In panic*) Do as he says, Terry. Please.

(**Terry** *allows himself to be pulled back to his seat.*)

Colonel I am glad you are being reasonable.

Burroughs There's no reason in this situation. You can't uproot children from their country and use them as brood mares. Have you no feelings, man?

Colonel I have a feeling for my homeland, Mr Burroughs. I wish to see it recover from the devastation caused by the powers that are hostile to us. I wish to see it great again. I wish to see it as a universal guiding force. As the only guiding force.

Burroughs And the rest of the world can go hang?

Colonel The rest of you can die out, Mr Burroughs. We have no desire to harm you.

Dr Ainsworth And, of course, we will die out without young women, won't we?

Colonel Exactly.

Dr Ainsworth And you have other raids planned on other groups?

Colonel You are the first. There are only a few others with suitable women. When we have visited them we shall leave you all in peace.

Mrs Burroughs To die.

Colonel It is the fate of all of us to die sometime, Madame.

Boyle It's a crazy plain, this idea of dominating the world. Do you think you can capture every woman in England, let alone the world?

Colonel We do not expect 100 per cent success. But the Federation will be the dominant power. It is historically inevitable.

Burroughs   Man, you're mad to think of power politics in a world catastrophe like this.

Colonel   (*Coldly*)   We are not mad, Mr Burroughs. We see the situation clearly. We intend to see that what emerges is a society to our liking.   (*Rising*)   And now, if you will excuse me, we must rest. The soldier here will remain on guard for one hour. Then he will be relieved for one hour. At the end of that time the young women must be ready to leave. Our helicopter is a large one, but as there will be other passengers there will be no room for baggage, only small items of a personal nature. Everything necessary will be provided for them in their new home.   (*To* **Burroughs**)   Do not be so foolish as to attempt an attack on the sentry. He has orders to shoot at the least threatening move. Be sensible and you will come to no harm.   (*To the* **Sergeant** *who is still eating*)   Turmi, ze soluti. [*Come, we will sleep.*]   (*To the* **Sentry**)   Pre dolantor.   [*Be vigilant.*]

(*He moves to the dormitory door followed by the* **Sergeant**.)

You have two hours, remember, to say your goodbyes.

(*He and the* **Sergeant** *exit. There is a pause. When the dialogue begins again it has a muted quality.*)

Terry What are we going to do? We can't let them get away with this.

Burroughs For the moment, we do nothing. Just sit and chat, or put in some hard thinking.

Boyle We could rush that sentry. He couldn't get everybody.

Burroughs We don't want any shooting. We don't want any unusual noise at all. It would bring out the other two and we'd be trapped. Just keep talking normally, about anything at all. We've got to keep things natural. Let the two in there get to sleep.

Lynda Talk naturally! When I'm about to be married off to one of those things!

Philip You prefer me, darling?

Lynda You know, I think I do.

Philip Victory!

Boyle Keep your voice down, Philip.

Philip Sorry.

Alan You were right, Mr Burroughs, when you said this fellow was mad. Whoever heard of conquering the world by capturing all the women?

Burroughs It's a new line in conquest, certainly.

Dr Ainsworth It's a load of fanatical eyewash. He couldn't possibly hope to capture all the women in Europe, let alone America and the rest of the world. This is just the Sabine Women all over again.

Tracy Who were they, Doctor Ainsworth?

Dr Ainsworth A group of women from way back who were in your position, Tracy.

Sharon Did they get out of it, Doc?

Dr Ainsworth I'm afraid not, Sharon. But we'll do our best for you.

Boyle It's a reversion to the primitive, isn't it? This notion of one tribe making off with the women of another tribe.

Dr Ainsworth That's the way I see it, Ted. I think this Colonel is in command of a group of men who haven't seen a woman for eight months. So he goes off raiding the first likely group he hears of.

Then he disguises what he's doing by calling it 'a blow for the Federation' or some such nonsense.

Burroughs   Maybe you're right, Jim. But the result's the same to us whether he's sincere or not.

John   Do you think there was any truth in what he was saying? About us starting the war?

Burroughs   We're never likely to know, John. Not for sure. You can be pretty sure that the whole damnable business was an accident or the work of a madman.

Dr Ainsworth   We've been on a knife-edge since Hiroshima, Adam. I always thought it was bound to happen sometime. I just hoped it wouldn't be in my lifetime.

John   If you thought that, why didn't you do something about it?

Alan   After all it's you older ones who got us into this mess.

Burroughs   We older ones as you call us, Alan, hadn't any say in the matter. Oh, we could vote at election-time and some people demonstrated pretty vigorously. My own son, when he was a student, spent half his time marching up and down with anti-Bomb posters. But it didn't affect the governments. They just went on building bigger bombs and better means of delivery. And the protesters got discouraged and the war-scares fewer, and people, and maybe governments too, swept the whole messy business under the mat and tried to forget about it.

Mrs Burroughs   Let's get back to the present, Adam. What are we going to do?

Burroughs   We can talk now, I hope. They should be dozing off and I don't imagine that sentry has any idea what we're saying. He hasn't shown the least flicker of interest. Has anybody any ideas? Apart from rushing him, because that's out.

Boyle   Where's your gun?

Burroughs   It's back in that drawer under the radio, but we can't start a shooting match. And I'm not so sure I could even hit him.

Terry   Couldn't we distract him somehow and take him from behind?

Dr Ainsworth   It needs to be quieter than that. I know what would do it if we could work the trick.

Burroughs   What?

Dr Ainsworth   One of my special pills. He'd just go drowsy, feel on top of the world and quietly die. Question is, how do we get him to take one?

Mrs Burroughs We could make a cup of tea and give him one. Will it dissolve in tea, Jim?

Dr Ainsworth Yes, they're soluble.

Susan Suppose he doesn't like tea?

Mrs Burroughs He drank it at breakfast. They all did.

Tracy What if he's not thirsty?

Terry We've got to try it.

Boyle He may not let us out of his sight to make the tea.

Burroughs Try clearing the table, Mary. See if he objects to that. One of you girls give her a hand. He may let women out, but not the men.

(**Mrs Burroughs** *begins clearing the table.*)

Tracy I'll give you a hand, Mrs B. I'll be glad to get out of sight of his gun.

(*She begins to help. The sentry eyes them watchfully, but makes no attempt to stop them.*)

Dr Ainsworth I have to get my bag.

Burroughs You'd better wait till the table's cleared. That fellow might be suspicious of too much movement.

Dr Ainsworth Yes, but he's suffering somewhat from fatigue, I think. That should help to dull his senses.

Boyle How are we going to get the tablet in his cup?

Dr Ainsworth Leave that to me. I'll pretend to take a headache tablet, but it really goes into a special cup. (*To* **Mrs Burroughs**, *who has returned*) Leave one cup with a spoon in it, Mary. Everybody clear on that? You leave the cup with the spoon strictly alone. See that Tracy knows, Mary. We hand them round, then give him one as an afterthought. If he sees us drinking he shouldn't be suspicious.

Mrs Burroughs I'll hand them round, including the sentry's.

Burroughs Mary, I think it would . . .

Mrs Burroughs No, Adam. It's safer if I do it. As you said, he'll be less suspicious of a woman.

Dr Ainsworth She's right, Adam. If *you* don't mind, Mary?

Mrs Burroughs No, Jim. I'll do it. (*She returns to the kitchen*)

Burroughs I don't like it, Jim. I'd rather it was you or me.

Dr Ainsworth It makes sense, Adam. We can't afford to fail. (*To the company*) I'm going to my bag now. I don't want anybody watching me. Talk naturally, even if it's nonsense. But keep talking.

(*He begins to move to the radio-table.*)

Susan I never could talk when I had to. Never knew what to say.

Sharon I know what you mean. Like having to stand up in class and give a speech.

Lynda Making speeches never bothered me.

Philip You never have been short of something to say, have you, Lynda?

Lynda I could always find the right words for somebody like you, mate.

(*During the dialogue* **Dr Ainsworth** *has reached his bag, opened it and produced a phial of white tablets. The* **Sentry** *follows his movements with his gun suspiciously.* **Dr Ainsworth** *looks up to see the pointed gun and reacts with mock astonishment, pointing to the tablets and then to his head.*)

Dr Ainsworth Tablets. Headache.

(*The* **Sentry** *relaxes as* **Dr Ainsworth** *moves away from his bag.*)

Burroughs Keep talking, if only about the weather.

John We haven't seen much of that recently, have we?

Gillian (*Nervously*) How was it up top, Terry? Was it raining, cold? What?

Terry The sun was shining. It was a warm, spring day. The trees were in bud, so there's life still going on.

(**Dr Ainsworth** *has moved back to the group and has shaken out a tablet from the bottle and placed it on the table. The bottle goes into his pocket.*)

Dr Ainsworth There's the pill. On the table. Don't look at it. Just leave it to me. For God's sake don't take the cup with the spoon in it.

(**Mrs Burroughs** *and* **Tracy** *come in with a tray of cups with the tea ready poured. One cup has the spoon in it. The tray is placed on the table near* **Dr Ainsworth**.)

Dr Ainsworth Oh, good. The tea. Now I can have my tablet.

(*He quickly drops the tablet into the cup with the spoon and stirs vigorously. He then takes another cup and mimes taking a tablet. People near the tray take cups. The remaining cups are handed round by* **Mrs Burroughs**.)

Burroughs If you can't drink without your hand shaking, leave it for the moment. Those who can drink look as if you're enjoying it.

Sharon My mouth's dry with excitement. I need a drink.

Alan It's nerve-racking. Has he taken a cup?

Terry Not yet.

Dr Ainsworth Keep your eyes on your own cup or on somebody else. And keep the talk going.

Gillian I hope it works. I want to get out of here, fast.

Terry How are we going to travel, Mr Burroughs? And where to?

Burroughs We'll use your old school minibus. It's still where Tom parked it that night he came back.

Alan Will it go?

Burroughs I've checked it a couple of times. Last time about a week ago. The engine's O.K.

John I hope it starts. We can't afford to waste time fiddling with an engine.

Burroughs It's a bit low on petrol, but there's enough to get us clear.

Tracy What happens if it doesn't start?

Burroughs We start walking. North. Till we pick up some other transport.

Mrs Burroughs (*To the* **soldier**) Tea? A cup of tea?

Soldier Prosiva. [*Thank you.*]

Mrs Burroughs (*With the spoon poised over the sugar bowl*) Sugar?

Soldier Nova. [*No.*]

> (*He takes the cup with his left hand, keeping a wary eye on the others. He then sits on the top step, his gun resting across his knee, and drinks.* **Mrs Burroughs** *sits.*)

Burroughs If we're forced to walk, we keep off the roads for a while. Keep to the hedges and the trees. Use what cover there is, in case that helicopter of theirs gets airborne.

Terry And if the bus works, where do we head for?

Burroughs The Lakes. In case there's any slip-up and we have to separate, we'd better make a rendezvous. Let's say Windermere. The landing stage at Bowness. That clear, everybody? The Bowness landing stage on Windermere.

Philip What's happening? I'm dying to look round.

Mrs Burroughs Nothing yet. He's taking his time.

Burroughs Where exactly is he, Mary?

Mrs Burroughs Sitting on the top step.

Dr Ainsworth If he falls down the steps there's bound to be some noise. We'd better be ready to catch him.

Burroughs Warn us, Mary, as soon as he begins to keel over.

Boyle How long does the pill take, Doc?

Dr Ainsworth Supposed to be about a minute, but he's taking his time drinking it.

Mrs Burroughs He's drinking it off now. Shall I take the cup from him?

Burroughs See if he puts if down first.

Mrs Burroughs Yes, he has. He's put it on the step.

Lynda This waiting! I feel like screaming.

Boyle Keep control of yourself, Lynda. Everything depends on our keeping things normal.

Mrs Burroughs It's beginning to take effect, I think. His head's nodding.

Burroughs Keep perfectly still everyone. Ted, you and I will go for him when Mary gives the word.

Mrs Burroughs (*Urgently*) Now. He's sliding down.

(**Burroughs** and **Boyle** *move swiftly to the steps and control the sliding body.* **Boyle** *grabs the gun. They ease the body clear of the steps.*)

Boyle I hope I know how to work this thing. (*He covers the dormitory door.*)

Burroughs Girls first. Quietly. Mary, you take them to the bus. Can one of you boys start the engine?

Terry I can.

Burroughs You take Gillian, Terry, and get the bus started. Don't use too much choke.

(*The girls and* **Terry** *are moving out quietly, shepherded by* **Mrs Burroughs**.)

The boys follow when the steps are clear. Keep it quiet.

(**Burroughs** *goes to the drawer of the radio table and takes out the revolver seen in Act One.*)

Dr Ainsworth (*Moving to the radio table*) I'd better have my bag.

Burroughs You see the boys out, Jim. Ted and I will wait until you've had time to get to the bus. If we don't appear in what seems to you a reasonable time, move off.

Dr Ainsworth Without you?

Burroughs If necessary. Get moving, Jim.

(**Dr Ainsworth** *follows the boys out.* **Burroughs** *and* **Boyle** *are left covering the door.*)

Boyle It sounds like a herd of elephants tramping out.

Burroughs Not really. Just seems that way.

Boyle I hope that bus starts. It was never noted for its reliability.

Burroughs If it gets us clear of the district, that's all we need. We can always hole up somewhere and move on when the coast's clear.

Boyle I see you've got your old gun. Remember when we had our little disagreement?

Burroughs Yes. I'm glad you all stayed, Ted. It's made the whole exercise seem worthwhile. Having the youngsters to look after and so on. I don't know about you, but it gave me a stake in the future.

Boyle I know what you mean, Adam.

Burroughs Of course, you're still young, Ted. It's your future as well.

Boyle Not a very bright one. Still, better than having no future at all.

Burroughs That's the way it would have been without the girls. (*There is a slight pause*) I think that's enough, Ted. We'll move out. You go first.

(**Boyle** *crosses to the steps and exits cautiously, followed by* **Burroughs**. *There is a long pause. The dormitory door opens and the* **Colonel** *enters. The emptiness of the room shocks him into wakefulness. He sees the* **soldier's** *body, draws his gun and crosses to the steps. He checks the man's heart, then goes swiftly back to the door, shouting through it.*)

Colonel Saporela! Turmi fedaste! [*Sergeant! Come quickly!*]

(*He throws open the other doors and takes a hasty look inside. The* **Sergeant** *runs in.*)

Che vegati. Ulmar rateba. Turmi. [*They have escaped. Ulmar is dead. Follow me.*]

(*He rushes out, followed by the* **Sergeant**.)

ACT 3

SCENE 1

An hour later. A hill-top. One corner of a bungalow is visible. The open door and damaged windows suggest that it is derelict. The roses climbing the trellis around the door are beginning to show leaves, but are not yet in flower. Two rustic benches stand in the garden, flanking the path. Two tubs, with shrubs, stand one on each side of the door. Upstage, steps lead to an entrance to another part of the garden, bordered by green hedging. Beyond the hedge is a stunted apple tree.

At the rise of the curtain the stage is empty. Voices are heard off.

Dr Ainsworth (*Off*) It's as good a place as we're likely to find.

Gillian (*Off*) I'm sorry to be such a trouble.

Dr Ainsworth (*Off*) It's no trouble, my dear. I'm used to it . . . or I was.

(**Dr Ainsworth** *enters followed by* **Gillian** *who is supported by* **Terry**. *She is in the first stages of labour.* **Terry** *leads her to the first bench where they both sit, holding hands.*)

Dr Ainsworth   Bring her over here, Terry and let her sit down.

Gillian   I'm sorry, Doc.

Terry   Don't keep apologising, love. It's not your fault.

Dr Ainsworth   No, it's that baby. The excitement must have been too much for him.

Gillian   Her. It's going to be a girl.

Dr Ainsworth   Him or her. It's a queer world to be born into.

(**Mrs Burroughs** *enters, followed by the girls.*)

Mary, I'm going to take a look inside. If it's clear, I want you and the girls to get a bed ready. Get a fire going too. We'll need some hot water.

Mrs Burroughs   When you're ready, Jim.

(**Dr Ainsworth** *goes into the house.*)

Sharon   What does he mean 'If it's clear'?

Mrs Burroughs   The previous owners may still be there, Sharon.

Sharon   Oh! You mean . . . dead?

Mrs Burroughs   They're not likely to be alive after all this.

Lynda   It's gruesome, isn't it?

Tracy It'll be like this wherever we go, won't it? Dead bodies all over the place. Skeletons!

Terry For God's sake, talk about something more cheerful. You'll upset Gill.

Tracy Sorry, Gill.

Gillian That's all right, Tracy. It doesn't upset me. I've other things on my mind.

Mrs Burroughs That's right, love. You concentrate on essentials. We'll soon have you into bed.

(**Dr Ainsworth** *appears at the door.*)

Dr Ainsworth You can come in, Mary. There's nothing to bother us here.

Mrs Burroughs (*Crossing*) I expect they left in a hurry.

Dr Ainsworth You're right. They didn't have time to wash the pots.

Mrs Burroughs Come on, girls. Let's get busy.

(*The girls, except* **Gillian**, *follow* **Mrs Burroughs** *into the house.*)

Dr Ainsworth You all right, Gillian? No more pains?

Gillian I haven't had a pain since we stopped.

Dr Ainsworth If you need me, send Terry.

(**Burroughs** *comes on followed by* **John** *and* **Philip**.)

Burroughs Will the house do, Jim?

Dr Ainsworth Couldn't be better, Adam. No mess to clear up. They seem to have had central heating, but there's one open fireplace. We'll need wood though. You lads collect some, will you? Anything that will burn. Fencing might be easiest. There's a shed at the back. Break that up if you can't find anything else.

Philip Come on, the demolition men.

(**Philip** *marches up the steps into the upper garden, followed by* **John**.)

Burroughs Do you need any help inside, Jim? I'm willing, but not very skilled, if you know what I mean.

Dr Ainsworth I don't need an engineer to help me deliver a baby, Adam. Have you nothing else to keep you busy?

Burroughs No. Ted and Alan are filling up with petrol. We managed to open up the tanks and found a semi-rotary pump. They can cope on their own.

Dr Ainsworth You'd better just sit it out then, Adam. I'll go and see how Mary and the girls are coping.

(*He goes into the house.* **Burroughs** *sits in the empty rustic seat.*)

Gillian Mr Burroughs.

Burroughs Um?

Gillian You're sort of . . . in charge of us all, aren't you?

Burroughs You could say that, Gillian. Though at the moment I think Dr Ainsworth is more the Captain of the ship than I am.

Terry Yes, but up to now you've been the boss, like Noah in the Ark.

Burroughs Quite an appropriate comparison, Terry. Adam's Ark, eh?

Gillian Well, we were wondering . . .

(*She is interrupted by* **John** *and* **Philip** *returning with wood for the fire.*)

Philip Make way for the woodcutters.

John Let's start on the shed. It'll be quicker than looking for dead stuff.

(*They go into the house.*)

Burroughs You were saying, Gillian?

Gillian Terry and I were wondering if you could . . . well . . . marry us.

Burroughs Marry you! I hardly think I'm qualified to . . .

Terry But you are really. Like the captain of a ship. You've power to do anything you want.

Burroughs I wouldn't know the words.

Gillian Just make them up, Mr Burroughs.

(**Mrs Burroughs** *appears at the door.*)

Mrs Burroughs We're ready if you are, Gillian.

Gillian Not just yet, Mrs B.

Mrs Burroughs Twenty minutes ago, you couldn't wait.

Burroughs These two young people have decided they want to be married, Mary. And they want me to perform the ceremony.

Mrs Burroughs Well . . . all I can say is . . . you've left it rather late.

Gillian We never thought of it before, Mrs B.

Terry And we wanted everything to be . . . well . . . legal.

Mrs Burroughs Do you remember the words, Adam?

Gillian He's going to make them up.

Mrs Burroughs Shall I call the others? We haven't much of a congregation.

Gillian I'd rather it was . . . quiet.

Burroughs (*Approaching them*) Well, I'll do my best. Can you stand, Gillian? Or shall I marry you sitting down?

Gillian I'll stand.

(*She struggles to her feet, helped by* **Terry**, *but has a spasm of pain.*)

Terry Are you sure you're all right, love?

Gillian Yes, I think so. It won't take long will it, Mr Burroughs?

Burroughs It'll be the shortest wedding on record, Gillian. Are you ready?

(**Gillian** *nods assent.*)

Do you, Terry, take Gillian to be your lawful wife?

Terry I do.

Burroughs Do you, Gillian, take Terry to be your lawful husband?

Gillian I do.

Burroughs By whatever power God or the Fates have granted me, I pronounce you man and wife.

(**Terry** *shyly kisses* **Gillian**. **Mrs Burroughs** *kisses them both.*)

Mrs Burroughs God bless you. Both of you. I hope you'll be very happy, in spite of everything.

(**Burroughs** *shakes* **Terry's** *hand and kisses* **Gillian**.)

Burroughs Well, it may not read like that in the book, but it's as legal as I can make it. I hope the baby brings you much happiness.

Mrs Burroughs The baby! Come on, Gillian. It's time we had you in bed.

(*She begins to lead* **Gillian** *off,* **Terry** *following.*)

You stay here, young man. This is women's business.

Terry I'd rather come in, Mrs B.

Mrs Burroughs We'll see what the doctor says. Come on then.

(**Gillian**, **Terry** *and* **Mrs Burroughs** *go into the house. There is a slight pause while* **Burroughs** *sits meditatively on the seat.* **Boyle** *and* **Alan** *come on.*)

Boyle   We've topped up the old bus. Filled some spare cans as well.

Burroughs   Good.

Alan   Where is everybody?

Burroughs   They're in the house, on urgent business connected with a baby.

Alan   All of them?

Burroughs   Philip and John are collecting wood. Breaking up the shed I gather. It must be a bit wet from the amount of smoke going up.

(*He looks at the roof of the bungalow.*)

Alan   Shall I go and help?

Burroughs   No, they'll manage. Sit down and wait. There's nothing to do now but wait.

(**Alan** *and* **Boyle** *sit.*)

Boyle   We parked the bus under the trees, a hundred yards back.

Burroughs   Good idea. You're thinking of that enemy helicopter, I suppose.

Boyle   Yes.

Burroughs   I've been thinking of that ever since we made a break for it.

Alan You mean we should have smashed it?

Burroughs Or made sure the Colonel and the Sergeant weren't able to follow us.

Boyle We should have killed them as well, you mean?

Burroughs If necessary. It would have been enough to take their guns, though. Render them harmless.

Boyle I'm glad we didn't try. I didn't feel very confident handling a tommy-gun.

Burroughs We'll just have to hope they're still sleeping. Or that they can't pick up our trail. Where's our gun, by the way?

Boyle I left it in the cab. I didn't think . . .

Burroughs It's safer there. We don't want young Philip playing with it. Or Alan for that matter.

Alan I haven't played cops and robbers for some time, Mr Burroughs. Real guns like that frighten me off.

Burroughs Noisy things. Anyway, I've still got mine. (*He takes it out*) Though I don't know whether I could hit the side of the house. I wasn't very accurate when I practised with it.

(*He puts the revolver away as* **Sharon**, **Lynda** *and* **Tracy** *come from the house.* **Sharon** *is still carrying her cassette recorder.*)

Sharon We've been sent out to join you.

Tracy No further use for our services.

Sharon Mrs B.'s kept Susan, though.

Lynda Well, we know when we're not wanted.

Boyle Could it be, Lynda, that Susan is just that bit more competent that the rest of you?

Lynda Oh, we know that. She was always teacher's pet.

Sharon We have other qualities, don't we, Alan?

Alan You may have. Can't say that I've noticed them particularly.

Tracy Hey, Mr Burroughs. Mrs B. said you'd married Gill and Terry.

Burroughs I did.

Sharon She didn't have a ring, though.

Burroughs The right words have been said, Sharon, so it's as legal as it can be. Ring or no ring.

Lynda They say weddings go in threes, don't they?

Boyle Do they, Lynda?

Lynda Well, lots of things do. Why not weddings?

Sharon I wonder who'll be next. Any ideas, Alan?

Alan You know, I never can make out whether she's joking or serious.

Burroughs Oh, serious, Alan. Women don't joke about marriage.

(**Philip** and **John** *come on.*)

Philip Still on about weddings? Hey, what about old Terry losing his liberty? Another bachelor bit the dust!

Boyle Don't be too confident, Philip. The girls say that weddings go in threes.

Philip (*Going down on one knee in a mock formal proposal*) Lynda, darling. Will you marry me?

Lynda Yes, I will.

Philip (*Jumping up in alarm*) You will!

Lynda You're as daft as a brush, but I reckon I can knock some sense into you.

Philip But I was only kidding. (*Pleading*) Lynda, you know we only make a joke of it.

John Another bachelor bit the dust!

(*They are shocked into silence for a moment by* **Gillian's** *scream from the house.*)

Tracy It's started, then.

Burroughs Does that tape recorder of yours still work, Sharon?

Sharon Yes, Mr Burroughs.

Burroughs Would you like to play something for us, Sharon?

Sharon I didn't think you were a pop fan, Mr Burroughs.

Burroughs Well, just this once, I think I'd like to hear you play it.

(**Sharon** *turns on a flood of pop. The girls dance to it in a half-hearted way.* **Burroughs** *and* **Boyle** *drift away to avoid the immediate impact of the noise. They talk with difficulty above the music.*)

Boyle How long do these things take, Adam?

Burroughs (*Not hearing*) What?

Boyle How long does it take for a baby to be born?

Burroughs I don't know, Ted.

Boyle I presume we'll have to stay here several days. Until Gillian's fit enough to travel.

Burroughs We could be stuck here for a week. Pity it had to be here. Far better if we'd been in a town where things were handy. We'll need food and bedding.

Boyle Will it be edible?

Burroughs (*Not hearing*) What?

Boyle The food. Canned stuff. Will it be fit to eat?

Burroughs We'll have to risk it.

(**Mrs Burroughs** *appears at the door, calling for less noise.*)

Mrs Burroughs Turn it down.

(**Sharon** *turns down the volume until* **Mrs Burroughs** *can be heard.*)

Mrs Burroughs It's hardly the time for a pop festival.

Burroughs My fault, Mary. I thought a bit of music might take our minds off the . . . situation.

Mrs Burroughs It needn't be so loud. Keep it down, Sharon.

(*She returns to the house.*)

Sharon Should I turn if off, Mr Burroughs? Seems a bit heartless . . . dancing while Gill's . . . you know.

Lynda Gill won't be bothering. She'll have her mind on other things.

Burroughs Keep it nice and low, Sharon. Just enough for us to be able to talk without shouting our heads off.

Tracy I wonder how long we'll have to wait.

Philip I'm getting hungry. When do we eat?

Lynda It's not two hours since you had your breakfast.

Philip Seems longer than that.

Alan How are we going to eat? There can't be much in the house.

Burroughs We'll send a party into town to collect some food when the baby's born. There's no point in going before. There'll be a long shopping list for the baby as well as food. I want Mary to go along for that.

Lynda We're going to be like millionaires, though, aren't we? Anything we want . . . there for the asking. Clothes, jewellery, anything you like to name.

Burroughs Maybe we shan't have time to enjoy all those luxuries, Lynda. Don't forget, we'll be farmers, growing our own food. We can't live on tinned stuff for ever.

Tracy I don't think I'm going to like our new world particularly.

Philip Oh, cheer up. It's better than being dead.

(*There is alarm as the* **Colonel** *and his* **Sergeant** *appear rapidly and cover the party with their guns.*)

Colonel Remain where you are.

(*He motions the* **Sergeant** *to one side where he crouches, covering the party with his gun. The* **Colonel** *crosses to the house door. The music is switched off.*)

Who is in the house?

Burroughs A baby is being born. The doctor and his wife are with the girl.

Colonel And the gun? Where is the gun you took after killing my man?

Burroughs It's in the bus. Up the road.

Colonel (*Relaxing*) Good. It would not be wise of you to begin a battle. You could expect no mercy after what you have done.

Burroughs We were only trying to protect ourselves. You couldn't expect us to let the girls go without a fight.

Colonel The fight is over and you have lost. You, as the leader, I hold responsible for the death of my man. I shall consider in time what is to be done with you.

Burroughs I accept the responsibility. I would do the same again.

Colonel Then you would be foolish. You cannot hope to evade the vigilance of the Federation. What kind of leader are you, I wonder? You gain a temporary advantage and then you send up smoke signals.

Burroughs We needed hot water for the birth. We had to take a risk. Otherwise you wouldn't have found us so easily.

Colonel (*Approaching him*) Eventually we should have found you. You had only one escape route. That we knew. Somewhere, sometime, you would have betrayed your presence.

Burroughs (*Wearily*)   All right. We'll accept for the moment, that you've won. What do you propose doing?

Colonel   The young women will be taken to our helicopter at once. Then we shall carry out the rest of our plan.

Burroughs   There's one girl who can't be moved. She's giving birth to her child.

Colonel   We will wait for the birth. Then we go.

(**Terry** *dashes in, unaware of the* **Colonel's** *presence.*)

Terry   Hey! It's a girl!

Colonel   Good. She will be the first of our young citizens.

Terry   What!

Colonel   It is important that we have plenty of girl children. They will be the mothers of our new world.

Terry   (*Furiously approaching the* **Colonel**)   You're not taking her. Neither the baby nor Gill. They're staying here with me.

Colonel   (*Raising his gun*)   Stay where you are. If you approach further I will shoot.

(**Burroughs** *takes out his revolver and shoots the* **Colonel** *in the back. Then he fires at and hits the* **Sergeant**.)

SCENE 2

As in Act Three Scene 1. Four days later. At the rise of the curtain the stage is empty. **Boyle** *and* **Alan** *come on and cross to the house.* **Boyle** *stays by the door.* **Alan** *goes in.*

Boyle   Get your stuff, Alan. Mine's in the bus already.

Alan   Won't take a minute.

(*He goes into the house.*)

Boyle   (**Calling into the house**)   Come on, everybody. The carriage is waiting.

(**Philip** *appears, carrying a heavy bag. He is dressed casually, as are all the young people.*)

Philip   Hello, Mr Boyle. Are we ready to move off?

Boyle   We are, Philip. We'd have been ready sooner if you'd been around to give a hand.

Philip   You've moved the helicopter on your own?

Boyle   Alan helped me. As a matter of fact, it was quite easy. It rolled down the slope and conveniently tipped over into the ditch. We didn't really need you. I just wondered where you'd disappeared to.

Philip   I've been packing.

(*He indicates the bag.*)

Boyle   What on earth have you got in there? The kitchen sink?

Philip   It's all the gear I brought back from town the other day. I needed some fresh clothes after all those months in school uniform. I didn't bring half as much as the girls.

Boyle   Get aboard then. I hope the bus will stand the weight.

(**Philip** *moves to go out.* **Sharon**, **Lynda**, **Tracy** *and* **John** *enter from the house with their luggage.*)

Philip   If it won't, we'll have to get another, won't we? There are plenty left parked around.

(*He goes out.*)

Lynda What's he going on about now?

Boyle I was wondering if the bus would take all this luggage you seem to have accumulated in a very short space of time. Philip suggests we find a bigger bus.

Lynda I've got bags of stuff.

Boyle So I see.

Sharon We found a smashing boutique.

Boyle Spare me the details. I can imagine. Get your luggage aboard . . . if you can carry it.

(**Sharon** *and* **Lynda** *move off.*)

Tracy (*To* **John**) If some people were gentlemen, they might give a girl a hand.

John Come on, then. I can manage one for you.

(*They move off.* **Alan** *enters from the house, carrying a small grip. He is followed by* **Dr Ainsworth**.)

Alan That didn't take long, did it? I haven't been grabbing everything in sight, like some I could mention.

(*He goes off.*)

Dr Ainsworth The others shouldn't be long, Ted. Mary's fussing over the baby like it was her own grandchild. Doesn't seem to think Gillian can handle it with any degree of safety.

Boyle Why are new babies always 'it'?

Dr Ainsworth I never stopped to think about it, Ted. I suppose it's because they all look alike.

Boyle How much travelling can Gillian stand?

Dr Ainsworth Oh, she'll stand the journey to the Lakes. Should be smooth going when we hit the motorway. Anyway, we can stop when we like. No need for panic now.

Boyle I suppose not. It's a relief to have that gang off our tails.

Dr Ainsworth Yes. Adam solved the problem very neatly. Though he doesn't see it like that.

Boyle It bothers him?

Dr Ainsworth Somewhat. Would it trouble your conscience, Ted?

Boyle Perhaps. For a while anyway.

(**Terry** *and* **Gillian** *come on from the house.* **Gillian** *carries the baby,* **Terry** *their luggage.*)

Dr Ainsworth Quite the young married couple. You could be off to Blackpool for your holidays.

Boyle Have you decided on the name yet, Gillian?

Gillian Margaret Mary. Margaret after my mother and Mary after Mrs B.

Terry We were going to call her Mary Margaret but Gill decided it was better the other way round, so Mrs B. had to take second place.

Dr Ainsworth Well, I don't expect she'll mind taking second place to your mother, Gillian.

Gillian I've a lot to thank Mrs B. for. And you too, Doctor.

Dr Ainsworth Oh, it was nothing, my dear. I must have delivered close on a thousand babies in my time and yours was one of the easiest, Gillian. We had more trouble with the father.

Terry I wasn't as bad as all that. A bit nervous, maybe.

Dr Ainsworth A case of acute neurosis. Prospective fathers are better off at home . . . or in the pub.

(**Susan** *appears carrying a small bag, and the baby's carry-cot.*)

Susan Mrs B. says she won't be long. She's tidying up. Though why she bothers, I don't know. The owners aren't likely to be back.

Dr Ainsworth Force of habit, Susan. Mary always was one for keeping the place tidy.

Boyle Do you need any help, Terry?

Terry No, I'll manage. Susan's bringing the carry-cot.

(**Terry, Gillian** *and* **Susan** *move off.*)

Boyle That bus is going to be bursting at the seams.

Dr Ainsworth We'd better pick up a good car as soon as we can. Relieve the congestion.

Boyle I'll go and see them packed in.

(*He goes off.*)

Dr Ainsworth Save me a seat. I'll join you in a moment.

(*He turns back to the house and calls through the door.*)

Mary! Adam! We're ready to move off.

(*He crosses and goes off.* **Mr** *and* **Mrs Burroughs** *come on from the house, carrying light luggage.*)

Mrs Burroughs   I'm sure to have forgotten something, Adam.

Burroughs   If you have, love, we can pick it up somewhere on the way. There's no shortage of anything now, except people.

Mrs Burroughs   I suppose so. You know, Adam, I was wondering what to get Gillian for the baby and then I realised that presents don't mean anything any more. Whatever she needs for the baby she can just nip out to the shop and get.

Burroughs   You can always knit.

Mrs Burroughs   I never was much of a hand at knitting. Not like your mother. Do you remember the things she knitted for David? How grateful we were?

Burroughs   We were struggling in those days, love, weren't we? When I was just starting. Now we're back struggling. It's ironic, isn't it? I go through thirty years of married life without harming a soul, so far as I can recall, and then in one day I poison one man and shoot two others.

Mrs Burroughs   You did right, Adam. And you didn't poison the other. I did. So we're both as guilty. It doesn't trouble my conscience, Adam.

Burroughs   (*Moving to overlook the upper garden*)   Still, there are two men buried out there who would be alive now if I hadn't pulled the trigger. You see, Mary, from one point of view it doesn't much matter who survives and multiplies, providing somebody does.

Mrs Burroughs   Sometimes I lose my patience with you, Adam. It's quite obvious to me that it's better for the English to survive. We all look after our own. After all, those aliens were doing just that. I was surprised you and Ted didn't finish off the job in the bunker. We'd have been saved this latest scare. I'm only thankful we came out of it as well as we did. And so are all the others.

(**Sharon** *comes on, crossing to the house.*)

Sharon   I forgot my tape-recorder. I know I can get another, but I thought I'd keep my own for sentimental reasons.

(*She goes into the house.*)

Mrs Burroughs Would you rather have Sharon and the rest in some communal baby factory?

Burroughs No. I know you've logic on your side, Mary. It just doesn't feel right, that's all, to be starting a new life on the basis of murdering your enemies.

Mrs Burroughs It was no murder, Adam. And anyway, what about all those millions they killed with their bombs, David among them?

Burroughs We don't know for certain, love, about David. We probably won't ever know.

Mrs Burroughs That's the worst of it, Adam. The not knowing. I could bear it better if I knew for certain he was dead. At the moment, I'm not disposed to be sentimental over three thugs who tried to wreck what future we might have. What you did was a perfectly justifiable defence of our own lives.

(**Sharon** *returns from the house with her tape-recorder and crosses.*)

Sharon Got it. You know, it's going to rain, I think. That's good, isn't it, Mr Burroughs? I remember Doc once saying the rain would wash the earth clean. Oh, Mr Boyle said to tell you we're all ready when you are.

(*She goes.*)

Mrs Burroughs It is looking black.

Burroughs It's already raining down in the valley.

(*A rainbow appears on the cyclorama.*)

Mrs Burroughs A rainbow. First we've seen for a long time.

Burroughs First rain we've had since we came up top.

Mrs Burroughs Remember the Bible, Adam?

Burroughs Not very well, love. Which part?

Mrs Burroughs The Flood. The rainbow . . . it was supposed to be a sign.

Burroughs What of?

Mrs Burroughs That God wouldn't destroy the world again.

Burroughs He did though, didn't he?

Mrs Burroughs Somebody did.

(*She takes his arm.*)

Come on, Adam. Forget the past. We've a future to think of.

Drama Activities

APPRECIATING THE PLAY

ACT I SCENE 1

1. Why do you think the play has been called *Adam's Ark*?
2. Imagine you are the director. What stage props would you need for the first scene in the bunker?
3. What causes the conflict between Boyle and Burroughs at the beginning of the play?
4. Why does the Deputy Controller's radio message increase the tension in the bunker?
5. 'Look, I've told you my orders. I shoot anyone invading this bunker illegally.' What do these statements reveal about the character of Burroughs?
6. Why can't Boyle and the students leave the nuclear shelter?
7. Why do a small group of boys and girls decide to leave the shelter?
8. Why do the people in the bunker have a good chance of survival?
9. Why does Dr Ainsworth enter the bunker 'looking grim and distraught'?
10. How does Dr Ainsworth's arrival increase the suspense in the play?

ACT I SCENE 2

11. How are the students feeling at the beginning of this scene?
12. What comments would you make about the character of Mrs Burroughs?
13. 'I'd never thought I'd miss washing-up.' What are the problems of living in the shelter?
14. How will the coming of the rains help to end the nuclear contamination?
15. 'If anyone else turns up now, Adam, we'd have to turn him out.' Why?

ACT II SCENE 1

16 What do the stage directions at the beginning of this scene reveal about the effects of the nuclear explosion?

17 The relationship between Boyle and Burroughs has changed since the beginning of Act I. Explain the change that has taken place?

18 What does the beginning of this scene show us about the relationship of Mrs Burroughs and her husband?

19 'He's been up since the crack of dawn. Not that we ever see dawn.' What does Mrs Burroughs mean by her last sentence?

20 In this scene, what evidence is there to show that the levels of radiation have fallen?

21 'Nobody had the right to keep us in if we wanted to leave.' What do these words of Terry reveal about his character?

22 Some of the characters complain about living in the shelter. What are some of these problems?

23 'It's touch and go for the human race.' What are some of the problems that the survivors may have to face?

24 'The door burst open and **Terry** is precipitated into the room at gunpoint by the **Colonel**. **Two soldiers** deploy to right and left.' What effect would the appearance of Terry and the soldiers have on the audience?

ACT II SCENE 2

25 How did the Colonel know that the nuclear shelter existed?

26 Why did the Colonel come to the nuclear shelter?

27 'Do not advance any further, or I may be obliged to shoot you.' What does this reveal about the Colonel's character?

28 'I have a feeling for my homeland, Mr Burroughs.' What is the Colonel's attitude to his homeland?

29 'At the end of that time the young women must be ready to leave.' What does this reveal about the Colonel's character?

30 Why does Burroughs decide not to rush the sentry?

31 'For God sake don't take the cup with the spoon in it.' How does the tension build up during this scene?

ACT III SCENE 1

32 Where does the action of this scene take place?

33 'Yes, but up to now you've been the boss, like Noah in the Ark.' In what ways has Burroughs been like Noah in the Ark?

34 How did the Colonel know where to find the survivors?

35 'You're not taking her. Neither the baby nor Gill. They're staying here with me.' What do these words reveal about Terry's character?

36 'Burroughs takes out his revolver and shoots the Colonel in the back. Then he fires at and hits the Sergeant.' What effect would Burroughs' actions have on the audience?

37 'It just doesn't feel right, that's all, to be starting a new life on the basis of murdering your enemies.' What does this reveal about Burroughs' character?

38 Comment on the importance of the rainbow at the end of the play.

39 If you were involved in a production of the play, which character would you like to play the part of? Why?

ISSUES FOR DISCUSSION

Here are some of the main issues that *Adam's Ark* explores. You may like to discuss them as a class or in small groups.

1 'My own son, when he was a student, spent half his time marching up and down with anti-Bomb posters. But it didn't affect the governments. They just went on building bigger bombs and better means of delivery.' How can ordinary people bring about the end of nuclear testing in the world?

2 'I got through thirty years of married life without harming a soul, so far as I can recall, and then in one day I poison one man and shoot two others.' Do you think Burroughs' actions were justified or not? Explain your viewpoint.

3 'Now look. This is just foolish. You can't go bringing loads of sick and wounded people back here. Don't you understand that you'll only be bringing them here to die? They can't possibly survive. This place is built to support about a dozen people, not an army.' Do you agree with these words of Burroughs or not? Why?

4 'He'll be dead anyway inside twenty-four hours. We can't afford to wait that long.' Do you agree with Dr Ainsworth's decision to kill Tom? Why?

5 'Your five girls will be the future mothers of our citizens and as such will be honoured.' What comments would you make about the Colonel's justification for taking away the five girls?

3

The Hood, the Sad and the Cuddly

by Robin George

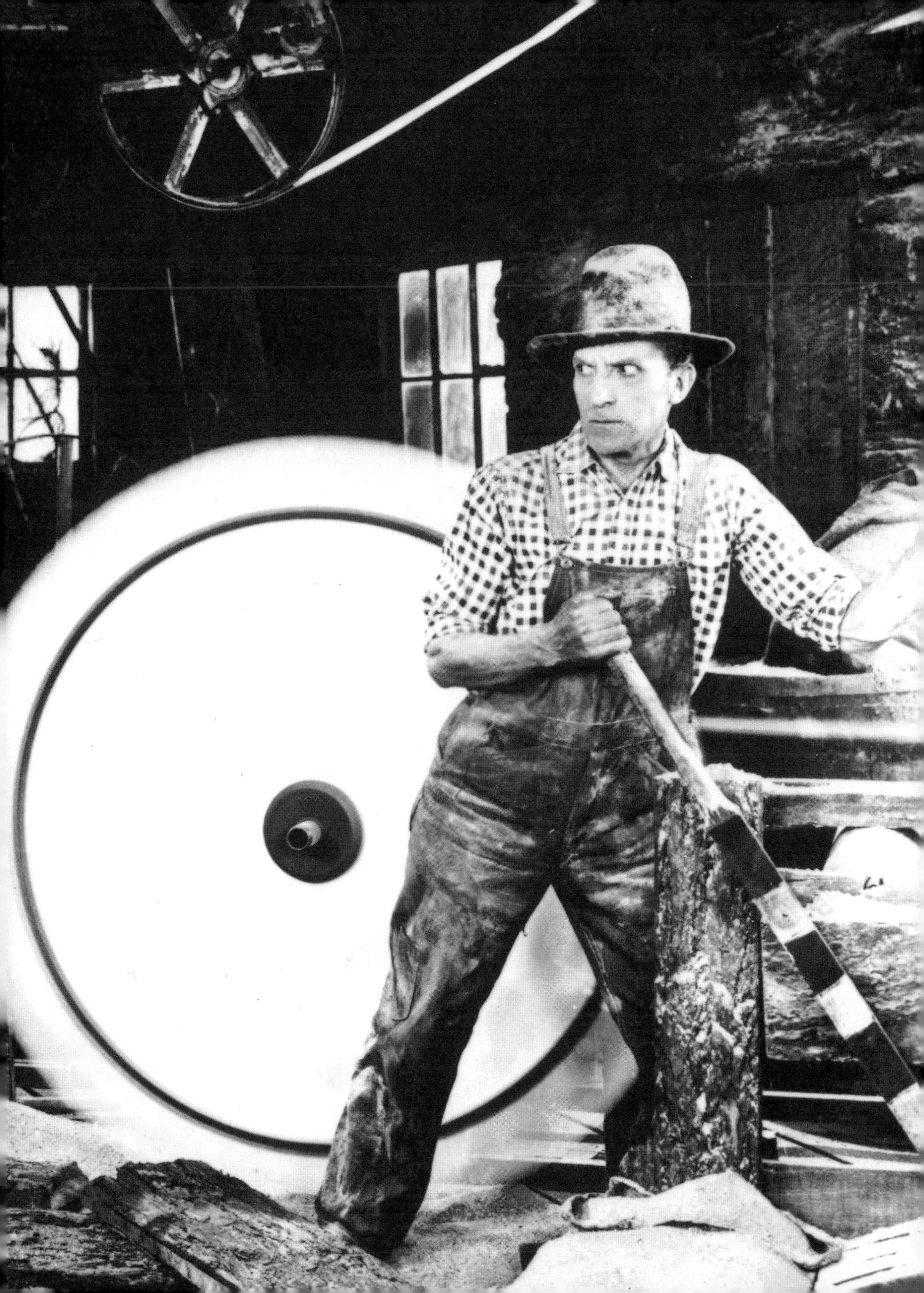

The Hood, the Sad and the Cuddly

by Robin George

a Modern Teenage Melodrama

THE play *The Hood, the Sad and the Cuddly* is a light-hearted play that contains aspects of the popular melodramas of the past. Bertha, the villain of the play, commits many dastardly deeds until she is utterly foiled in the final scene. On the other hand, Vincent and Fanny are pure of heart. The humour comes from the ridiculous situations in which the characters find themselves and the exaggerated ways in which they react to the events. The play ends on a happy note with Fanny getting her man and Bertha being completely reformed.

CHARACTERS

VINCE	Straight, conservative, sporty.
FANNY	Sweet, naive, sheltered girl. Has freckles and wear glasses.
BERTHA	Extremely tough and aggressive girl. Knows what she wants and is determined to get it.
LEECH	Bertha's bumbling cronies.
SPUD	Cowardly but with a tough facade. Fearful of Bertha.
EUGENE	As the other two but a real 'crawler'.
VINCE'S MOTHER	Sickly old lady
BERTHA'S MOTHER	Tasteless, loud person. Gaudy clothes. Protective of Bertha.
SOCIAL WORKER	A hippy. Changeable: sympathetic to intolerant.
CHARLOTTE	Precocious school girl.
PRUDENCE	Opposite of Charlotte.
NARRATOR	Flamboyant, showy, confident.

(OTHER STUDENTS IN THE LIBRARY IF NECESSARY.)

SCENE 1

Narrator *enters. Rock and roll music is heard in the background.*

Narrator Well hidy-hi all you young boppers out there. We're gonna tell you a story now 'bout a chick called Fanny. She was plain – I mean squaresville man! One day she met this dude called Vince and did she go ape. I mean she wanted him BAD! Trouble was, Vince, that's the dude's name, he didn't know she existed. This is what happened.

The playground. **Fanny** *enters and notices* **Vincent** *reading a book.*

Fanny (*To audience*) Gee! Look at that boy! Isn't he handsome. He must be the new boy who arrived yesterday. Oh, I wonder if he'll talk to me and be my . . . boyfriend. I'll have to use my old-fashioned charm and my pearly whites which, incidentally, I brush everyday with Macleans Toothpaste.

Fanny (*She sits next to* **Vince**.) Hello. I'm Fanny Windsor. What's your name?

Vince (*Continuing to read*) Vincent.

Fanny Vincent. That's a nice name. You're new here aren't you Vince? . . . Where do you live Vince? . . . Are you staying here long? Vince? . . . What class are you in Vince? . . . Do you believe in God? I'm agnostic myself. Are you academically minded Vince? I am . . . Do you like Shakespeare? I saw Macbeth last night. It was so . . . (**Vince** *leaves*) (*To audience*) Don't you just love the silent type! But I knew he wouldn't like me. I don't know why boys aren't attracted to me. Mummy always tells me to start with small talk such as the Iranian arms deal or domestic politics or Einstein's theory of relativity. I suppose I need some advice. Of course! Charlotte and Prudence know a lot about boys. They can coach me. Then I'll return, sweep Vince off his feet and he'll be my . . . my steady. (*Giggles.*)

(*Exit.*)

SCENE 2

The Library. **Fanny** *is sitting alone reading* Everywoman.

Charlotte Hi, Fanny, whatcha readin'?

Fanny Oh, nothing.

Charlotte (*Grabbing the book*) You're kiddin'? (*Laughs.*)

Prudence　Really, Fanny. That's disgusting! You're too young to be reading that sort of thing. You'll get perverted.

Fanny　How old do I have to be for goodness sake!

Prudence　At least twenty-one. My parents still haven't read it.

Charlotte　Where'd they get the info then. Back of a Cornflakes packet?

Prudence　Well I never. (*Shocked.*)

Charlotte　I know. And you probably never will.

Fanny　Go argue somewhere else will you.

Prudence　What's the matter, Fanny? You look so glum.

Fanny　I am . . . I'm in love.

Charlotte　In love! Who with?

Fanny　Vincent. (*Dreamily.*)

Both　Vincent!

Fanny　But he could never love me. I'm too plain. He doesn't even know I exist.

Charlotte　Looks like I found you just in time. I remember when I knew nothing about the opposite sex. Of course, that was years ago. It was so long ago, it's hazy.

Prudence　Oh, really Charlotte!

Charlotte　Oh, really Prudence!

Fanny　Please you two. I need help.

Charlotte　Yeah, I can see that. (*Inspecting her clothes.*)

Prudence　Charlotte, don't be such a bitch. There's nothing wrong with her clothes.

Charlotte　You're just saying that 'cos you get your clothes from the same place . . . the museum. Fanny you have to wear something sexy. Try a pair of skin-tight jeans and a very short, very lacy crop-top. You'd look stunning!

Prudence　(*Sarcastic*)　Mmm, just out of this world.

Fanny　What do you think, Prudence? Should I change my fashion?

Prudence　No, certainly not. Stay just the way you are. That's the best way to impress a man – just be yourself. We don't want to lose the Fanny we all know and love. You must remember that love is not merely a physical attraction. Why, my boyfriend, Randal, says he's in love with my mind.

Charlotte (*Laughs hysterically.*)

Prudence What's so funny.

Charlotte I was just imagining Randal taking you back to his place and making wild, passionate love to your brain.

Fanny But how will I approach him. I wouldn't have a clue how to talk to a boy. I've never liked someone this much before.

Charlotte (*Dramatically*) Oh, be still my heart!

Fanny Please, Charlotte. Don't make fun of me.

Charlotte OK. I'm sorry. All you have to do is walk up to Vinnie Baby and say, 'Hey, you're cute. How'd ya like me to show you a good time.' But make sure you wiggle ya hips. Like this. (*She demonstrates.*)

Prudence That might work with the kind of people you mix with. Fanny, if you take her advice he'll either jump on you or spit on you. Just be yourself.

Fanny Are you sure? He'll probably just ignore me.

Charlotte Of course he would. We're talking about dull and boring Fanny here, remember.

Prudence How could you say such a thing. She's upset enough as it is.

Fanny Don't worry. I know you didn't mean it. I'll just finish this book then I'll go home and probably kill myself.

Charlotte Good idea! Can I have that English essay of yours? You know, seeing ya won't be here tomorrow.

Prudence (*Grabbing* **Charlotte**) Come on. Bye, Fanny and don't worry so much. It'll give you wrinkles.

(*Both exit.* **Fanny** *examines wrinkles.*)

Fanny God, I feel bad! Everyone else can get a boyfriend except me. It makes me so angry!

(*Dramatic love music plays in background.*) (*Exit.*)

Narrator Man, what a bummer! Fanny reckons she's got trouble now but she don't know that another chick called Bertha has got the hots for Vince as well. I'd better split – here comes Bertha now.

SCENE 3

Bertha's hideout. The scene begins with Leech, Spud and Eugene doing a dance to dance music. When finished, they exit. **Bertha** *enters.*

Audience   Boo! Hiss!

Bertha   (*To audience*)   Arr, shut ya face! Eugene! Spud! Leech! Get here! Where are those brainless head-bangers!

Eugene   (*Off stage*)   Coming Bertha.

(*They race in, colliding into each other.*)

Bertha   Any of yous seen that new spunk at school?

Eugene   Yeah, Bertha. I believe his name is Vincent.

Spud   Van Coff.   (*Laugh.*)

Bertha   Shut up. I like the look of him and I plan to make him mine . . . any way I can.

Eugene   What's the plan, Bertha, ay. What's the plan?

Leech   Hey Bertha, why don't we kidnap him.

Spud   Yeah, or tie him to the train tracks.

Bertha   Nah! I've gotta impress him with me charm, wit, sophistication and sensitivity.

Eugene   Yeah, sounds good, Bertha.

Bertha   Course it does. And if that doesn't work, I'll pull his tongue out with me teeth!

Now here's me plan.   (*All gather around*)   I walk up to him and ask if he'll help me with me homework.

Leech   But you never do any homework, Bertha.

Bertha   (*Grabbing his nose*)   I know you idiot. It's just an act, made up, pretend, make believe . . . got it!

Leech   Got it.

(**Bertha** *lets go violently.*)

Eugene   Do you want me to send him a message Bertha?

Bertha   Nah, leave it to me. Now Spud and Leech, go find out his timetable so's I always know where to find him.

Both   Right, Bertha. (*Exit.*)

(**Bertha** *proceeds to pretty herself up in mirror.*)

Eugene Oh boy, Bertha! You are one smooth operator. By the time you're finished with Vince, he'll be putty in your hands. He won't stand a chance. He'll be beggin' you to go with him.

Bertha Tell me something I don't know.

Eugene Just one thing, Bertha.

Bertha What's that.

Eugene What if he gives you the cold shoulder? What if he doesn't fall head over heels in love with you?

Bertha (*Grabbing* **Eugene** *by the throat*) Are you sayin' I'm not pretty . . . and sweet . . . and charming . . . and sexy.

Eugene Course not, Bertha. You're all of those things.

Bertha Say 'em.

Eugene Sweet.

Bertha Yeah.

Eugene Charming.

Bertha Yeah.

Eugene Pretty.

Bertha Yeah.

Eugene (*To audience*) Pretty ugly!

Bertha I heard that.

Eugene And . . . and sexy.

Bertha That's better . . . (*Let's go.*)

Eugene But what if he doesn't go out with you.

Bertha He will. But if he doesn't . . . (*She sings: 'I'm gonna knock on his door, ring on his bell'.*)

(**Eugene** *and* **Bertha** *do a choreographed sequence to the first verse of this song. Song finishes as Leech and Spud race in knocking* **Bertha** *over.*)

Bertha Good one you morons!

Leech Sorry, Bertha. Don't hit me, Bertha. It was an accident.

Spud Calm down, Bertha. We've got some news for ya. Vince's got a free period five and so have you. Talk about luck!

Bertha Good, good, very good! Anything else?

Leech (*To audience*) She's gonna love this!

Bertha Well – What!

Spud (*Excited*) Vince and his mum are renting a house.

Bertha So what! Do you have any idea how many people are renting houses in Melbourne, bird brain!

Eugene I don't know why you bother with them sometimes, Bertha.

Bertha You're right. I think it's time for a thick ear. One each.

Leech No wait! There's something special about this particular house.

Bertha What?

Leech Your mum owns it.

Bertha (*Freezes in disbelief*) My mum? Are you sure?

Eugene They made it up so's they wouldn't get a belting. It's obvious.

Bertha Who told ya?

Leech Vince did. We asked him where he lives and he told us . . . just like that.

Spud So we went around and checked. It belongs to your old cheese alright, Bertha.

Bertha (*Can hardly contain herself*) Excellent! Excellent! I do believe I have Mr Vincent Van Coff exactly where I want him and before long he will be mine. Spud, I'm sorry I doubted you. Come over here. (**Bertha** *bops him on the head*) That's for calling me muvver an old cheese. Follow me gang – to the playground. (*Exit.*)

(*Dance music is heard.*)

SCENE 4

The playground. **Vince**, *as usual, is sitting and reading.* **Bertha** *oozes in with her cronies.*

Audience Boo! Hiss!

Bertha (*To audience*) Cool it ya morons! Now pay attention. Ya might learn something. (*To cronies*) You three stay out of sight. (*They hide*) Hi there, Vince.

Vince Hello.

Bertha What've ya got for lunch today?

Vince Nothing.

Bertha I've got asparagus, jam, brussel sprouts and sardines.

Vince (*Turning to* **Bertha**) You have four sandwiches for lunch?

Bertha Na, just the one. Gotta watch the old figure ya know. Ya want a bit?

Vince (*Retreating*) No thanks.

Bertha It's really good tucker and ya did say ya didn't have any lunch today.

Vince I'm really not hungry, thanks all the same.

Bertha (*After a pause*) Nice day.

Vince Yes.

Bertha Don't get weather like this much, do we.

Vince I guess not.

Bertha Seen any good movies lately?

Vince No, not really.

Bertha Hey, what kinda music do ya like? Bought this grouse record yesterday. (*Sings.*)

> 'Gonna eat my Grampa for breakfast
> Gonna eat my Aunty for brunch
> Gonna put my sister in a kitchen Wizz yeah and suck her through a straw for lunch.'

Vince Very nice.

Bertha Yeah, not bad ay? (**Vince** *leaves*) Where ya goin? Hey, come back. Snob! You're makin' a big mistake puke face! (*Yelling*) I hope ya like sleeping under the stars!

Vince (*Returning*) What's that supposed to mean?

Bertha Just that my muvver happens to own the house you're renting and if you don't agree to be my steady within twenty-four hours, you're out.

Vince But my mother is very ill. She wouldn't last a night on the streets of Lilydale.

Bertha (*Aside*) Good! So he loves his mother. Very rare in this day and age.

Vince Of course. I would do anything to keep her safe and well.

Bertha Anything? (*Sleazing up to him.*)

Vince (*Breaking away*) Well, almost anything.

Bertha You've got twenty-four hours. If you're stupid enough to say no, garbage will be your pillow, if you get my drift.

Vince You wicked, evil, despicable witch.

Bertha So, you do love me.

Vince My mother has taught me that evil can never triumph over virtue. The forces of goodness and niceness will overcome . . .

Bertha Alright already! I get the picture. Don't forget, twenty-four hours. (*Exit.*)

Vince (*Downcast*) Sob! Sob! What am I gonna do. I can't love Bertha . . . Nobody could love Bertha. Fido, my bull terrier couldn't love Bertha. It's Fanny that my heart really yearns for. I guess I'm doomed. Maybe I'll feel better after a good work out.

(*Exit.*)

SCENE 5

The playground. It is the next day and **Vince** *is engrossed in his book as* **Fanny** *enters.* **Bertha** *is spying from the wings. As* **Fanny** *enters, she trips.*

Vince Are you alright. Here, let me help you up.

Fanny No it's OK. (*Picks up books, changes her mind and throws them down again*) Well, if you insist. (*As* **Vince** *picks them up, she savours his closeness.*)

Vince You should watch where you're going. You might hurt yourself. After all, a man like me may not always be around.

Fanny Golly, I'm such an idiot. I could kill myself.

Bertha (*To audience*) We should be so lucky!

Fanny Well, I'd better get going. (*Turns sharply and drops books*) Oh, no.

Vince Let me help you. After all, you're such a delicate, fragile little thing.

Bertha (*To audience*) Doesn't it just make you want to puke!

Fanny I'll be alright.

(*As they stand,* **Vince** *gives* **Fanny** *her books and as he does, he touches her hand. Their eyes meet.*)

Vince Are you sure you'll be alright?

Fanny Yes, I'm fine thanks.

(*Stare into each others eyes for a long time.*)

Vince Fanny. ⎱
Fanny Vince. ⎰ together

Vince Yes. ⎱
Fanny Yes. ⎰ together

Vince You go first.

Fanny It's nothing important. What did you want to say?

Vince Just that . . . you're standing on my foot.

Fanny Sorry. Guess I'll see you around.

Vince Guess so. Bye.

(*They begin to exit at opposite ends, they stop, turn for one last look then exit.*)

Bertha (*Addressing audience*) Ya think I'm worried, don't ya. Well I'm not. Vince loves his mum too much to see her freeze to death in the gutter. You'll see. He'll dump that little mush-bucket like a hot potato and then he'll be mine. All mine! (*Manic laugh. Exit.*)

(*Dance music is repeated.*)

Narrator Hey! Hey! Hey! Looks like Vince and Fanny have really got somethin' going here. Did ya feel those heavy vibes?! Of course, there's still the problem of Bertha and her cronies. Let's visit Vince and see how he breaks it to his old cheese.

SCENE 6

Vince's house. As the scene begins, **Mrs Van Coff** *is heard wheezing and coughing in the back. She enters in dressing gown and shawl, takes bottles of pills from pockets and places them on table then sits.*

Vince (*Enters depressed. Kneels by her chair*) Hello, mother. It's me, Vince.

Vince's mother Did you (*Cough*) have a (*Cough*) nice day dear? (*Cough.*)

Vince Quite nice, thank you Mother. It's good to see you're on the mend.

Vince's mother Yes, I'm really feeling much better today. That blood transfusion did me the world of good. (*Cough*) (**Vince** *is pensive*) What's the matter, Vincent?

Vince Why, nothing at all Mother. (*Aside*) I must put on a brave front for my mother's sake. What I have to say might kill her.

Vince's mother Now don't go putting on a brave front for my sake, Vincent. What you have to say won't kill me.

Vince It's a girl.

Vince's mother (*Clutches her chest. Gags. Pops a pill*) So you're in love. How nice. I remember the first time I fell in love . . . Arthur was his name . . . We'd both had a triple by-pass operation and . . .

Vince No, Mother. I'm not in love . . . at least not with this person. There's this brute of a girl at school. She's forcing me to go steady with her.

Vince's mother But you can't force people to love you. What's this girl's name?

Vince Bertha.

Vince's mother Bertha?! Sounds more like a dog.

Vince Looks more like a dog too. Mother, I am deeply troubled. Bertha's mother owns this house and she's threatened us with eviction if I don't agree to be her steady.

Vince's mother You mean they'll throw us out into the cold, cold snow!

Vince That's right.

Vince's mother And me already close to death?

Vince Yup.

Vince's mother With one foot in the grave?

Vince You bet.

Vince's mother Shortly to tap on those pearly gates?

Vince Aha. But I know you wouldn't want me to give in to that evil person.

Vince's mother (*Aside*)   I wouldn't?!

Vince   You've brought me up to believe in honesty, sincerity, goodness and virtue.

Vince's mother (*Aside*)   I did? What an idiot!

Vince   So I refuse to weaken and fall into her arms just because she threatens to tear the roof away from over our heads.

Vince's mother (*Aside*)   I was afraid he was going to say that.

Vince   What did you say, Mother?

Vince's mother   Nothing dear. I'm proud of you for standing up to that . . . that creature. You just do what you have to do. I'll be alright. (*Violent coughing fit.*)

Vince   Gee, thanks Mother. (*Starts to exercise with dumbells.*)

(*Heavy knock on the door.*)

Vince   Will you get that Mother. I'm busy.

(*Mum, crippled with coughing fit, opens door.*)

Vince's mother   Yes sir, can I help you?

(**Bertha** *enters.*)

Audience   Boo! Hiss!

Bertha   No thanks, I'll help myself . . . to your son.

Vince's mother   You keep away from my Vincent. He's told me all about you and your threat.

Bertha (*Pushing her into chair*)   Take a seat granny. (*To* **Vince**)   I didn't see a removal van outside so I take it you've changed your mind.

Vince   We don't need a removal van for two suitcases. Anyway, what are you doing here. I've still got twenty hours.

Bertha   I just thought you might have decided already, seeing how your mum's so sick and all.

(*Mum nods agreement.*)

Vince   Well I haven't. So if you'll kindly leave.

Bertha   Sure I'll kindly leave but I'll be back you little spunk (*Smacks his bottom*) . . . with an eviction order. (*Laughs.*)

(*Exit.*) (*Dance music.*)

SCENE 7

Bertha's house.

Bertha (*Pacing inside her house*)   I've gotta think of a way to get Vinnie-poo and his old cheese evicted. (*To audience*)   Got any ideas? Course not. What am I askin' you for anyway. I've got it! I'll go up to me old muvver and tell her that he punched me. Yeah. Then she's sure to kick 'em out. But she'll want to look at the evidence. Soon fix that.   (*Punches herself in the arm*)   There that should do it.

(**Bertha's mother** *enters.*)   How was your day Mother?

Bertha's mother   Fine dear and how was yours.   (**Bertha** *is busy rubbing eyes.*)   Bertha, are you alright?

Bertha   Sure Mother, I'll be fine.

Bertha's mother   It's that Fanny girl again, isn't it. She's nothing but a trouble maker. I've got a good mind to tell her mother how much she's hurt you.

Bertha   No Mother, it's not Fanny this time. It's Vince.

Bertha's mother   Vince! That nice boy who lives with his mother in our house!?   (**Bertha** *nods*)   Beatrice, you're blushing! Are you in love with Vince?

Bertha   Certainly not, Mother. In fact, it's the opposite.

Bertha's mother   Well?

Bertha   Mother, it was horrible. I've never been hurt so bad in all my life.

Bertha's mother   The beast! What did he do?

Bertha   (*Bursting into tears*)   He hit me.

Bertha's mother   My poor baby. Where?

Bertha   Right there. It really hurts. I think it's broken.

Bertha's mother   Let's have a look. (*Examines it*)   What sort of an animal would do that to a defenceless girl. He ought to be locked up. Just wait till I tell Mary and Daphne and Judy and Dorothy and . . .

Bertha   Mother!

Bertha's mother   What dear?

Bertha   What are you going to do?

Bertha's mother Well, what can I do?

Bertha (*To audience*) Wait for it. (*Back*) Well, you could throw them out of your house.

Bertha's mother Don't you think that's a teeny weeny bit drastic?

(**Bertha** *flinches and cries.*)

Alright dear. Perhaps you're right.

Bertha Oh thank you Mother. Thank you. You're the bestest mother any girl could wish for.

Bertha's mother I know.

Bertha Listen, Mother, I just have to pop out for a while. Bye!

Bertha's mother (*Calling after her*) Bye dear. (*Looks at audience*) So, what are looking at me like that for. Look, I know she's a bitch but what can I do? I'm her mother.

(*Exit.*)

SCENE 8

Vince, *his* **mother** *and the* **social worker** *appear from between screens as if they're coming out of the front door. Mum is sobbing.*

Social worker There there Mrs Van Coff. It's not as bad as all that. Life is full of little knock-backs. Life goes on. Laugh and the world laughs with you – cry and you cry alone. (*Crying continues*) Shut up ya sook!

Vince Everything will seem better in the morning, Mother.

Vince's mother I'll be dead by the morning.

Social worker (*To audience*) With a bit of luck!

Vince Isn't there something you can do for us?

Social worker But of course! I'm a social worker, remember. It's my duty to help the poor underprivileged and dispossessed souls in our society. Besides, if I didn't, I'd get the sack.

Vince's mother Good, then you can get us a house.

Social worker A house! A house! There are thousands of homeless people out there, starving, in need of medical attention and you have the nerve to ask for a house! Hang your head in shame! (*They do*) However, (*they look up*) I do know of a place that's vacant at the moment, nothing flash mind you but it's cosy and dry.

Vince   Good, good, we'll take it.

Social worker   Very well, follow me.

(*Exit.*)

(*The three re-enter. It's darker.*)

Social worker   Well, here it is.

Vince's mother   (*Looking around*)   Where?

Social worker   There.   (*Pointing.*)

(**Vince** and **his mother** *look down, then at each other and cry.*)

Social worker   Now don't start that again. A lot of people would give their right arms to sleep in one of these. I notice it's the deluxe model too.

Vince   How can you tell?

Social worker   Someone's thrown in a newspaper. It'll keep you nice and warm.

Vince   But it's an industrial waste bin!

Social worker   That's right sonny Jim. What'd you expect – the presidential suite at the Hilton?!

Vince   No, just something bigger.

Social worker   It's this or the gutter. Now what's it gonna be?

Both   This.

Social worker   Right then. I'll see you later. Sleep tight.

(*She exits, they squeeze in.* **Vince** *spreads newspaper over* **his mother**. *They doze off.*)

(**Bertha** *enters with candle.*)

Audience   Boo! Hiss!

Bertha   (*To audience*)   Did you ever see anything more pathetic in all your life? I almost feel sorry for them . . . almost.   (*Approaches and knocks.*)

Vince   (*Wakes*)   Who is it?

Bertha   Well it's not bloody Avon calling!

Vince's mother   Go away you brute!   (*Cough.*)

Bertha Is that any way to talk to your guardian angel? I thought you might be a trifle nippy so I brought you a candle. Here, I'll light it for you.

(**Vince** and **his mother** *huddle around.*)

Vince's mother Thank you Bertha, that was very thoughtful of you. (*Sneezes and blows out candle.*)

Bertha Oh what a shame. And that was my last match too. Oh well, see ya.

Vince Bertha.

Bertha Yeah Vinnie-poo.

Vince I've decided to . . .

Bertha Yes?

Vince To . . .

Bertha To what?

Vince To stay here a while. Nice neighbourhood this.

(**Bertha** *exits.* **Fanny** *appears round corner.*)

Fanny Psst!

Vince Did you say something, Mother?

Vince's mother No dear.

Fanny Psst! Psst!

Vince Fanny! It's you! How did you find us?

Fanny Ssh! Bertha might still be around. I followed her. Quick, bring your mother. You're staying at my house.

Vince We wouldn't dream of it.

Fanny There's food.

Vince and Mother Food?

Fanny Warmth.

Vince and Mother Warmth?!

Fanny Beds.

Vince and Mother Beds?! (**Vince** *grovels, kissing her.*) Oh thank you, thank you, thank you.

Fanny Vince, stop it! (*To audience*) There'll be time for that later. Come on. Let's go.

(*Exit.*)

Narrator Oh boy that Bertha is one mean cat. I'm talking cruel with a capital 'K'. The situation looks bad for poor old Vince and Fanny – I mean desperationville. But can things get worse? You bet your sweet bippy they can. Just watch!

SCENE 9

Dark alley, **Eugene**, **Leech** *and* **Spud** *repeat their dance wearing stockings over their heads.* **Fanny**, **Vince** *and his* **mother** *are struggling along when* **Bertha**, **Leech**, **Spud** *and* **Eugene** *jump out.*

Eugene Hold it! Stop right there! Don't move! This is a mugging! (*Turns to* **Bertha**.) Did I do it good Bertha, ay? Did I do it good?

Bertha You idiot, Eugene. You said my name. Now they know who I am.

Leech But, Bertha, you just said Eugene's name. Didn't she, Spud. She did, Spud, you heard her.

Spud Der, yeah that's right. Bertha, you did say Eugene's name.

Bertha You idiots! Now they know who we all are.

Vince What do you think you're doing. My mother can't stand out here in the cold all night. Let us pass. (*Tries to push past but is pushed back.*)

Fanny You tell them Vince.

Bertha Yeah Vinnie-poo. You tell them. (*Laughs.*) I have given you twenty-four hours to be my boyfriend so now I'm taking you . . . by force!

Vince I'm not going to go with you. No matter what you do.

Bertha What if I threatened to cut your heart out and use it for a football.

Vince Then I'd go.

Vince's mother You despicable little girl. You kick us out of our house in the middle of winter and now you want to kidnap my son.

Bertha Shut ya mouth, granny.

Eugene Yeah, you tell 'em, Bertha. You tell 'em.

Vince You have no right to speak to my mother like that. It looks like I'm going to have to teach you a lesson. I pump iron, you know.

Bertha
Eugene ⎱ Oooh, he pumps iron!
Leech ⎰
Spud

Bertha Hold me up Eugene, I think I'm gonna faint. (*Laughs.*)

Fanny You'd better laugh while you can, Bertha. My Vince has a fist of iron.

Bertha Listen here sweet little Fanny, if you'd kept your nose out of Vince's life, his mum would've been in a nice, warm house and Vince would've been my boyfriend.

Fanny He would never agree to that.

Bertha Do you know karate?

Fanny No.

Bertha Good (*Bops* **Fanny** *on the head. She collapses.*)

Vince You just try that again. Go on. Just try it one more time.

Bertha OK. (*Bops* **Vince's mother** *on the head.*) Alright guys, grab him. Take him to the hideout. (*To audience*) I told you I'd get even. Tonight Vince and me are gonna make beautiful music together . . .

  (*Exits.*)

  (*Repeat dance music.*)

  (**Fanny** and **Vince's mother** *regain consciousness.*)

Vince's mother Ohh! My head!

Fanny Are you OK, Mrs Van Coff?

Vince's mother Ohh, it's my head. My heart. My kidneys. My toes. My back.

  (**Fanny** *puts a hand on her shoulder.*)

  Ohh, my shoulder. Quick, get my pills from my handbag.

  (**Fanny** *finds the pills, and* **Vince's mother** *swallows one.*)

  Ahh, that's better. Who are you?

Fanny I'm Fanny.

Vince's mother That's a fanny name.
    (*Giggle.*)

Fanny Hasn't Vince spoken of me at all?

Vince's mother Vince? Who's Vince?

Fanny Your son.

Vince's mother Oh yes. Now that you mention it, that's all he ever does. It's always Fanny this and Fanny that. It's very nice to meet you. Speaking of Vince, where is he? My son!

Fanny My love! Bertha must have taken him.

Vince's mother My only son! My life! My world! My everything! My intestines!   (*Pulling at sausages from dress.*)

Fanny What can we do? Who can we turn to?

Spud Never fear, Coco's here. Try Kellogg's Coco Pops and you'll never be in the depths of despair.

Fanny Hey, do you smell something?

Vince's mother No. Wait a minute. I do. It smells like, it smells like, like . . .

Fanny BO.

Vince's mother (*Sniffs*)   Did you shower today my dear?

Fanny Of course I did. It smells more like Bertha.

Vince's mother I have an idea! Why don't we follow the scent. It will lead us to Bertha and to my beloved son. This play's going to have a happy ending after all.

Fanny (*Grabbing her*)   Come on then. I think it's this way.

   (*Exit.*)

SCENE 10

The hideout. **Vince** *is shoved inside.*

Bertha Guys, tie spunk features to that chair over there.

Eugene Right, Bertha. (*They busy themselves, winding a rope around* **Vince**. '*Here we go round the mulberry bush . . .* '.)

Bertha What are you doing?

Eugene Just what you said, Bertha. Tying up Vince and putting him in the chair.

Bertha I said tie him to the chair. Otherwise he'll escape. Understand?

Eugene That's a very good idea, Bertha. Gee, it's easy to see why you're the brains of this outfit. Always thinking aren't you, Bertha.

Bertha Shut up for a while and start tying! (*To* **Vince**.) Vincie-poo, I know you don't like me. I know you think I'm cruel and mean and all those nasty things but I'm not. Deep down I'm a warm (*Snigger*) sensitive (*Snigger*) loving. (*Snigger*) Do you mind! Caring human being. I know you could learn to love me. So whadaya say, Vinnie-poo.

Vince Get lost! My heart yearns only for Fanny.

Bertha (*With great control*) OK, Vince, if that's the way you want it. Eugene! (*He races over*) Go get that tape I bought the other day.

Eugene Which one Bertha?

Bertha Barry Manilow. (*Incredible fearful reaction.*)

Eugene Bertha. You wouldn't! Not that! Boil him in oil, drag him round the block in ya mum's panel van but . . .

Bertha Get it!

(**Leech** *and* **Spud** *are cowering in the corner while* **Vince** *is struggling to free himself.*) (**Eugene** *returns, holding it at arms length, gives it to* **Bertha** *who waves it in front of* **Vince**.)

Of all the devilish, evil, destructive, inventions created by man, this, the Barry Manilow tape, would have to be the worst. Vincie-poo, prepare to die.

Bertha (*Bertha places the tape in a cassette player.*) Eugene, Leech, Spud, take these ear plugs. They'll protect you from the deadly air waves. (*They insert plugs.*) Music starts 'I can't smile without you', **Vince** screams and struggles as if electric shocks are running through him. Gradually, he weakens and slumps in chair.

Fanny (*Bursting in*) Alright, Bertha. It's all over. Now turn that thing off. (**Bertha** *laughs.*)

Vince's mother (*Entering*) Oh what lovely music. (*Starts grooving.*)

Fanny Alright, I'll do it myself. (*She struggles closer but music forces her back.*)

Fanny (*To mother*) It's no use. Wait a minute. It doesn't seem to be harming you. Quick, turn it off.

Vince's mother Mellow out Fanny. Get down! Boogie!

Fanny Listen to me! Your son is dying. You must do something!

Vince's mother (*Grudgingly*) Oh, alright. (*She walks towards* **Vince**. **Bertha** *tries to stop her*. **Vince's mother** *hits* **Bertha** *with stick*. **Bertha** *falls, the impact knocking out her ear plugs*.)

Bertha (*Scrambling round on all fours*) My ear plugs! They've fallen out! Help me!

(*Meantime*, **Fanny** *unties* **Vince** *and covers his ears. He starts to regain consciousness. While* **Vince's mother** *wards off* **Eugene**, **Spud** *and* **Leech** *with a stick,* **Fanny** *finds ear plugs, inserts them and grabs the cassette player. She approaches* **Bertha** *who is now totally unhinged*.)

Fanny Right, Bertha. You're going to do exactly as I say.

Bertha Anything! Just kill that music!

Fanny You're going to leave Vince and me alone. No more interference or dirty tricks.

Bertha Sure! OK! Whatever you say!

Fanny And you're going to give up your evil ways and be sweet, just like me. Promise?

Bertha Just like you?

Fanny Just like me.

Bertha Don't you think that's going just a bit too far?

(**Fanny** *turns up volume*.)

Bertha Alright! You win. (*Music stops*.)

Vince Fanny!

Fanny Vince. (*They embrace*.)

Bertha's mother (*bursts in*.) Bertha!

Bertha Mother!

Bertha's mother You've been a naughty girl, Bertha. This sweet little social worker told me all about it.

Bertha (*To the* **social worker**) So you had to open your big fat . . . I mean, yes, mother. I have been naughty. But I've changed. I've learnt my lesson and from now on I'm going to dedicate my life to helping others.

Bertha's mother Oh, Bertha!

Bertha Oh, Mother! (*Embrace*) Guys, can you ever forgive me. I've treated you unfairly.

All Unfairly!

Bertha Cruelly?

Spud That's more like it.

Bertha Anyway, I'm sorry. Can we be friends?

(**Eugene**, **Spud** and **Leech** *go into a huddle. Mumble, mumble.*)

Eugene OK.

Bertha I think I'm gonna cry.

Fanny So am I.

Vince's mother So am I.

Vince I'm not.

Leech I am.

Social worker Me too.

Fanny (*Downstage*) Oh I'm so happy now that I've got my man.

Bertha I've got my friends. (*Hugs them.*)

Bertha's mother I've got my daughter.

Vince Oh, Fanny, whenever I'm with you I just want to sing.

All No!!

Narrator I've got a better idea. Let's boogie!

All Yeah!!!

(*Everyone goes into general unchoreographed rock'n'roll dance to bright dance music. Towards the end, they take their bows in pairs and exit.*)

(*The end.*)

• Drama Activities •

APPRECIATING THE PLAY

1 Bertha is the villain of the play. What are some of the wicked things she does?

2 What does the audience do to show its disapproval of Bertha?

3 Fanny is the heroine. What is her attitude to Vince?

4   What are Vince's feelings towards Bertha?
5   Why is Bertha confident that Vince will be hers?
6   How does the dramatist exaggerate the sickness of Vince's mother?
7   What suffering does Vince and his mother have to endure?
8   How does goodness triumph over evil at the end of the play?
9   What examples of exaggeration can you find in the play?
10 What scenes of the play did you find humorous?

MELODRAMA

Melodrama portrays the triumph of good over evil. Characters are either very good or very bad; with the main characters being the hero, the heroine and the villain. Melodrama is full of impossible events and situations and elements are often intensified and exaggerated. In this play the hero and the heroine suffer distress, persecution and separation and their suffering continues until just before the final curtain when they are miraculously united happily together.

The villain is completely heartless, unscrupulous, hateful and entirely evil. The villain always gets his or her just desserts. On the other hand, the hero and the heroine are as pure as the driven snow.

The sympathy of the audience is always with the hero and the heroine, but its antagonism is directed at the villain. Consequently, in a melodrama, the audience cheers the hero and boos the villain.

Pathos or the way the play evokes emotion in the audience is very important in melodrama. It is used continually to arouse sympathy for the misfortunes that beset the hero and his acquaintances. Emotive words such as 'miserable', 'poor', 'lonely', 'unhappy' and 'despair' are used to arouse the audience's pity.

FOILED AGAIN!

Now write your own piece of melodrama. To help you write your own script, here are your characters, your plot or story, and some words and expressions you might like to use in your play that are typical of the language of melodrama.

Remember that in melodrama, the three main characters are always a beautiful but helpless heroine, a handsome hero and a cunning and ruthless villain. The audience often hisses and boos the villain and cheers on the hero.

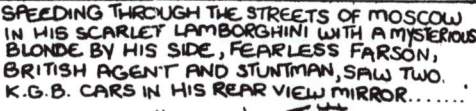

CHARACTERS

SIR RUDOLPH	The wicked landowner
SILAS	Sir Rudolph's vile gamekeeper
FANNY	The beautiful young heroine
MOLLY	Her poor and helpless mother
CLIVE	Her old, sick father
ARTHUR	The strong, handsome hero
SERGEANT SLOGGER	Police officer
CONSTABLE CLIVE	Police officer

PLOT

Sir Rudolph and Silas arrive at Clive's and Molly's miserable little cottage to collect the rent. When they find they can not pay, Sir Rudolph threatens to evict them into the snow unless they give him their beautiful daughter, Fanny. They have to agree.

> As Fanny is carried off by Sir Rudolph and Silas, her screams for help are heard by her beloved Arthur. He rushes to the police and explains what has happened.
>
> Meanwhile, Fanny rejects Sir Rudolph's insincere marriage proposal and escapes from his clutches only to fall headlong over a railway line as she runs away. To punish her for rejecting him, Sir Rudolph and Silas tie Fanny across the railway lines.
>
> As the train thunders towards her, Arthur arrives and unties her in the nick of time. Fanny and Arthur melt in each other's arms and they agree to marry, while Sergeant Slogger and Constable Clive arrest Sir Rudolph and Silas and lead them off to prison.

WORDS AND EXPRESSIONS

penniless and starving	hiss the villain!
I am promised to another	unhand me!
merciful heaven	lying rogue
at his mercy	help a maiden in distress
a heart of gold	vile creature
wretched rascal	to the rescue!

Here are some opening lines that you could use to begin your play.

FOILED AGAIN!

Silas (*knocking*) Open up! Sir Rudolph is here to collect the rent.

Molly (*opening the door*) I am sorry Sir Rudolph but we are poor and penniless since my husband, Clive, fell ill and . . .

Sir Rudolph Ha. So you will not pay your rent. Ha. Then out in the snow with you and all your sticks of furniture and your pitiful possessions. (*Hisses and boos from the Audience.*)

Molly I beg you, Sir, to have mercy. Give us one more week. We'll get the money somehow.

Audience Yes! Yes!

Silas I will throw them out in the snow right now.

Audience Shame!

Sir Rudolph Wait. (*peering*) Who is that beautiful girl I see.

Molly and Clive That is our daughter, Fanny.

Audience Aaaaahhhhhh.

Sir Rudolph Ha. Well don't stand there like a couple of nitwits! Introduce me!

NOW IT'S OVER TO YOU

Continue with the script to complete the plot. When you have finished, choose characters to act out your melodrama for the class.

4

Dracula

Adapted by Tom Hayllar

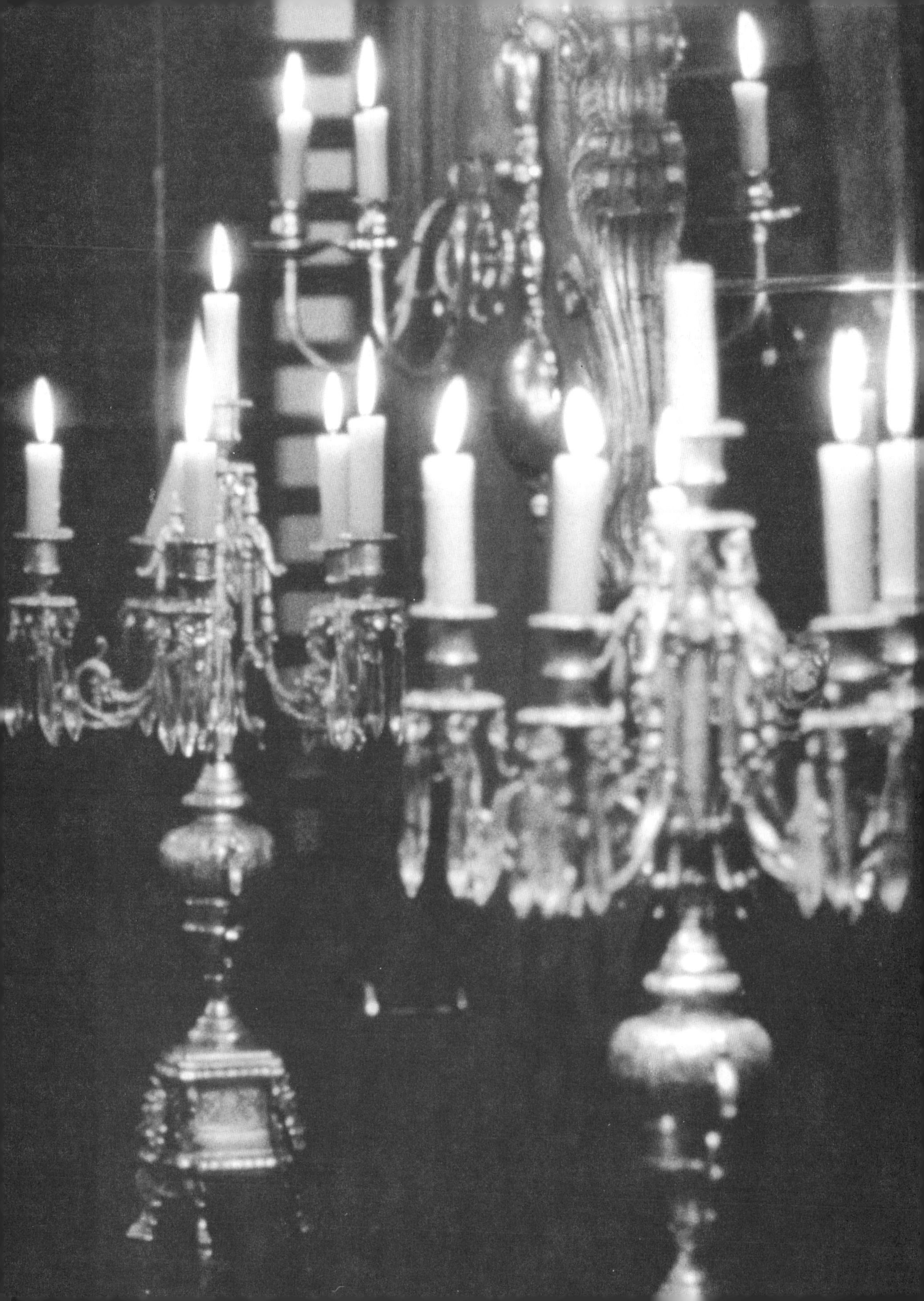

Dracula

by Tom Hayllar

adapted for radio from the novel *Dracula*
by Bram Stoker

In his famous Gothic horror novel, *Dracula*, Bram Stoker has created a monster in human form who changes himself into a vampire. As you read and act out the parts in this radio play, you will notice that many special sound effects are needed. A tape recorder and plenty of imagination will ensure that the play becomes as suspenseful and eerie as possible.

CHARACTERS

Narrator	
Jonathan Harker	A young London lawyer
Mina	A lovely young lady who is also Jonathan's fiancée
Old Innkeeper	
Coachman	
Count Dracula	An ancient vampire in human form
Dark haired woman	
Red haired woman	Three beautiful but deadly vampire sisters
Fair haired woman	
Lucy	An attractive woman who is Mina's best friend
Old lady	Lucy's servant
Arthur	A doctor, Lucy's husband
Professor Van Helsing	A medical man and a vampire specialist

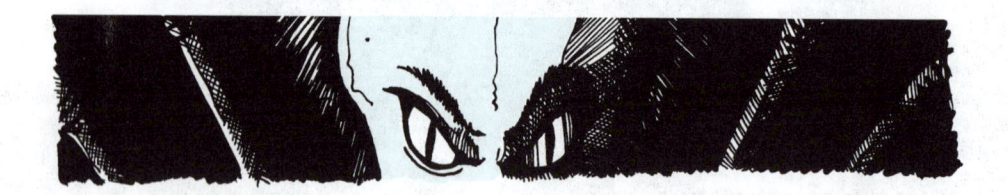

ACT 1

Castle Dracula.

Narrator As the play begins, Jonathan Harker, a young solicitor who works for a law firm in London, has received a letter from the far-off country of Transylvania. He discusses the surprising invitation it contains with Mina, his fiancée.

Jonathan You remember I mentioned that we have a wealthy client named Count Dracula who lives somewhere called Transylvania?

Mina Didn't he ask you to find him a big, old house in London?

Jonathan He's the man. Now he has sent me a letter asking me to meet him in Transylvania, all expenses paid, so that I can show him personally all the documents on the house. Of course, I won't go.

Mina Why not? Jonathan, you must take this opportunity to please such an important client. The firm might promote you. And, darling, I hate to say this but I do think you need a holiday.

Jonathan Well, I suppose I'd only be gone for a couple of weeks. It can't hurt, can it?

Mina Darling, I know you've made the right choice. Come on, I'll help you pack.

Jonathan By the way, where is Transylvania?

Narrator Transylvania is a remote country in Eastern Europe. Its landscape is misty and mountainous with ancient castles and thick forests through which packs of wolves roam and howl at the moon. It took Jonathan a week by train to reach Bistritz, the closest town to Count Dracula's residence. From there he had to travel by public coach to Borgo Pass, high in the Transylvanian mountains. From Borgo Pass, Count Dracula had arranged for his own coach to pick up Jonathan and take him to 'Castle Dracula'. Jonathan found he had time to have a meal at the Inn in Bistritz before the coach left for the pass.

Old Innkeeper Here is your lunch, sir. It's a tasty venison stew.

Jonathan (*Hungrily*) Ah, yes, this will keep me warm on my journey into the mountains.

Old Innkeeper And where will you be travelling to, sir?

Jonathan To 'Castle Dracula'.

Old Innkeeper (*In a shocked whisper*) 'Dracula'. Did you say the name, 'Dracula'?

Jonathan Yes . . .

Old Innkeeper (*Clutching his arm*) 'Dracula' is not a good name in these parts, young sir. Turn round and go back home!

Jonathan Don't be silly. I don't believe in gossip and, anyway, I've come too far to turn back now.

Old Innkeeper (*Rummaging in his pockets*) Then take this gold cross and chain to wear round your neck. Use it if you have to.

Jonathan I thank you for the gift but how will I use it?

Old Innkeeper May that terrible time never come, but if it does you will *know* how to use the cross! I hope you enjoy your lunch, young sir.

Narrator The public coach took Jonathan up into the mountains. At first, it was a beautiful, sunny afternoon but when the sun set the mountains became dark and menacing shapes. Jonathan shivered as wolves began to howl in the dark forests all around.

At Borgo Pass, the coach stopped to allow Jonathan to alight. The coach driver handed down his luggage and the coach rattled away leaving him alone in the night. Suddenly, Jonathan saw the outline of another coach, with four black horses, silently waiting beside the road.

Coachman (*Calling*) Are you the Englishman? The guest? Count Dracula's personal coach is waiting to carry him to Dracula's Castle. Ha Ha Ha Ha Ha . . .

Jonathan (*Hesitating*) I am the Englishman that Count Dracula is expecting.

Coachman Pass me your luggage and climb up beside me. Through the dark night we go with the wind! Hold tight, Englishman. Ha Ha Ha Ha . . .

Narrator As the coach rushed through the darkness, Jonathan was alarmed.

Jonathan Coachman, we have no lights. How can you be sure of the road?

Coachman The horses know the way.

Jonathan What are those dark shapes running along the road behind us?

Coachman Wolves and other creatures of the night. Nothing to be frightened about, Englishman – unless we stop. Ha Ha Ha Ha . . .

Narrator After many hours of travel the coach, much to Jonathan's relief, rattled over cobblestones and he realised they were in a courtyard. The great dark mass of a castle rose before them.

Coachman We have arrived, Englishman. Ha Ha Ha Ha . . .

Jonathan Thank you.

Narrator A great wooden door creaked open and a very tall, white haired man held up a lamp. His eyes seemed to glow in a face that was as pale as moonlight.

Dracula I am Count Dracula. Welcome to my castle, Mr Harker.

Jonathan Call me Jonathan, Count.

Dracula (*Shaking his hand*) Jonathan, I notice you are shivering. I ask you to pardon my icy hand, sometimes my circulation is very bad. Now you must come with me. I will show you your bedroom and then you will eat a good supper. But first we climb this spiral staircase . . . down several long passages, damp and mossy I am afraid – we have much rain in Transylvania. Now here (*Throwing open a creaking door*) is your bedroom.

Jonathan If you don't mind, Count, I think I'll go straight to bed. I'm not feeling very well . . .

Dracula No! You must eat now. You must keep up your strength. Transylvania can be bad for the health if you are not strong.

Narrator Jonathan could not refuse. He began to eat and found he was hungry. The Count who did not eat, gradually moved closer to his guest. Jonathan noticed how red the Count's lips were and how long and sharp his teeth were. An unpleasant smell seemed to fill the room. Despite the castle's thick walls, Jonathan could hear wolves howling.

Dracula We call our wolves, 'the Children of the Night' and their howling is the night music of Transylvania.

Jonathan Count Dracula, you have been most kind but I am very tired.

Dracula How thoughtless of me. Of course you must go to your bed. We will talk in the morning. Pleasant dreams!

Narrator Jonathan's sleep was filled with nightmares in which he heard wolves howling and terrible shrieks of laughter.

Jonathan (*Waking up*) I feel terrible. I must get up and shave. That's odd, there's no mirror. It's just as well I have a portable mirror in my luggage. (**Jonathan** *starts to shave.*)

Count Dracula (*Entering the room quietly*) Good morning, Jonathan.

Jonathan (*Startled*) Count Dracula! I didn't see you behind me. You, er, didn't seem to appear in the mirror.

Dracula Arrrrghhhh. You have cut yourself, Jonathan.

Jonathan Yes, you startled me and . . . COUNT DRACULA! Why are your eyes glowing red?

Count Dracula (*Furiously*) Aaaaarrrgghhh.

Jonathan And why are your hands moving towards my throat.

Count Dracula I NEED YOUR BL . . . Ahhhhh. (*Leaping back.*)

Jonathan (*Surprised*) You touched the gold cross I wear around my neck!

Count Dracula (*Recovering*) Please forgive me. I am not myself this morning. Jonathan I do not wish you to have a mirror in Castle Dracula. It is something we are not used to. We have no need to beautify ourselves here. Ha Ha Ha! Here is what I think of mirrors! (*He throws the mirror out of the window.*) And beware of cutting yourself again. It is dangerous for your health, Jonathan.

Now, today I have to be absent for a while. After you have eaten your breakfast, why not amuse yourself by looking around my castle? Of course, you will not wish to enter those rooms with locked doors. They are places where no guest would wish to go.

Narrator   Feeling anxious about what had happened and what Count Dracula had said, Jonathan ate very little breakfast. He had lost his appetite. Restlessly, he wandered through the castle. There were many locked doors. He looked out of every window he passed but the ground was always far below. In the cold and gloomy atmosphere of Castle Dracula, Jonathan began to feel more like a prisoner than a guest.

The days passed. Count Dracula had signed all the papers for his purchase of the London house yet he would not let Jonathan leave the castle.

Count Dracula   I wish to delve into your thoughts. I want you to tell me all you know about England.

Jonathan   (*Wearily*)   I will do my best. However, I long to return to England – to Mina, my fiancée, and to my job as a lawyer.

Count Dracula   You are unhappy here?

Jonathan   (*Fearful of Dracula's temper*)   NO! It's . . . just that I often feel so tired.

Count Dracula   It must be the climate. But seriously, my young friend, do not go to sleep in any other part of the castle. It is old and has many memories and there are bad dreams for those who sleep unwisely. Sleep only in your own room. If you do not . . .   (*The* **Count** *made motions with his hands as if washing them.*)

Narrator   The Count's warning frightened Jonathan and for several days, when he felt tired, he quickly returned to his room. Then, he grew careless. One day, late in the afternoon, he found a door which seemed to be locked but opened when he pushed hard. The room he entered had ancient furniture but all covered in dust. There was a big window with a view but it was obscured by cobwebs. Jonathan found a couch, blew off most of the dust, cleared the window of half its cobwebs and relaxed to enjoy a view of the mountains . . . but I will allow Jonathan to describe what happened next.

Jonathan   I suppose I must have fallen asleep. I hope so, but I'm afraid it was all real. I opened my eyes. The room was moonlit. I was not alone. Three beautiful women dressed in long, white robes, stood in front of me. I spoke to them.

Who are you?

Dark haired woman   I am one of Count Dracula's relatives. As you can see, my hair is jet black, and my eyes . . .

Red haired woman   Her eyes are piercing and just like mine, they have a beautiful, reddish glow. Look deeply into them.

Fair haired woman   And look at me! Unlike my two sisters, I have long golden hair. But my eyes, too, are piercing yours to your soul.

Jonathan   All three of you are very beautiful and, yet, I feel dreadfully afraid of you.

Dark haired woman   Our lips are ruby red . . .

Red haired woman   Our teeth are pearly white . . .

Fair haired woman   And very, very sharp.

Jonathan   Please leave me alone . . .

Dark haired woman   Do not be afraid of us. All we want to do is give you our kisses.

Red haired woman   Long, lingering kisses.

Fair haired woman   Kisses so sweet they will be painful.   (*Leaning to kiss him.*)

Narrator   As the woman bent over him, Jonathan smelled the sweet fragrance of her breath and saw that her red lips were open. He felt her teeth brush his throat with a touch that made his skin tingle. He felt faint. His heart began to beat faster. Her teeth were just about to draw blood when the mighty voice of Count Dracula filled the room.

Count Dracula   (*Shouting*)   HOW DARE YOU TOUCH HIM! THIS MAN BELONGS TO ME!

Fair haired woman   (*Furious*)   We have fallen in love with him!

Red haired woman   And, he has fallen in love with us!

Red haired woman   We need to kiss him and he needs our kisses!

Count Dracula   I will give you this promise. When I have finished with him, you three will have your turn. Now, I have to wake him up. There is work to be done. You three, GO!

Narrator   As Jonathan looked up at them, the three women disappeared. They faded into the moonlight. Then horror overcame Jonathan and he sank into deep unconsciousness.

Count Dracula Wake up, Jonathan. You have been tossing and turning and calling out. You must have been dreaming. WAKE UP!

Narrator Jonathan woke slowly and fearfully and was amazed to find he was back in his own room. Count Dracula must have carried him there. He knew he had not been dreaming. Somewhere in the castle there were three beautiful but terrible women who were waiting to drink his blood. Meanwhile, Count Dracula was waiting to tell him something.

Count Dracula My dear friend, I have to leave the castle for a little while but you will remain here as my honoured guest.

Jonathan Count Dracula, I must return to England! To Mina, my fiancée.

Count Dracula Impossible. My coach driver and horses are away on a mission.

Jonathan I will walk. I want to leave at once.

Count Dracula What about your luggage?

Jonathan I won't worry about it. I'll send for it some other time.

Count Dracula I like your spirit. 'Welcome the arrival, speed the parting guest.' I will not allow you to remain here a moment more against your will. Come along, I'll show you to the front door.

Narrator Walking slowly, Count Dracula, holding up a lamp, led Jonathan to the great, wooden front door. Suddenly, he held up his hand.

Count Dracula Listen.

Narrator From the other side of the door came the howling of many wolves. It was just as if they had started up when Dracula raised his hand. Then he drew back the bolts on the door, unhooked its heavy chains and pulled the door open. Immediately, wolves, howling angrily, poured through the opening. Their red jaws were filled with champing teeth and their claws scoured the wooden door. Jonathan was horrified. He screamed.

Jonathan SHUT THE DOOR! I'll . . . I'll go in the morning.

Narrator Jonathan covered his face with his hands to hide his tears of bitter disappointment. Dracula, with one sweep of his mighty arm, caused the wolves to cower and back away. He threw the door shut and the great bolts clanged and echoed through the hall as they shot back into their places. Dracula, holding high the light, led Jonathan back to his room.

Count Dracula Goodnight, my friend. You had better remain here till my return. Then we will discuss plans for your departure.

Narrator A red light of triumph shone in Count Dracula's eyes as he smiled and left the room, closing the door behind him. Jonathan was about to lie down when he thought he heard a whispering behind the door. He crept softly to it and listened.

Count Dracula Back! Back to your own place! Wait. Have patience. Tomorrow night he is yours!

Dark haired woman I can hardly wait! My lips are red!

Red haired woman My teeth are sharp!

Fair haired woman Blood! We need blood!

Narrator Jonathan must have fainted with horror. When he came to, seconds later, it was to hear Dracula's footsteps echoing off down the corridor.

Jonathan I must follow Dracula and see how he leaves the castle. This may be my last chance to escape (*Opens the door cautiously*).

Dark haired woman (*Laughing*) We see you!

Red haired woman We are licking our lips!

Fair haired woman And we are sharpening our teeth!

Narrator Jonathan nearly fainted again, but before he could react the three beautiful but deadly women vanished, laughing.

Jonathan After Dracula! It's my only chance to survive!

Narrator Dracula hurried along several cold, stone corridors until he stopped and opened a door. When the door had closed behind him, Jonathan crept up and tried it. It was locked. He put his ear to the wood.

Jonathan I can hear a window being opened. If I look out of an opening in the corridor I may be able to see Dracula's room. (*He ran along the corridor until he found an opening*)   Yes, there's Dracula's room. The window is open but nothing is moving. Wait! There's something coming out. It's Dracula and he's coming out head first! I can't believe this! Now, the whole man emerges and begins to crawl downwards. It's horrible! His cloak is spreading around him like wings, his hands and feet act like claws. He is crawling down the wall like a huge bat. What kind of man is this? Or what kind of creature that looks like a man? I feel the dread of this horrible place overpowering me. Fear is making me tremble fearfully. How can I escape?

Narrator Jonathan needed the keys to the outer door of the castle. He realised that the keys might be in Count Dracula's locked room and that there was only one way of entering. Jonathan made his preparations. He returned to his own room, put some food and his most valuable possessions in a small, cloth bag and hung it by a cord around his neck. Hoping Dracula had not re-entered his room, he went back to the opening in the corridor and leaned out of the opening. The ground was far beneath him.

Jonathan I must climb from the opening in the corridor to the window of Dracula's room. It's a long way down. If I can lean out and grasp the stones and don't look down   (*He climbs, desperately using his hands and feet*)   . . . Three more steps and . . . Ah AhAh . . . (*Breathing heavily*)   some of the stone broke off – but I'm nearly there. Now, I can just reach the window, and pull myself over the sill. At last, I'm in Dracula's room.   (*Looking around with relief*)   and he's not here . . . Good heaven's, it's completely empty except for a great pile of golden coins in the middle of the floor. Dracula's gold. I'll scoop up a handful to help me in my escape. Now, let me see. There are two doors. One, I know leads out into the corridor but the other?   (*He tries it*)   It is unlocked and opens to reveal . . . a narrow, stone passage leading into an old chapel   (*He goes ahead and looks around*).   What a monstrous sight! The floor has been turned into a graveyard! There are fifty coffins, all with their lids open and all of them filled with earth — except one. I have to lift the lid and look in it. I must know what is in there. I will regret it but I have to look . . .

Narrator Full of dread, Jonathan lifted the coffin lid. He was horrified at what he saw. There lay Count Dracula – his face evilly twisted in a frightful grin!

Jonathan   The eyes are staring at me yet they do not seem to see me. The hair has changed from white to dark grey and the pale skin is rosy with health. He leers even in his sleep. The teeth are sharp. The mouth is red and on the lips are drops of fresh blood! Dracula is a vampire who has just been drinking!

Narrator   Jonathan was still staring at Dracula's hideously bloated face when the sudden sounds of banging doors made him slam the lid back on the coffin and leap away to hide just as a gang of workers entered the chapel and began closing the lids of the dirt-filled coffins and carrying them away. Jonathan managed to escape from Count Dracula by covering himself with the dirt in one coffin. Choosing his moment carefully, he climbed out of the coffin after it had been carried outside and ran into the mountainous countryside of Transylvania. A week later, forty nine coffins filled with earth and one containing Dracula, were loaded onto a ship bound for England.

ACT 2

Dracula in England.

Narrator In London, Jonathan's fiancée, Mina, waited anxiously for news of him.

Mina (*Talking to her friend,* **Lucy**) I'm very worried about Jonathan. What has happened to him? He should have returned to England weeks ago. I haven't even had a letter.

Lucy There probably isn't any mail from a place as wild and remote as Transylvania.

Mina (*Beginning to sob*) I don't know what to do.

Lucy (*Comforting her*) I have a feeling that he is going to be alright. While you are waiting to hear word from him, why don't you come and stay with me down at my cottage in Hythe. It's a beautiful spot, close to the sea, with plenty of healthy walking along the clifftops. The sea air would be so good for you. Arthur is in Holland at the moment visiting his old teacher, Professor Van Helsing, so you will be doing me a great favour by keeping me company.

Narrator Mina took up Lucy's offer and for the first few days of her stay in Hythe, Lucy and she walked the cliff paths. One of Lucy's favourite walks was through the old churchyard with gravestones that clustered around the Old Hythe Church set in the smooth, green meadows behind the clifftops. Then, on the night of the third day, something strange happened.

Mina What woke me? It's the sound of footsteps coming from Lucy's room and passing my bedroom door. I'd better go and see if she's alright.

Lucy Ohhhh, the gravestones are calling me . . . calling me.

Mina She's sleepwalking! (*Taking her by the arm*) Let me lead you back to your bed.

Lucy (*Waking*) Thank you. I don't know what came over me. I was having a weird dream in which I was told to leave my bed and walk to the churchyard.

Mina It was just a bad dream. Here's your bed. I'm sure you'll sleep well now.

Narrator The next night, a great storm hit Hythe. Lightning seared the sky and thunder shook the cottage walls. Neither Lucy nor Mina could sleep so they sat up and watched the sudden displays of lightning. Spray from the giant waves crashing at the foot of the cliffs, lashed the cottage. Mina felt terrified but Lucy's eyes gleamed with an odd excitement. The storm passed on but that afternoon Lucy's old servant told Lucy and Mina that a shipwreck had occurred during the storm. Lucy eagerly questioned her.

Lucy Did any living creature reach the shore?

Servant Curious that you should ask that, ma'am. The village folk saw a big, black dog jump off the deck of the wrecked ship and swim to the beach. But before they could catch it, the creature ran off howling. Nobody's seen it since.

Lucy And what about the ship's cargo?

Servant Now there's something that gives me the creeps, ma'am. All that could be found was a cargo of coffins! One of them broke open as they were being salvaged and what do you think was inside?

Lucy Earth.

Servant (*Surprised*) How did you guess that, ma'am?

Lucy (*Shaking her head*) I don't know . . . it just came into my head like a picture.

Servant When all the coffins were stacked on the beach, they were claimed by a bunch of foreigners who had them taken away to London in carts.

Mina (*Shivering*) How weird.

Servant (*Crossing herself*) Nothing like today's going on has ever been seen in Hythe before. And where are all the sailors, poor things?

Lucy Only the big, black dog escaped. Only one living thing escaped and it was the big, black dog . . .

Narrator Lucy went sleepwalking again that night. Mina woke to find her friend had left the house. Very worried, Mina searched in the moonlight. She could find Lucy nowhere but eventually she thought of Lucy's favourite place – the churchyard. She saw her half collapsed over a tombstone and as Mina hurried towards her friend she thought she saw a long, black shape bending over her. However, it had vanished by the time she reached Lucy and she thought it must have been only a shadow.

Mina Lucy! Are you all right?

Lucy It's my throat.

Mina There are two red marks on it. (*Shuddering*) I wonder . . .

Narrator For several days Lucy sickened. Her face grew paler and paler. Then she seemed to be recovering until, one awful night, Mina saw a great black bat with glowing red eyes flapping out of Lucy's window.

Mina (*Rushing into her friend's room*) Are you hurt?

Lucy No, I don't think so . . .

Mina (*Screaming*) There are two wounds on your neck and they're bleeding!

Narrator Mina was shocked and worried but suddenly she had no time to think about what she had seen. Her own life was about to change.

Mina It's a letter from Jonathan! He's alive!

(*A few days later, they met in London.*)

Mina My dear Jonathan, how wonderful to see you but how thin and pale you are!

Jonathan I lived through a nightmare in Castle Dracula.

Mina Tell me what happened.

Jonathan I can't. If I did you would also experience the nightmare and I can't do that to you.

Mina We must forget the past.

Narrator Mina and Jonathan soon married. But even the happy occasion at the church was shattered when Jonathan recognised a man in the crowd of well-wishers.

Jonathan That tall man walking quickly away from the church – it's Count Dracula!

Mina He's stopping and turning around. He's smiling at us. It's . . . it's an evil smile.

Jonathan The red lips, the sharp, white teeth. How well I remember fearing them to the depths of my soul.

Mina He's turned and vanished into the crowd.

Jonathan What is that monster doing here at the church?

Mina Remember, he has a house in London.

Jonathan Ah, yes.

Narrator While Jonathan and Mina were in London, Lucy, in the cottage at Hythe, took a turn for the worst. Her husband, Arthur, returned from Holland to be with her.

Arthur My dear Lucy, you look so pale and thin. As your husband and as a doctor I must ask you tell me everything.

Lucy My dear husband thank heavens you are here. Every night I have had dreams in which I see red eyes emerging from a cloud of golden dust moving slowly through the air towards me.

Arthur (*To himself*) Golden dust? Red eyes? I must get the advice of my old medical school teacher, Professor Van Helsing.

Narrator The professor, an expert on vampires, arrived with all possible speed. He was shocked by Lucy's appearance and – and the cause behind it.

Van Helsing Gott in Himmel! She looks terrible! She needs a blood transfusion immediately!

Arthur I will give her my blood.

Lucy (*Dreamily*) I love the gaze of the red eyes and the feel of the golden dust.

Van Helsing The marks on the throat and the loss of blood indicate that Lucy is the victim of a vampire.

Arthur What can be done, Professor?

Van Helsing There is an old-fashioned remedy that I hope will work.

Arthur What is it?

Van Helsing Garlic. It has a powerful smell that is extremely hateful to vampires. In its presence they begin to feel heavy and helpless. I am going to place several garlic plants in the room (*He places the pots*) Now I place this wreath of garlic flowers around Lucy's neck.

Arthur I pray that the cure will be successful, Professor.

Narrator The cure was successful – for two days.

Arthur I only left Lucy alone for an hour or two. I had to visit a patient.

Van Helsing I fell asleep in a chair in the next room. Suddenly, I heard a sound. I rushed into Lucy's room. The bedroom window was shattered and Lucy lay on the floor. There was glass all round her and the wreath of garlic had been ripped from around her neck. The other garlic plants were trodden into the floor. Lucy's eyes were closed. Then Arthur rushed in.

Arthur What's happened? LUCY!

Van Helsing (*Kneeling*) There's still a pulse but it's very weak.

Arthur (*Wringing his hands*) Is she going to recover?

Van Helsing No. She is dying. However, we must not let her die in a coma.

Narrator At that moment, Lucy's eyes opened.

Arthur Lucy, my darling, what happened?

Lucy (*Softly and slowly*) I was awakened by a flapping sound at the window pane. At first it was a big bat with sharp white teeth and red eyes. I was terrified until I saw I had been mistaken. It was not a bat at all but a tall man with a very white face. He called my name and his voice was so persuasive and hypnotic but when I still would not open the window he smashed it. For a moment there was the smell of garlic which seemed to grow stronger then it faded. Red eyes came close to mine through golden mist.

Narrator As she finished speaking, Lucy raised herself towards Arthur who was bending over her. Her mouth opened. Her lips were very red and her teeth were very sharp and very white.

Van Helsing (*Pulling* **Arthur** *away from* **Lucy**) That's not Lucy anymore!

Arthur What . . . what do you mean?

Lucy (*Suddenly angry and vicious*) COME HERE TO ME! . . . I NEED THE STRENGTH YOUR BLOOD CAN GIVE ME! YES, QUICKLY, YOUR BLOOD! AHHHHHHhhhhhhh . . .

Narrator Lucy was dead. Van Helsing would not allow Arthur to kiss his wife on the lips. He kissed her hands instead.

Arthur Is she at peace now?

Van Helsing I do not think so.

Arthur What? I don't understand.

Van Helsing If the tall man who came through her window was Dracula then he has been drinking her blood and she is also a vampire.

Narrator A month passed and apparently Lucy was resting in her grave. Then, around the quiet little seaside village of Hythe, children began to vanish. Later, each child was found at dusk in the old churchyard among the gravestones, unharmed except for two little, red bites on the neck. Each child said that a beautiful dark-haired lady had smiled, spoken softly and given him or her a hug until unconsciousness came.

Jonathan The red bites and Hythe churchyard – I'm afraid Lucy has emerged as a vampire!

Mina We must get in touch with Professor Van Helsing again. He is the only one who can tell us for sure.

Jonathan And we need his advice.

Narrator When Van Helsing arrived he demanded immediate action.

Van Helsing There is no doubt that a vampire inhabits Lucy's body and that poor Lucy herself is a restless spirit.

Mina How horrible!

Van Helsing We must destroy the vampire and allow Lucy to rest in peace.

Jonathan (*Grimly*) What is the plan, Professor?

Van Helsing We must go to Lucy's tomb, open her coffin and without hesitation, drive a sharpened stake into the heart of the thing we find lying there. We must then cut off the creature's head.

Mina Can we do these terrible things?

Jonathan When can we tell Arthur about his wife?

Van Helsing We must go to Hythe immediately.

Narrator Arthur was horrified but he accepted the fact that Lucy's body had been captured by a vampire and that they had to kill it. Using lanterns and carrying a cross, a sharp wooden stake, a hammer and an axe, they made their way to Lucy's tomb in the old churchyard. It was an eerie place.

Arthur I last saw this tomb in sunlight when all the flowers were fresh. Now they are withered and the stone and ironwork of the tomb are throwing monstrous shadows.

Mina Although it is quite a warm night, there's a weird chill surrounding the tomb.

Jonathan The hair on my head is rising. I can't help it.

Van Helsing I am pulling open the door to the tomb. The coffin rests inside. Jonathan, lift the lid!

Mina (*Gasping*) It's empty!

Arthur Where's Lucy?

Van Helsing The vampire is away hunting a victim. We will wait for it to return.

Narrator They left the tomb, closed the door and waited. All around them, the old tombstones looked ghastly white; the trees hanging over them were black and twisted. Even the grass rustled with a threat of doom. Suddenly . . .

Van Helsing SHHHhhhhh. (*He pointed.*)

Jonathan A figure dressed in white is coming towards us through the tombstones.

Mina A dark-haired woman.

Jonathan Her lips are crimson. It's fresh blood!

Arthur LUCY! (*He began to move towards her.*)

Van Helsing NO! (*Restraining him*) Look, her eyes are blazing with hell fire!

Jonathan The Lucy creature is rushing with open arms toward Arthur.

Lucy Come to me, Arthur. Leave these others and come to me. My arms are hungry for you. Come into my arms, my husband. COME AND KISS ME!

Mina (*Horrified*) Arthur is running to meet her. He seems to be under a spell.

Jonathan The Lucy creature is leaping towards him!

Van Helsing (*Running between them and holding up a golden cross*) STOP!

Lucy AHHHHHhhhh. Keep it away! Don't show me the cross!

Narrator Lucy, who was really a vampire, stumbled back from the upraised cross. She shrieked in fear and rage and rushed towards the tomb.

Arthur (*Bewildered*) Please, Lucy, wait for me!

Jonathan The tomb door is closed.

Mina No, there is a tiny crack and she is disappearing into it!

Van Helsing Now, we must be strong and enter the tomb. Bring the hammer, the stake and the axe.

Narrator They opened the door and entered the tomb. The professor lifted the lid off Lucy's coffin. They all gasped . . .

Mina It's Lucy but . . .

Arthur Is this really Lucy's body or only a demon in her shape?

Van Helsing It is her body that is now possessed by a foul thing. Soon you will see her as she was and is. Who will change Lucy from an unholy vampire to a holy person? I am willing . . .

Arthur No! I must do it. How will I kill the vampire?

Van Helsing Your decision is both right and brave. To kill the vampire and allow Lucy to rest in peace, you must take this pointed stake in your left hand and this hammer in your right. Place the point over the body's heart.

Arthur   Like this?

Van Helsing   Yes. Then, when you hear us begin to pray, hammer in the stake with all your strength.

Arthur   (*Softly*)   I understand.

Van Helsing, Mina, Jonathan   We pray for the soul of Lucy . . .

Van Helsing   NOW!

Arthur   DIE YOU VAMPIRE!   (*He hammers at the stake*)

Lucy   AHHHHHHHhhhhhhhh.

Narrator   The Thing in the coffin writhed and a hideous blood-curdling screech came from the opened red lips. The body shook and quivered and twisted in wild contortions. The sharp, white teeth clamped together.

Arthur   Take that! And that!

Narrator   And then the writhing and the quivering of the body became less and the teeth ceased to clamp and the face to quiver. Finally IT lay still. The terrible job was done. Arthur collapsed. The others hid their faces. Only the professor continued to stare into the coffin. Then he shouted . . .

Van Helsing   Look, LOOK!

Jonathan   It's Lucy – she's no longer the foul thing that we hated.

Mina It's the Lucy we loved in her life. See, her face has become sweet and pure.

Arthur (*Wonderingly*) Now, there is a holy calm that lies like sunshine over her features.

Van Helsing Arthur, can you forgive me for what I have done?

Arthur Forgive? Bless you for giving my dear Lucy her soul back and for giving me peace.

Van Helsing Arthur, you may kiss her. Kiss her lips because she is no longer a grinning devil and a foul thing for all eternity.

Narrator Arthur bent and kissed Lucy. Then the professor tapped him on the shoulder . . .

Van Helsing Now, leave the tomb while we finish our work. (*Arthur leaves*) Jonathan, break off the stake level with the body.

Jonathan (*Doing it*) There, it is done.

Narrator They replaced the coffin lid and left the tomb. Outside, now in bright morning sunshine, they clasped hands.

Van Helsing My friends, one step of our work is done but there remains a greater task. We must find the grand master of all the vampires.

Jonathan Count Dracula himself!

Van Helsing We MUST stamp him out. However, it will be a very difficult and dangerous task. Dracula can change himself into a huge, black dog or a monstrous bat. He can vanish into a golden mist and he can see in the dark with the great, red eyes of a vampire. Yet, both the crucifix and the garlic take away a vampire's power. A sharpened stake and a special, sacred bullet fired through him as he lies in his coffin can kill him forever. Are you still with me in our great task of finding and killing the monster, Dracula?

All YES!

Narrator Jonathan knew that Dracula had bought a house somewhere in London. The professor suspected that the coffins filled with earth that had been washed onto the beach at Hythe during the shipwreck had been taken to Dracula's house. However, when Jonathan tried to remember the address he found his mind was a blank.

Van Helsing Dracula has done this. Tell me, do you still possess any object that was with you in Castle Dracula?

Jonathan   Only this gold cross and chain that I wear around my neck.

Van Helsing   (*Taking the cross*)   I am going to swing this cross back and forwards, very slowly, in front of your eyes. As you feel yourself getting drowsy, allow your mind gradually to form a framed space in which pictures may appear.   (**Jonathan** *nodded*) . . . I want you to form a picture of yourself in your room in Castle Dracula.

Jonathan   (*Hesitating*)   Yes . . . yes, I see myself in the room.

Van Helsing   Count Dracula is calling you. You must go to him.

Jonathan   No, no! Please, I can't!

Van Helsing   Be strong. All he wants from you are details of the house you have selected for him in London. Go to him.

Jonathan   (*Trembling*)   Now, I see myself sitting with Count Dracula. I am showing him a picture of the house.

Van Helsing   Describe the house you see in the photograph.

Jonathan   It is very old and covered in ivy – like an ancient church. There is a great arched doorway and a dim hallway. Upstairs there are many rooms. From the ground floor, mossy steps lead down to a damp cellar. Outside, a high stone wall surrounds the house.

Van Helsing   Is there an address?

Jonathan   There is . . . but it is blurring rapidly. A golden mist is spreading across the photograph. I can only make out the word 'Purfleet'.

Van Helsing   Nothing else?

Jonathan   A pair of red eyes are emerging from the mist.

Van Helsing   Enough! Wake up! Dracula knows we are spying on him!

Narrator   They made plans to hunt down Dracula, the greatest vampire of all, and destroy him. Mina agreed to wait for them. The professor assured her she would be safe in her room as long as she did not open the door or window to anyone – or anything. The vampire hunters hurried to the London suburb of Purfleet where they walked the streets until at last, after dark, they found the high walls and the old, ivy-covered house beyond. The rusted iron gates in the wall were unlocked and soon they were walking a weed-covered path to the high arched, wooden front door.

Jonathan   It's locked.

Van Helsing   Use your skeleton key.   (*The door creaks open*)   Now let's light our lanterns and hold them high and follow me down the hall. Walk quietly!

Arthur   The walls are covered with spider webs and the floor is thick with dust.

Jonathan   But there are footprints.

Van Helsing   (*Stopping*)   A table and on it a big bunch of keys and each key has an old, yellow label. We want the one that says 'Chapel'.

Jonathan   Here it is.

Van Helsing   Where is the chapel, Jonathan?

Jonathan   (*In a trance-like voice*)   The door at the end of the hall leads to the chapel.   (*Taking the keys and going forward*)   I will unlock it.

Narrator   As the door swung open, they staggered back coughing. The air that rushed out of the chapel was stagnant and foul.

Arthur   The stench is horrible!

Van Helsing   It is the hideous odour of blood!

Jonathan   (*Holding up his lamp*)   Look! Rows and rows of coffins!

Van Helsing   Each coffin is waiting for a victim who will become another vampire. Put your handkerchiefs over your noses! We must enter and put garlic leaves in all of the coffins. No vampire can stand the presence of garlic.

Narrator   They moved among the coffins throwing garlic leaves into them until they came to the last one. Jonathan was just about to throw garlic leaves into this one too when he suddenly swayed as if about to faint.

Arthur   (*Grabbing him*)   What's the matter?

Jonathan   I . . . I can feel my energy being drained out of me . . . Something is happening to Mina. I . . . I feel that great danger is approaching her.

Van Helsing   Somehow Dracula has found out where she is staying. We must leave at once!

Arthur   What about the last coffin?

Van Helsing   There's no time! Away!

Narrator   Mina was indeed in great danger. Here she describes in her own way how ultimate terror reached out for her.

Mina When the men had gone, I was preparing to go to bed when I realised that everything was so silent. I looked out of the window and saw that a fog had gathered on the lawn. I went to bed but then I saw that fog had entered the room. It was pouring through the door's keyhole! Suddenly, the mist changed into a tall thin man wrapped in a black cloak. In the dead, white face the eyes glittered with fiery specks, the nose was long and thin and the red lips parted to show sharp, pointed teeth. It was Dracula himself! I would have screamed only that I was paralysed with fear. For an instant my heart stood still.

Narrator Dracula bared her throat with his hands saying as he did so . . .

Dracula (*Laughing mockingly*) Ha, ha, ha. First a little refreshment to reward my efforts to reach you.

Mina Strangely enough, I did not want to hinder him. I suppose it is part of the horrible curse that he places on his victim. Then, oh heaven, heaven pity me! He placed his lips upon my throat. I was half fainting. I felt the last of my strength draining away. How long this horrible thing lasted I do not know. But, it seemed a long time before he took his awful, sneering mouth away from my throat and then I saw it drip with fresh blood! He spoke again . . .

Dracula You, the loved one of my pursuers, will soon be the blood of my blood and the flesh of my flesh. You will become my relative!

Mina Have mercy on me!

Dracula NO! You have helped my enemies, your husband and his friends, in thinking to destroy me. Very soon you will always obey my call. When my brain says, 'Come!', you will cross land or sea to obey me. You will do this because now you will drink *my* blood and become part of *me*!

Mina (*Pleading*) Please spare me. I will never plot against you again.

Dracula SILENCE!

Narrator Meanwhile, Jonathan, Arthur and the professor had rushed across London to reach Mina. Now they burst through the door of her room . . .

Jonathan What we saw horrified us. Dracula had Mina's head clasped to his chest. Bright, red blood stained his shirt.

Van Helsing The Count turned his face towards us and a hellish look seemed to leap into it.

Arthur His eyes flamed red with devilish anger.

Jonathan The white, sharp teeth behind the full lips of the blood-dripping mouth clamped together like those of a wild beast. With the mad energy of a demon, he turned and sprang at us!

Arthur However, the professor was ready for him. He ripped a golden crucifix from his pocket and held it high.

Van Helsing All of you – hold up your crucifixes! Back, Dracula, BACK!

Narrator Mina's three rescuers held high their golden crucifixes. Dracula cowered further and further back. Then, suddenly, he was not there at all. In his place, a cloud of vapour swirled across the floor towards the door and vanished through the keyhole. At the same time, something rose past the bedroom window.

Arthur Did you see that? It was a huge bat!

Van Helsing It was Dracula.

Narrator Now, Mina gave a scream that was so wild and so piercing that the others will remember it till their dying day. Jonathan rushed to her side.

Jonathan (*Wringing his hands*) Her poor face is ghastly.

Arthur Blood smears her lips and trickles from her throat.

Jonathan (*Seizing her hands*)   Her eyes are mad with terror.

Mina   Don't touch me! I am unclean . . . UNCLEAN!

Jonathan (*Embracing her*)   Come to me, my love . . .

Mina   Dracula forced me to drink his blood and now I am your worst enemy.

Jonathan   No . . .

Mina   Yes . . . Wait.

Narrator   A dreamy look came into her face.

Mina   I can hear the rush of water, the sound of waves. I see a coffin. The lid is on it but I can see inside and there lies Dracula, his hands crossed on his chest and a smile on his face. The coffin is being lifted from a small boat. It is being handed up into a ship.

Narrator   Mina's vision faded.

Van Helsing   Now she will sleep. There is nothing more we can learn from poor Mina until she wakes again.

Arthur   Our troubles are over! Dracula is leaving England.

Van Helsing   Now, more than ever we need to find the fiend and destroy him even if we have to follow him into the jaws of hell – Castle Dracula.

Jonathan   Why not just let him leave?

Van Helsing   Because, Dracula has lived for centuries and can live forever and Mina, with some of Dracula's blood flowing in her veins, will be an ageless vampire too if she should die before Dracula is destroyed. We must reach Castle Dracula first. Once inside his tomb in Castle Dracula he will be safe from us. Let us make our preparations for a speedy departure from England.

Mina (*Waking suddenly*) I am coming with you.

Van Helsing No. You might . . .

Mina You think I might reveal your plans to Dracula?

Van Helsing Dracula can see into your mind.

Mina If you hynotise me I will be able to resist Dracula's invasion of my mind and yet I will still be able to see into his.

Van Helsing You're right. You must come with us.

Narrator They rushed across Europe by train. At the Transylvanian border, Mina, under hypnotism, disclosed that they were winning the race with the ship carrying Dracula in his coffin, still at sea . . .

Mina I can hear the sounds that Dracula can hear. Waves are lapping against the side of the ship. Sails are cracking and the wind is howling.

Jonathan Dracula is still lying in his coffin in the ship that is taking him to eastern Europe.

Van Helsing Now we must hire some vehicle to take us up into the mountains of Transylvania to Castle Dracula.

Arthur The race is on!

ACT 3

Dracula's tomb.

Narrator A coach pulled by four galloping horses took them on their way to their final meeting with Dracula. Mina in her hypnotised state, again revealed the sounds that Dracula heard . . .

Mina The wheels rumbling over a rough road, wind rushing through trees, wolves howling. I see Dracula . . . he is still lying in his coffin with his arms crossed on his chest but his eyes are open. They are glowing red and his mouth is parted to show his shining, pointed teeth.

Jonathan Dracula has landed!

Arthur He is on his way to the castle.

Van Helsing We have no time to lose.

Narrator They raced up to the Borga Pass which was only a few hours travel from Castle Dracula. But by then it was dark, a mist had closed in and it had begun to snow. They realised they would have to wait 'till daylight. Because they were so close to Dracula, they took precautions . . .

Van Helsing I will mark a big circle around us with garlic leaves. None of us must go outside it if we value our lives.

Jonathan Listen to the wolves (*Wolves howling*). I'll light a fire. Mina must remain next to it.

Arthur The horses are restless. I'll look after them.

Narrator Soon they wrapped themselves in blankets and slept. Towards midnight the horses began to scream.

Arthur Look at the horses! They are cowering lower and lower to the ground and screaming, moaning and rolling their eyes in absolute terror.

Van Helsing Everyone remain inside the circle and stay close to Mina. I fear for her safety.

Mina (*Suddenly no longer under her hypnotic spell*) Fear for *me*? There is no one safer in all the world than I am from *them*.

Jonathan My love, what do you mean?

Mina (*Pointing*) What do you see out in the mist and snow?

Jonathan What are they . . . whirling shapes?

Arthur There are three of them and they are taking on human form.

Jonathan (*His voice full of fear*) I know who they are . . . the three beautiful women from Castle Dracula. They are dressed in long, white robes. One has golden hair, one has jet black hair and one has fiery red hair. All of them have full, red lips and sharp, white teeth. Now they are smiling and beckoning to Mina.

Van Helsing They are Dracula's creatures! Vampires!

Fair haired woman Come sister . . .

Red haired woman Come join us in a beautiful life . . .

Black haired woman Of seeking victims with . . .

Fair haired woman Rich, red flowing blood . . .

Red haired woman The glorious taste, the pleasure of hunting victims.

Fair haired woman Come, join us sister and know all this.

Mina I am very attracted and yet I also fear . . .

Narrator All the rest of the night, the three beautiful sisters kept up their gestures and enticements: twining their arms, laughing, pointing to Mina and beckoning. The men seized burning branches from the fire to ward them off. They held Mina back whenever she tried to rush from the circle to the vampire women. Even their golden crosses seemed to be powerless against the vampires in the darkness of mist and snow. Only the circle of garlic leaves kept the three beautiful sisters from sweeping Mina off into their twilight, vampire existence. At last, with the coming of dawn, the three beautiful women melted back into the whirling mist and snow to become wreaths of transparent gloom that moved away towards Castle Dracula and were lost to sight.

Jonathan (*Sighing with relief*) The three horrible but beautiful vampires have gone. Snow is falling and there is a strange excitement in the air. Mina, are you well?

Mina (*Shakily*) Yes . . . but I feel there are dangers to us from all sides.

Arthur Far off, the wolves are howling. The snow brings them down from the mountains.

Van Helsing The horses are nearly ready and we will soon be off. This morning we ride to certain death but whose and where and when it will take place we can not know. Jonathan, please make sure you have your shotgun loaded and ready for instant use. And everyone make sure to have your sharpest knife in your belt.

Jonathan My gun is loaded and ready to use, Professor.

Narrator Just as they were getting ready to ride the last short distance up the mountain to Castle Dracula, a rough farm wagon, pulled by two sweat-streaked horses galloping and madly whipped by two shaggy haired and bearded men rushed past. Through the flying mud and stones the professor and his friends caught sight of a huge black box roped to the back of the wagon.

Van Helsing After them! Count Dracula lies in the box!

Narrator As they dashed wildly after the cart with its doom-filled load, they looked up and saw Castle Dracula perched on the mountain's summit, sheer cliffs on three sides. It seemed to overwhelm them with its wild and uncanny atmosphere. All around they could hear the wolves howling and the sound though coming muffled through the deadening snowfall, was full of terror. Soon, the great iron gates of Castle Dracula came into view.

Jonathan Look! The great gates are swinging open on their own to allow the cart to pass through into the courtyard!

Van Helsing Close up to them! Follow them through! We must stop Dracula from reaching his tomb in the castle. Once there nothing can harm him and the world of the vampires will be safe forever!

Narrator They were just too late. The horses reared up as the iron gates clashed together in front of them. It took them valuable minutes to prise the gates apart just enough to squeeze themselves through. The cart stood in the middle of the courtyard. The bearded men and the huge, black wooden box were gone. They ran up steps that led to the castle's huge wooden door.

Arthur (*Trying the iron handle*) It's bolted from the inside.

Van Helsing (*To* **Jonathan**) Shoot it open!

Jonathan (*Firing his shotgun*) That's got it!

Narrator But as they force the door open, Mina screams, falls and writhes on the ground . . .

Mina AHHHHHHHHHhhhhhhhh.

Jonathan What is it? Speak to me my love! What is it?

Mina Unseen evil is pouring from the castle. It is in my throat . . . my head . . . my soul!

Arthur We must leave her behind.

Narrator Suddenly the howling of the wolves was much louder.

Van Helsing No. She would be in danger from the wolves and besides she is drawing away some of Dracula's evil energy. It might make all the difference. We must carry her in with us.

Narrator The professor went first, Jonathan and Arthur followed supporting the swooning, moaning Mina. Jonathan pointed the way to the old chapel and the graveyard. With the howling of the wolves in their ears they descended the dank, stone steps into the depths of Castle Dracula. The foul smell of opened graves rose to meet them. Huge bats swooped around them. At one point, they recoiled in horror as the shape of a huge black dog with burning eyes sprang at them with open jaws and blood-stained teeth. But the professor lifted his golden cross and it sprang right through them! Trembling, they pressed on till the graveyard stretched out in the gloom before them.

Jonathan Over there! They are working furiously to open the huge, black box.

Arthur See where they have placed the box – at the entrance to a great stone tomb.

Jonathan And there is only the one word carved on the tomb, in tall letters: DRACULA.

Van Helsing Dracula must stay in his coffin. (*Shouting to the bearded men.*) Stop! Do not open that box!

Arthur Too late. They have lifted the lid . . .

Van Helsing We must force them to close it again.

Narrator But as they advanced, the two bearded men sneered at them and shook their fists. Van Helsing turned to Jonathan . . .

Van Helsing Fire your gun . . .

Jonathan Bullets are useless against the vampire . . .

Van Helsing Warn those ruffians to get away. Fire a shot into the air.

Narrator At the shattering sound of the shot, the bearded ruffians ran wildly away into the gloom. But the delay had given Dracula the time he needed . . .

Mina OHHHHhhhhhhh . . . like a grotesque and gigantic bat, Dracula is crawling from his box. His head is turning towards us . . .

Jonathan His face is dead white. He snarls at us and shows his long, pointed fangs . . .

Dracula Stay back, you feeble worms, and let all your actions be stilled. Once I am in my tomb waves of vampires will fly forth to seek you out and suck you dry of blood! HAAA, HAA, HAAAaaaaaa!

Arthur His eyes are as red as leaping flames.

Van Helsing Waves of evil sweep towards us from his eyes and force us to stand still as stone, unable to move a step or lift a hand.

Arthur In his cloak he flaps towards the base of the tomb. His fingers are shaped like claws as they scrape and pull him forward over the floor.

Jonathan And look, a great stone slab is rising away from the floor to reveal a yawning entrance with a glimpse of grinning skulls and piles of bones with shreds of clothing still clinging to them.

Narrator Suddenly three shapes sprang into existence – the three vampire sisters, amazingly beautiful yet deeply evil. Around them wolves leap and bats flit.

Fair haired woman (*Holding out her hand*) Take my hand, O my Lord Dracula, and let me help you into your tomb.

Red haired woman (*Bending*) I lift your arm to help you forward, Lord Dracula.

Black haired woman (*Pulling*) Now that we are about to enter your great tomb, O Dracula, I am heaving your shoulders over the threshold and . . .

Mina (*Screaming and leaping forward*) NOOooooooo! You will not escape, because I share your mad and evil blood I am not paralysed by your stare. And this golden cross (*She lifts it high*) protects me.

Narrator Like a screaming, vengeful arrow, Mina sped straight to Dracula sprawled at the threshold of his awful tomb. The three beautiful sisters shrieking with rage, shot out their arms to stop her, the wolves leapt at her and the bats swooped at her head. She swept them all aside and flung herself upon the evil form of Dracula.

Narrator With superhuman strength, Mina smashed down even Dracula's talons and swiftly smeared garlic leaves over his face and mouth.

Mina Taste the bitter vampire poison of garlic leaves, you fiend!

Dracula They seem to crack my brain and bring on terrible sickness. Take them away!

Narrator Mina shouted in triumph and held her holy cross up to his eyes.

Mina See the cross and shudder for the cruelty you have inflicted on humanity. Think of poor Lucy!

Dracula Take away the cross! Take it away! It ices my blood. It will crush my immortality. Take it away!

Narrator Suddenly the professor, Jonathan and Arthur found they were able to move their limbs again. Dracula's attention was elsewhere.

Van Helsing We must rush forward together and strike with our knives. Lift your crosses high as you run – when I say the word . . . NOW!

Narrator But like some terrible fence, the vampire sisters, now screaming and clawing the air in front of them, the wolves leaping and snarling and the bats fluttering and showing their needle teeth stood between the running men and Dracula now squirming under the attacks of the frenzied Mina.

Van Helsing Strike at them with your crosses!

Jonathan Make way, you hideous creatures!

Arthur (*Thrusting with his cross*) Ah, that's better.

Narrator The vampire forces cringed and whimpered before the sacred power of the gleaming crosses and the three men broke through.

Van Helsing Now only Dracula himself lies before us. Let us do our terrible deed quickly and rid the world of this bloodthirsty monster – FOREVER!

Jonathan (*Pulling* **Mina** *aside*) Come, my love, you have done enough.

Van Helsing I lift my knife for the fatal blow.

Dracula (*Choking with hate*) You . . . you may kill my body but in the course of years my soul will work its way into other times and other bodies and I will return as Dracula again and the blood of your descendants will flow into my veins. You can not kill the immortal one!

Van Helsing Die, foul monster. Die!

Narrator Unable to help themselves, Jonathan, Mina and Arthur shrieked with horror as they saw the professor's great knife gleam in the air, descend into Dracula's body. A last look of such pure hatred flashed from the eyes that they will never forget it.

Van Helsing Quickly, destroy the heart!

Narrator Both Jonathan and Arthur recovered from their shock sufficiently to raise their own knives and plunge them into Dracula's heart.

Jonathan (*Astounded*) What kind of miracle is this? The body is crumbling.

Arthur Into horrible pieces.

Narrator And, at the same time, all around them, each of the three beautiful sisters froze, withered into ancient bodies and crumbled to pieces.

Van Helsing And now Dracula becomes dust that shivers on the floor.

Jonathan   And blows away into . . .

Mina   Nothingness.

Narrator   And, around them, the three vampires sisters sagged into columns of collapsing dust, the leaping wolves hit the ground and became dust swirls and the circling bats flicked into puffs of dust and were gone in an instant.

Van Helsing   Dust to dust . . . and the world is saved.

Mina   We must pray that it remains so forever.

Narrator   So there, in that ghastly place before the gaping tomb of DRACULA they knelt, held hands and prayed.

All   God, in heaven, preserve us from all evil, visible and invisible . . .

• Drama Activities •

DRAMATISING DRACULA

Imagine you are playing the part of Dracula in a stage production.

1   How would you dress for the part?

2   What colours of face paint would you choose to apply? Explain your choice.

3 What aspects of Dracula's character would you emphasise?

4 How would you inspire fear in the play's other characters?

5 What sound effects would you like to accompany each of your appearances on stage?

6 How would you indicate to the audience that you are changing into a vampire?

7 What feelings would you show and how would you show them when the cross is raised to ward you off?

SETTINGS AND ACTIONS

Write down the most important actions that take place at each of the settings below.

Setting
- The Inn at Bistritz
- Borgo Pass
- The entrance to Castle Dracula
- Jonathan's bathroom
- The dusty room
- The window of Dracula's room
- The coffin in the old chapel
- Hythe churchyard at night
- Outside Lucy's tomb
- Inside Lucy's tomb
- The chapel in the Purfleet house
- Mina's room
- In the forest clearing
- The stone steps leading to the depths of Castle Dracula
- At Dracula's tomb

EXCLUSIVE INTERVIEW WITH COUNT DRACULA!

You are a newspaper reporter who manages to sneak into Castle Dracula in an effort to try to get an exclusive interview with the notorious Count Dracula. Count Dracula grants you an exclusive but terrifying interview. Write about your experience in a newspaper article with the above headline.

5

The Cowpokes of Calico

by Bill Condon

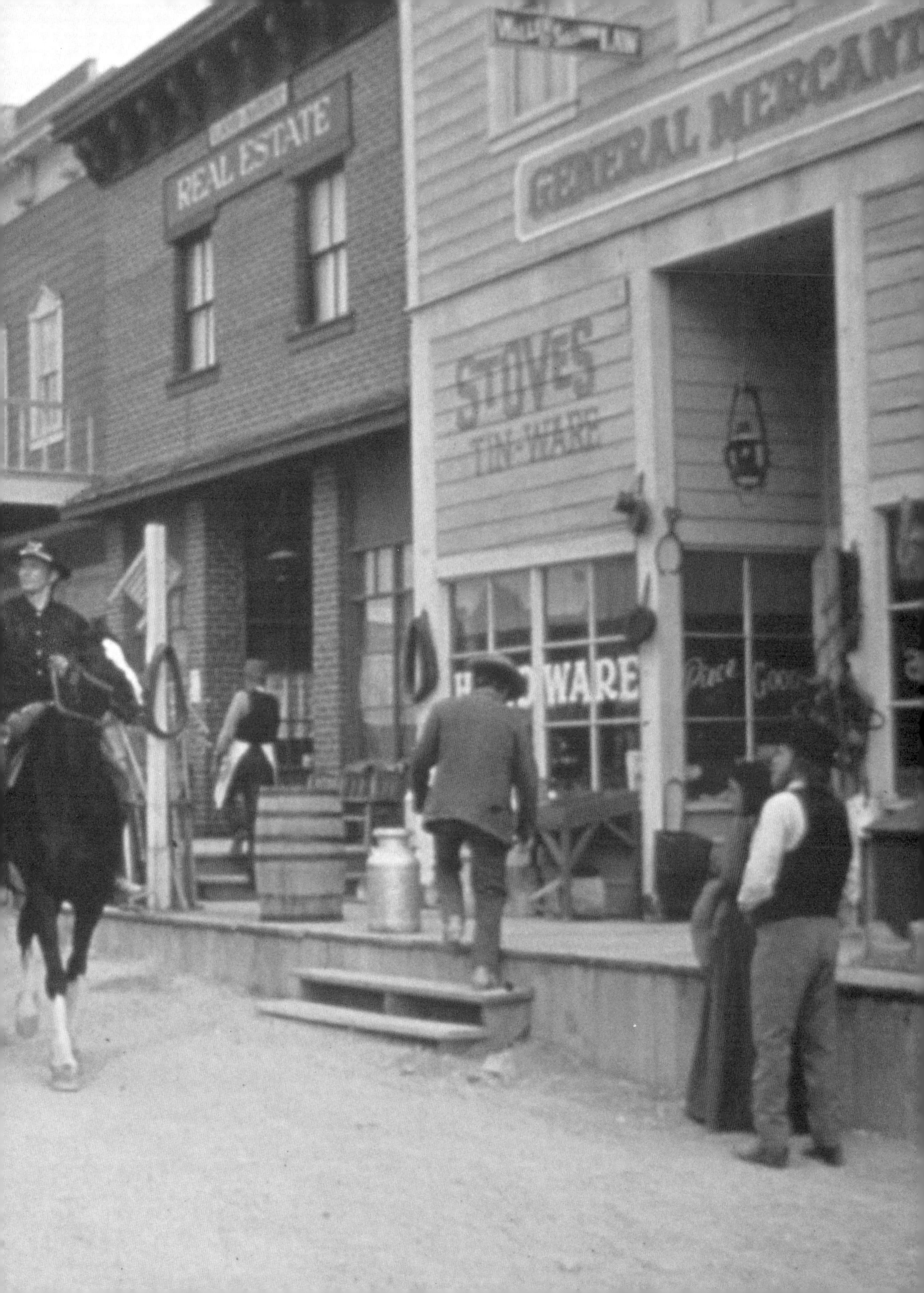
REAL ESTATE
GENERAL
STOVES
TIN-WARE

The Cowpokes of Calico

by Bill Condon

The play, *The Cowpokes of Calico*, mocks the world of the old wild west. Exaggeration and jokes abound and there is plenty of rip-roaring fun. The notorious new sheriff, hired by the good folk of Calico to bring peace to their town, shoots everyone in sight. However, in the end, Sheriff Cactus Calhoun himself turns out to be a coward. As the characters act out their comic roles, much of the fun comes from the western clichés that run through the dialogue and action.

CHARACTERS

Sheriff Cactus Calhoun
The Mayor
Belle Brown
Annie
Redeye
Rosie
Bobby Ray
Jessie
Pecos
Junior
Polly
Bertha
Al Hoot
Chief Brown Cow
Several Indian Braves
Several Townsfolk

SCENE 1

*The **Mayor** stands on a table addressing the townsfolk.*

Mayor   This here meetin' of the townsfolk of Calico is declared open.

Belle   I'm Belle Brown and I'm speakin' on behalf of the women of Calico.

Mayor You go right ahead, Belle.

Belle I'm here to complain about the no-good cowpokes we got in this town.

Annie You're durn tootin', Belle.

Redeye That means she agrees, Mayor.

Mayor I know what it means, Redeye – I ain't no city slicker. Say your piece, Annie.

Annie It's gettin' so a lady ain't safe to walk to church without some sidewinder firin' a shot at her.

Rosie There's bushwhackers behind every tree.

Bob'ray That's because we don't have enough toilets in Calico. Get it? They go behind the trees . . .

Mayor That's a good one, Bobby Ray.

Jessie We don't want no joshin', Mayor, we want action!

Pecos Jessie's right. Rustlers steal my cattle!

Junior Poachers steal my eggs!

Bob'ray I reckon anyone who poaches eggs should be fried! Get it? It's a joke . . .

Redeye I vote we hang Bobby Ray.

Bob'ray OK, OK. I can take a hint – no more jokes.

Belle Well, Mayor, what are you gonna do to clean up Calico?

Mayor I already done it, Belle.

Annie What do you mean?

Mayor The roughest, toughest, meanest, uncleanest cowpoke who ever rode the wild west is gunna be our new sheriff.

Pecos You mean . . .

Mayor Yes! Cactus Calhoun!

Polly Why I hear tell he shot his own grandma in the back for ten dollars.

Mayor That ain't nothin' but a dirty rotten lie!

Polly You sure about that?

Mayor Positive . . . he got twenty dollars.

Rosie Is it true he shot eight men before his 21st birthday?

Mayor No! That's another durn lie. He shot eight men on his 21st birthday – to celebrate.

Rosie A critter like that will sure keep the peace.

Junior I'll feel a whole lot safer when he comes to town.

Belle We're all much obliged to you, Mayor.

Mayor Think nothin' of it. And now, without further ado, let me introduce the man himself – the one, the only, Sheriff Cactus Calhoun!

Cactus *enters to applause.*

Cactus Hot diggety dog! That sure is a might neighbourly welcome.

Belle We want you to feel right at home, Cactus.

Cactus Why, thank you, ma'am.

Redeye We're right behind you, Sheriff!

Cactus *spins around, draws his gun and shoots behind him. Two bystanders fall . . . then crawl off stage.*

Mayor Why'd you do that, Cactus?

Cactus He said they were right behind me – I figured he meant outlaws.

Redeye I said *we're* right behind you.

Cactus *spins around, draws his gun and shoots again. Two more fall . . . then crawl off stage.*

Cactus Thanks for tippin' me off, Mister.

Redeye But I said . . .

Junior Better not say it, Redeye.

Mayor If there's anything I can do to help, please let me know, Cactus.

Cactus Now as a matter of fact, there is, Mr Mayor. I want you to pass a law that no guns be allowed in town.

Mayor Anything you say, Cactus. Everyone throw down their guns.

Several guns drop to the floor.

Cactus I don't want to see any weapons of any kind.

Bertha You mean like knives?

Cactus I mean anything that could be used as a weapon; newspapers, umbrellas, false teeth, concealed machine guns . . .

Mayor You heard the man, folks. Throw down your weapons.

Several knives, newspapers, umbrellas, sets of teeth, hit the floor.

Cactus (*Pointing*) You!

Mayor Me?

Cactus Yes, you Mr Mayor! Hand over those braces – they could be used as a slingshot!

Mayor But my pants will fall down.

Cactus Do it now or I'll fill you full of lead.

Mayor All right! All right!

He hands over his braces and his pants fall down.

Cactus That's better. Now me and my pistol packin' deputy here – where is my pistol packin' . . .

Al Hoot *enters*.

Hoot Sorry I'm late. I was just checkin' my bags again – I packed everything but my pistols.

Cactus As I was sayin' – me and my deputy –

Hoot Al Hoot.

Cactus Who *sometimes* remembers to pack pistols – we don't take no chances. Ain't that a fact, Al?

Hoot I sure reckon. Why once Cactus here shot a varmint because he figured he was about to sneeze on him.

Cactus It was self defence; he had a real bad cold.

Mayor But Cactus, we brought you here so's we could have a nice peaceful town.

Belle The Mayor's right. We don't want to be afraid to sneeze.

Cactus I ain't a'fixin' to do you folks no harm. You just abide by the rules and there won't be no trouble.

Redeye What in tarnation is the rules?

Cactus Tell 'em, Hoot.

Hoot Everyone is to be off the streets by six o'clock. There's to be no more gamblin' and drinkin' –

Cactus Or loud singin' in church.

Polly We can't even sing in church?

Hoot Nope.

Cactus I run a real quiet town – that way I can hear anybody whose a'talkin' about me behind my back.

Hoot Cactus has got mighty fine ears.

Junior But you can't do this!

Cactus Strange how my trigger finger starts itchin' when folks say I can't do somethin'.

Mayor You can do anything you like, Sheriff.

Cactus That's better. Now you folks go and have yourself a good ol' time – you got nothin' to worry about no more.

The **townsfolk** *exit.*

Hoot Looks like we can relax now, Cactus.

Cactus Relax? That's what Spotted Pete was doin' when they plugged him. How come you want me to relax, Hoot?

Hoot You gotta get some shut-eye.

Cactus Deadeye Dillon was gettin' some shut-eye when he done got drilled. How come you want me to sleep?

Hoot No reason. Honest.

Cactus I ain't slept in ten years, and I ain't gunna!

Hoot I heard you snorin' last night.

Cactus You callin' me a lowdown, no good, yellow-bellied liar?

Hoot No! No! I'd never do that!

Cactus You been plottin' against me all the time, haven't you, Hoot?

Hoot No! I promise I haven't!

Cactus I can see dishonesty and treachery written in your eyes.

Hoot My eyes ain't big enough to have words like that written in them.

Cactus At the count of three I'm a'gunna draw. One . . .

Hoot Cactus, you're makin' a big mistake. I'm your best friend!

Cactus Two . . .

Hoot Don't be crazy!

Cactus That does it! No one calls me crazy! Three!

He shoots. **Hoot** *falls.*

Cactus I sure am sorry, Hoot. I liked you almost as much as my hoss.

Hoot Why didn't you just wing me, Cactus?

Cactus I figured the least harmful place to shoot you was between the ears – everyone knows you ain't got nothin' between your ears.

Hoot Well, a man's gotta do what a man's gotta do.

   The **townsfolk** *enter.*

Belle We heard a shot.

Cactus Thank goodness you're here. Get this man to an undertaker before it's too late.

   Cactus *exits.* **Al Hoot** *is carried off stage.*

Annie He shot down his own deputy.

Mayor The sheriff's plumb loco, folks.

Polly We gotta do somethin', Mr Mayor.

Belle You got us into this mess, you gotta get us out of it.

Mayor Let me think . . . I know! We'll scare Cactus out of town!

   Cactus *enters.*

Cactus Did I hear you folks talkin' about me behind my back?

Mayor No, Sir, Mr Sheriff.

Cactus I heard somethin' about tryin' to scare me out of town.

Rosie I can explain that. I said the Injuns attackin' might scare you out of Calico.

Mayor And I said nothin' would scare ol' Cactus.

Cactus Injuns? No one told me there was Injuns in these here parts.

Polly Sure is, Sheriff. The hills is alive with the sound of war dances.

Pecos Them painted savages collect scalps the way some folks collect stamps.

Cactus I can rassle grizzly bears, sleep on an ant hill, and eat porridge without a blindfold – but I sure ain't partial to Injuns. I'm leavin'!

   A very, very old **Indian** *staggers in.*

Chief How.

Cactus An Injun!

Chief Pleased to meet you. Chief Brown Cow's my name. How.

Cactus Have you Injuns got us surrounded?

Chief Heck no. I'm the only Indian in town. All others on reservation.

Cactus But I thought the Injuns were attackin'.

Chief Who ever told you that spoke with a forked tongue; I only a'tackin' when I'm puttin' down carpet in the tepee.

Bertha Sheriff, the chief here is about 120 years old. He don't know what he's sayin'.

Redeye It's just one of them there Injun tricks, Sheriff.

Cactus Oh it's a trick all right – but it's you folks who is doin' the trickin', not my red brother here . . .

Junior Don't you go gettin' riled Sheriff.

Cactus The last fella who tried to trick me is admirin' the view from Boot Hill.

Bob'ray But there ain't no view at Boot Hill. That's a –

Jessie Hush up, Bobby Ray.

Mayor We didn't mean nothin', Cactus.

Cactus You better say your prayers, Mayor.

Pecos He's gunna shoot him!

Annie Wait! The Durango Kid sure won't like it if you shoot the Mayor – they's related.

Mayor We are?

Annie Sure your are.

Cactus The Durango Kid? Sounds like a mighty tough owlhoot.

Annie There ain't no one faster on the draw –

Bertha 'Ceptin' maybe you of course, Sheriff.

Junior Then again, maybe Durango is even faster than the Sheriff.

Jessie I hear Durango's never been beat in a shootout.

Polly I hear tell he plugged a hundred men – or was that two hundred?

Cactus Hmm . . . this is your lucky day, Mayor. I'm not gunna shoot you after all. Good day, folks.

    Cactus exits.

Mayor Thank heavens!

Annie He fell for it!

Mayor You mean I'm not related to The Durango Kid?

Annie There ain't no Durango Kid. I made it up to scare him.

Rosie It sure did work.

Redeye He let out of here like a turkey on Thanksgivin' Day.

Pecos Shh! He's comin' back!

    Cactus returns.

Cactus I been thinkin' it over. If I leave now, some of you folks might get to thinkin' I'm scared of this here Durango Kid.

Bertha We wouldn't think that, Sheriff.

Cactus Maybe, maybe not. But I've decided to publicly challenge The Durango Kid to a shootout at high noon on Main Street.

Annie What if he don't show up?

Cactus Then I'll just have to shoot the Mayor here – he ain't much, but he's better than nothin'.

Mayor Thanks, Cactus.

Cactus I'll be moseyin' along now. See you folks at high noon.

    Cactus exits.

Mayor Help!

Jessie Don't panic. We'll think of somethin'.

Pecos We gotta find us a gunslinger.

Rosie There must be someone who's brave enough to help.

Belle Who'll be the first to volunteer?

Annie I will. I made up this Durango Kid story so it's only fittin' that I follow it through.

Rosie What do you mean, Annie?

Annie I'm strappin' on a shootin' iron. This Cactus fella ain't gunna bully me no more!

SCENE 2

Cactus *enters*.

Cactus It's high noon. That means it's time for me to teach The Durango Kid a lesson. (*Shouting*) Where are you, Durango? Come on out you sneaky prairie dog. Come on out and fight me like a man!

Annie *enters*.

Annie I'm The Durango Kid. And I'm gunna fight you like a woman.

Cactus Well if that don't beat all!

Annie May the best woman win, Cactus.

Cactus Now lookie here, little lady. I don't want you to worry none about gettin' shot and all. I'm gunna see to it that you get a mighty purdy funeral.

Annie Anytime you're ready.

Cactus At the count of three . . .

The **townsfolk** *enter. They all have guns.*

Belle You'll have to shoot me too, Cactus.

Rosie And me.

Polly Me too.

Junior Don't forget me.

Redeye You'll have to shoot the whole durn town.

Cactus Hot diggety dog! I don't mind if I do! I've taken on a whole town lots of times. My six-shooter is gunna blow you to pieces – and that could be a might painful.

The **chief** *and several* **Indians**, *giving war whoops, enter.*

Chief How!

Cactus Injuns!

Chief How you going to beat all of them, and all of us, pale face?

Cactus I reckon I ain't.

Annie Get on your hoss and hightail it out of town.

Chief If you not go, my braves make you cactus, Cactus.

Cactus Goodbye, Chief. Goodbye, folks. Here's my sheriff's badge. This town's too tough for me!

He exits.

All Hurray!

Mayor A mighty fine piece of work. Much obliged.

Annie Aw shucks, 'twern't nothin'.

Belle It surely was! I reckon we just found ourselves a new sheriff.

Annie You mean me?

Belle No! I mean Chief Brown Cow!

Chief How about that!

Mayor I've only got one thing to say to you, Chief.

Chief What's that, Mr Mayor?

Mayor How now, Brown Cow?

• Drama Activities •

APPRECIATING THE PLAY

1 What is the play's setting?

2 Much of the humour of the play comes from the dialogue. Why is this so?

3 Imagine you are the director of this play. What stage props would you need?

4 As director, what instructions would you give to the actor playing the part of Belle?

5 As director, how would you tell Cactus to play his part?

6 Do you think audiences would enjoy seeing a production of this play? Why?

7   The playwright has used many examples of exaggeration to create humour. What are some examples of exaggeration?

8   If you were the actor playing the part of the Mayor, what would you wear?

9   Which scene in the play do you think is the most humorous? Why?

10 Do you think the ending of the play is a good one? Why?

11 What do you think are the strengths and weaknesses of this kind of play?

12 If you were given the opportunity of acting in this play, which part would you choose? Why?

DIALOGUE

The dialogue adds interest and humour to the play. On the left are pieces of dialogue from the play. Opposite each, write down the normal language equivalent.

Western dialogue

- *You're durn tootin', Belle*   **You are quite right, Belle**
- *I ain't no city slicker*
- *We don't want no joshin', Mayor*
- *That sure is a might neighbourly welcome*
- *Thanks for tippin' me off, mister*
- *I'll fill you full of lead*
- *I ain't a 'fixin' to do you folks no harm*
- *My trigger finger starts itchin'*
- *You gotta get some shut-eye*
- *You callin' me a lowdown, no good, yellow-bellied liar?*

- *The sheriff's plumb loco, folks*
- *I can rassle grizzly bears, sleep on an ant hill and eat porridge without a blindfold but I sure ain't partial to Injuns*
- *Don't you go gettin' riled Sheriff*
- *There ain't no one faster on the draw*
- *I heard tell he plugged a hundred men*
- *I'll be moseyin' along now*
- *We gotta find us a gunslinger*
- *I'm strappin' on a shootin' iron. This Cactus fella ain't gunna bully me no more!*
- *Get on your hoss and hightail it out of town*

6

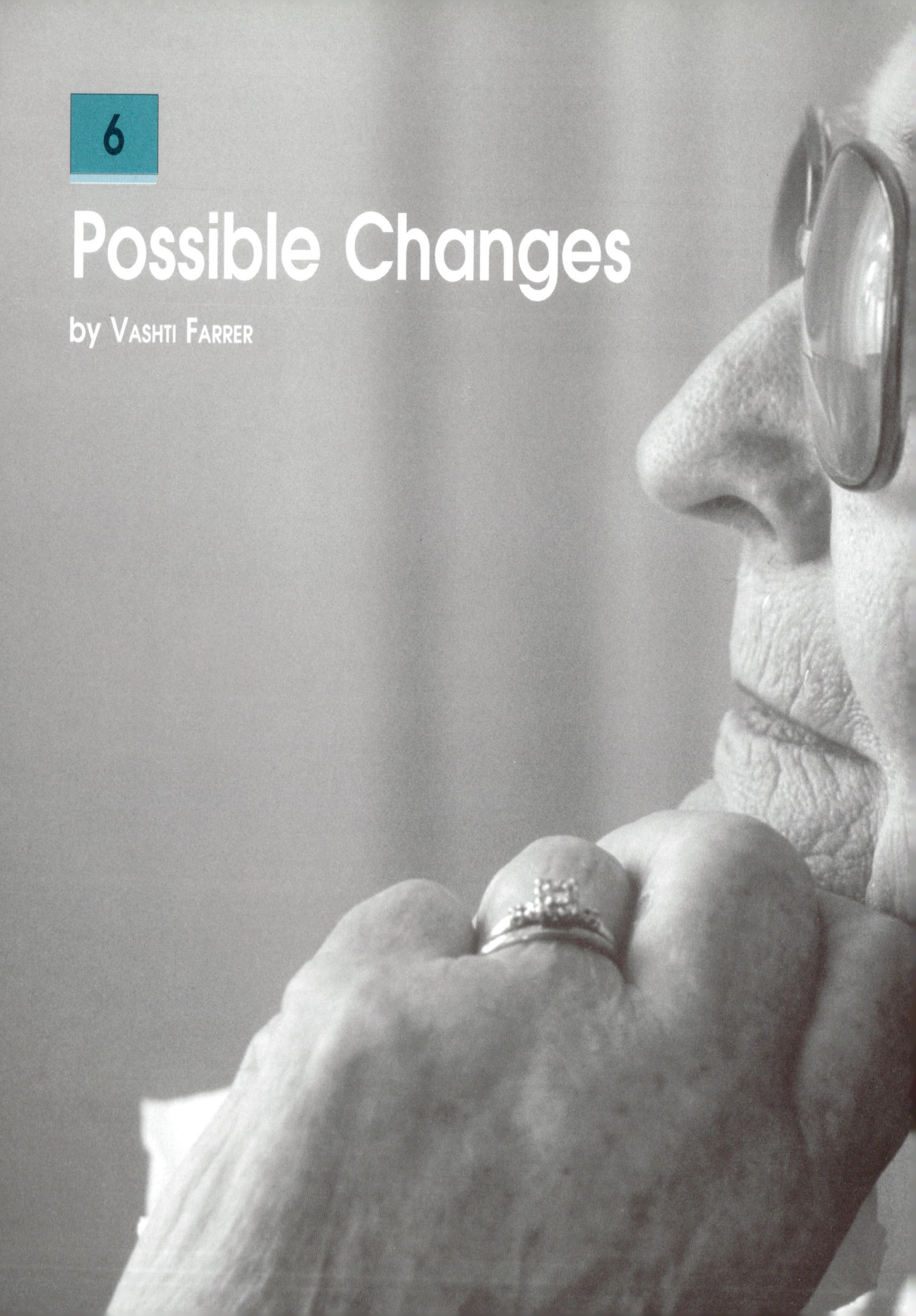

Possible Changes

by Vashti Farrer

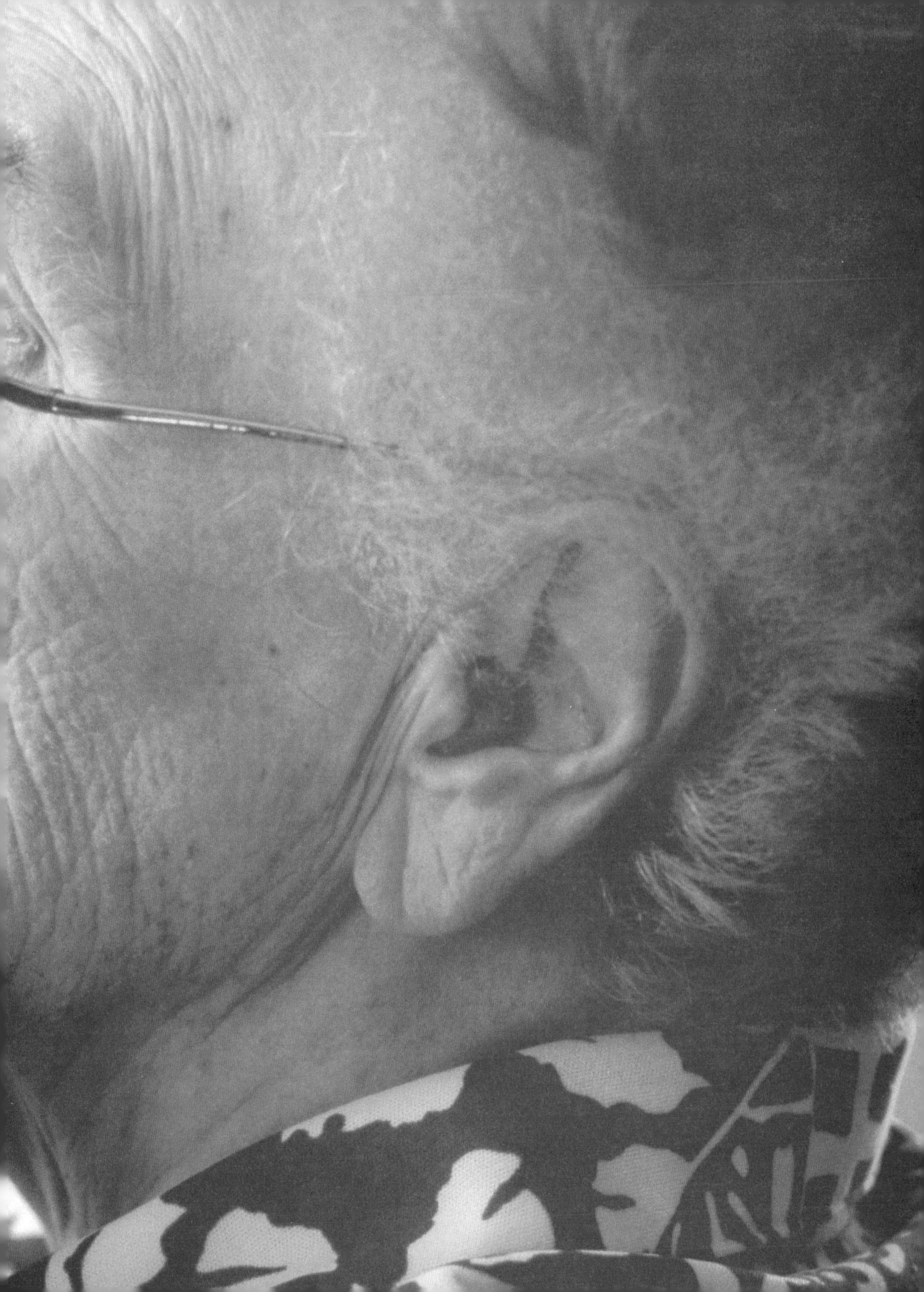

Possible Changes

by Vashti Farrer

The play *Possible Changes* is a play that explores important issues such as racial prejudice and the horror of war. The dramatist, Vashti Farrer, uses the enactment of a daydream to resolve these issues.

CHARACTERS

Sheila	In her late seventies
Judy	Sheila's daughter; in her fifties
Greg	Judy's son; in his twenties
Kasumi	Greg's girlfriend; in her twenties
Frank	Sheila's late husband; as he was in his late twenties

SCENE 1

Suburban sitting room, front door/porch side on. Comfortable old-fashioned couch, coffee table and armchair. Small table for telephone and framed photo of man in Australian World War Two uniform. Archway through to kitchen. At side of stage, another chair, table and telephone. Tea tray with cups, saucers, Anzac biscuits.

Mid-morning. Doorbell rings, **Sheila** *is slow to answer it.*

Sheila   (*Opening door*)   About time you got here!

Judy   (*Entering*)   Sorry I'm late, Mum, I was held up in traffic. Anyway, what's the matter?

Sheila   Matter?

Judy   You sounded distraught on the phone. Has something happened?

Sheila   Yes, I've got new neighbours.

Judy   I know.

Sheila   Well – didn't you notice?

Judy Notice what?

Sheila They're Asian.

Judy Mum! You didn't drag me all the way over here just to tell me that? I thought it was something serious.

Sheila It *is* serious. They're taking over. Suburb by suburb. You wait. It'll be your turn next.

Judy Oh, for heaven's sake! Don't be so racist.

Sheila I'm not racist!

Judy Yes, you are.

Sheila Anyway, it doesn't count. They're Japanese.

Judy It does, and they're not. They're Chinese.

Sheila How do you know? Have you spoken to them?

Judy Of course. Mrs Lee was hosing her garden when I pulled up. And she's very nice. She said what a lovely garden you have.

Sheila There! What did I tell you? Can't wait to buy me out.

Judy Mum, you're being ridiculous! They're just a harmless young couple, with young children. I would have thought you'd be pleased having kids around again. It means you won't be lonely any more.

Sheila Who says I'm lonely? And anyway, what would you know about it? You've got Greg.

Judy When I see him. You forget he's 23 now, he's got a life of his own. During the day he's at work, and he's out most nights.

Sheila Hrrrmph! At least he still lives at home.

Judy For the moment. But he's thinking of moving out. He's got a new girlfriend and he's pretty keen. They're thinking of moving in together.

Sheila It wouldn't have happened in my day.

Judy No, maybe not, but things have changed. A lot of kids try living together first, before settling down. Anyway, that's not why you rang me. What about the neighbours?

Sheila I don't want them next door. Not after what they did to your father.

Judy (*Exasperated*) Mum, the neighbours didn't do anything to Dad. They weren't even born then. Besides, it was the Japanese.

Sheila You don't know what those POWs went through.

Judy Yes, I do. There were some horrible things happened. But war's war. It's always horrible. And it was a long time ago.

Sheila Not for me it wasn't.

Judy No, but feeling this way won't bring Dad back. You have to move on, Mum.

Sheila (*Holding back tears. Defiant*) You'll never catch me driving a Japanese car.

Judy No, you prefer a clapped out Morris Minor that every time you park it, you have to put a bucket underneath the radiator.

Sheila Don't you criticise my car!

Judy Well, don't you criticise the neighbours. They've done nothing to you. (*Gently*) Look, Mum, I'm sure it'll all work out fine.

Sheila I miss him. Still.

Judy I know. But he was my father too remember. Sometimes I think you feel you're the only one allowed to grieve.

Sheila They beat him to death, in that camp.

Judy (*Sighs*) Yes, I know that too, but you're only punishing yourself. If he had come back, who's to say you would have stayed together? People change. A lot of those wartime marriages didn't last.

Sheila (*Fiercely*) Ours would have. We weren't like these flibbetigibbets now, hopping from one bed to another.

Judy Well, it's not quite as bad as that, but in any case, things change (*Drops voice slightly*) and some of us move with the times.

Sheila What was that?

Judy Nothing. Look, Mum, I'd better be going. Just take it one step at a time with the neighbours. Say hello when you see them. You don't have to ask them in for a three-course meal. (*Pause*) Although a cup of tea might be nice.

Sheila (*Stubbornly*) Oh, all right. I'll try.

Judy Good for you.

Sheila And Judy. Tell Greg to ring me, will you?

Judy I will.

Sheila   Better still. Tell him to bring this new girlfriend round to meet me, will you?

Judy   Oh. If you like.

Sheila   He's not ashamed of me, is he?

Judy   Of course not. Don't worry, I'll tell him. Bye Mum.

(*Lights fade on* **Sheila** *and* **Judy**.)

SCENE 2

Lights up on same setting. Mid-afternoon. **Greg** *rings doorbell. Door opens.*

Greg   (*Hiding* **Kasumi** *behind him*)   Here, let's play a trick on her. You hide behind me.

Kasumi   (*Giggling*)   But Greg! What will she think?

(*He just gets her hidden when door opens.*)

Greg   Hi, Gran.   (*Bends down and kisses her.*)

Sheila   Greg! How lovely to see you! But you're a naughty boy. You should have rung to say you were coming. I would have made you a chocolate cake.

Greg   Mum said just to surprise you, and talking of surprises, here – (*pulls* **Kasumi** *forward*)   I'd like you to meet my girlfriend, Kasumi. Kasumi, this is my grandmother.

Sheila   (*Silence while she looks at her*)   You didn't tell me she was one of them.

Greg   One of them?   (*Embarrassed*)   I didn't think it was necessary.

Sheila   You realise her lot killed my Frank.

Greg   Gran!   (*To* **Kasumi**)   Look, I'm awfully sorry about this, Kasumi. You see, her husband died on the Thai Burma Railway.

Sheila   You mean, he was *killed*.

Kasumi   (*Puzzled*)   On the railway?

Sheila   Yes. He was a prisoner-of-war. And those bastards worked the poor buggers till they dropped.   (*Addresses* **Kasumi**)   Murdered them. As good as. Starved and beat them to death.

Kasumi   (*Defensive*)   I don't know of such things.

Sheila No, I'll bet you don't. They kept them hidden. Denied them even. None of it taught in the schools just as if none of it ever happened, but it did!

Greg Look, Gran, maybe this wasn't such a good idea. I'll come back some other time. On my own.

Sheila No! I want to hear what she has to say about it.

Kasumi I am sorry if your husband died. But I was not a part of it. My grandfather, he died also.

Sheila Died? Oh, did he now? Not in Thailand, I'll bet.

Kasumi No, in Australia.

Sheila (*Puzzled*) But – he couldn't have. The war didn't come down that far. Darwin, yes. It was bombed, and Townsville too, pretty badly, although they hushed it up at the time. Then there were those minisubs that sneaked into Sydney Harbour. But not what you'd call a 'real war'. Not the war our POWs had.

Kasumi My grandfather also was a prisoner.

Sheila Nonsense. They were stopped. I tell you. Up north. And we didn't have prison camps.

Greg Yes, we did, Gran. Don't you remember, Cowra?

Kasumi That is the name. Cow-ara.

Greg Cowra. It's out west from Sydney. Way out west.

Sheila You don't mean the break out?

Greg Yes.

Sheila Oh that! That was just a handful of – troublemakers. Nothing more.

Greg No, Gran. It was pretty big, really. Well over a thousand prisoners. It was the biggest prison breakout, ever.

Sheila Hrrrmph! Nonsense. I'm sure we would have heard more about it at the time.

Greg That's just it, it was hushed up, from the public. Even years later, they still tried to keep it quiet.

Kasumi My grandfather was a pilot. He was shot down over Darwin. My grandmother thought he had been killed. It is what she was told.

Greg You mean, she didn't know he'd been taken prisoner?

Kasumi No. His funeral was held in our village. There is a plaque in the family shrine.

Sheila (*Shows just the faintest sign of softening*) Well, we can't stand here on the doorstep all day. The neighbours might see us. You'd better come inside. I suppose you want a cup of tea?

Kasumi (*Very polite*) Oh, no, please, I do not wish to give trouble.

Sheila It's not trouble. I'd just boiled the kettle when you knocked. It'll only take a minute. I've got some biscuits too, somewhere. Anzacs. Greg's favourite. They were his grandfather's too.

(*Exits through archway in direction of kitchen.*)

Greg (*Hugs* **Kasumi**) Please, don't mind her. It'll be all right, you'll see. She's not such a bad old stick, really, when you get to know her. A bit gruff, but she's had a hard life. She took Grandad's death pretty badly, so I guess she's a bit . . .

Kasumi Prejudiced.

Greg (*Embarrassed*) Well, yes.

Kasumi I understand. These things cause much pain.

Greg You never told me about your grandfather.

Kasumi My family do not wish to speak of him.

(**Sheila** *enters carrying tea tray with plate of Anzac biscuits.*)

Sheila Here we are. Help yourself to milk and sugar. I'm sorry, I didn't catch your name.

Kasumi Kasumi.

Sheila Quite pretty, really. So, tell me about your grandfather?

Kasumi In Japan there was Bushido (*She looks to Greg for help in explaining.*) A way . . . ?

Greg A way of life, a code of behaviour.

Kasumi Yes. Honourable to die, shameful to be held prisoner. Not only for the prisoner. For his family, also it meant great shame. Prisoners felt they were dishonoured for life. Some changed their names.

Greg So their families wouldn't know?

Kasumi Yes.

Greg And your grandmother? When did she find out?

Kasumi Many years after a man came to see her. He knew my grandfather in Cow-ara.

Sheila You know it's strange. When our boys were captured, the first thing they did was notify their families. So they'd know they hadn't been killed. They wanted to stick it out, survive, till the end of the war. Many of them didn't, of course. (*Wipes away a tear.*)

Kasumi My grandfather, he wanted to die, not to bring shame on my grandmother or his son.

Greg Your father. So, what happened?

Kasumi The prisoners felt shame inside them. Growing, burning inside. Two years later it was still burning. They wanted to . . . (*She looks to Greg again*) Setsujoku? It is a ritual.

Greg You mean, a ritual killing? Like a mass suicide?

Kasumi (*She nods*) Yes.

Sheila What are you talking about? Suicide? What suicide?

Greg Well, they had knives and clubs, all homemade of course. And when the time came, they just hurled themselves at the barbed wire only to be mown down by machine guns.

Sheila Rubbish! Our boys would never have shot in cold blood.

Greg Of course they would. It was wartime. Gran, remember? If prisoners escape and attack the guns, what do guards do? Shoot!

Sheila Well, anyway they weren't all killed.

Greg No, but about 230 of them were. And another hundred were wounded. Some of our blokes were battered to death, defending the guns.

Sheila (*Shudders*) That'd be right.

Greg Oh, come on, Gran. Don't you think our lot would've done the same, if they'd had the chance?

Sheila (*Indignant*) No, I don't.

Greg Anyway, some of them got away and managed to stay out for a week or more.

Sheila But not your grandfather, right?

Kasumi No, he was killed the first day. He wanted to die. To end his shame.

Sheila And your grandmother?

Kasumi It was very hard for her. Bringing up my father with no money.

Sheila Yes, but what did she think when she found out he'd been a prisoner?

Kasumi She was angry. Very angry.

Sheila Angry?

Kasumi Yes, ashamed, embarrassed.

Greg For the family.

Kasumi And for my father. He was a young man then. She did not know what the villagers would say. But my grandfather's friend told her not to be ashamed, that he was no longer ashamed he'd been a prisoner. He said, 'Do not worry. Your husband was a soldier. He fought like a soldier. Be full of pride for him.'

Greg Has she been out to Australia? To see his grave?

Kasumi No, she is dead now. But I have been to see it. My father said I should be the one to come, for the family.

Greg (*Puts arm around her*) And I'm glad he sent you.

Kasumi Greg! Your grandmother.

Sheila Oh, don't mind me. He's been able to wrap me round his little finger, ever since he was a toddler. Got away with murder, he did.

Kasumi (*Slightly alarmed*) Murder?

Greg (*Grins*) I'll explain later. (*Looks at watch*) Look, Gran, I'm sorry but we have to be going. We want to take in a movie and I didn't realise how late it was.

Sheila That's all right. You run along. And Greg, come again soon, won't you?

Greg (*They stand up*) Sure, Gran. (*He kisses her on cheek.*)

(*He and **Kasumi** move towards door.*)

Kasumi (*Holds out her hand*) Thank you, for having me.

Sheila (*Looks at the hand, hesitates, then slowly offers hers. **Kasumi** bows her head as they shake.*)

(*Lights fade.*)

SCENE 3

This scene takes the form of a daydream, or an examination of **Sheila's** *thoughts. The effect is slightly ritualised. Sheila is not mad. She knows Frank is dead and has been for many years, but it's as if, in her loneliness, she imagines how he would think and react if he were still alive. Stage is in darkness except for two spotlights on* **Sheila** *(L) and* **Frank** *(R) sitting on bar stools. They address their lines straight to the audience.*

Sheila I miss you, Frank. Still.

Frank I know you do, love.

Sheila It's been years now, yet, sometimes when I look at your photo, it seems only yesterday. Remember, how we stood on the wharf, and I held Judy up? She was so sure you could see her, but there were hundreds of men crowding the decks of that troopship.

Frank I saw you both, and when things got really bad, that was what I tried to keep in my mind, the sight of you both standing there, waving.

Sheila I had photos of you in uniform, of us. And young as she was, Judy can still remember how you swung her up in the air and kissed her goodbye. Then you walked up that gangway. We never saw you again.

Frank When we were captured, they confiscated everything. All our personal belongings. I managed to hide your photo, in my boot until it rotted, like everything else in the jungle.

Sheila How did you die, Frank?

Frank Who knows? Cholera, probably.

Sheila Cholera?

Frank Well, it was rife. But it could have been anything. Starvation, overwork, beatings, there are many ways to kill a man.

Sheila I didn't think anything would kill you. You seemed so strong.

Frank I thought it might be a bullet. I never thought of fever. I was sure I'd come back. But as the months wore on, I grew weaker and weaker. In the end, I just wanted to die.

Sheila And the Japs? Didn't you hate them?

Frank At first, yes. We all did. But after a time we realised we were all stuck there, waiting for the war to finish.

Sheila But the men dying of malaria, starving. Surely you blamed the guards?

Frank A lot of guards were Korean. The officers were Japanese. But when you're struggling to survive, finding something to eat becomes more important than anger. You talk of food, dream of food. You search for things to eat, grass, hibiscus leaves, anything green, that's edible.

Sheila I don't understand. You had such cause.

Frank Hate drains you, saps all your energy. It eats in like tropical ulcers, festering away inside. In the end, there's no point. To survive, you have to put it behind you, get on with the business of living.

Sheila I've never thought of it like that.

Frank Think of the future, Sheila. Don't live in the past.

(*Lights fade.*)

SCENE 4

Spotlight on **Greg** *standing at the phone table on stage apron. Phone rings in Sheila's sitting room. She enters from wings and answers it.*

Greg Hi, Gran.

Sheila Greg! How nice.

Greg I'm going to be over your way tomorrow, I was thinking of popping in to see you. Will you be there?

Sheila Of course, I will. And this time I'll make you a chocolate cake.

Greg Don't go to any trouble.

Sheila Oh, it's no trouble. I like doing it. Oh, and Greg. I was thinking of asking you and Kasumi to lunch. So you'd better tell me what she eats.

(*Fade.*)

SCENE 5

Lights up on **Sheila** *seated, making phone call. Phone rings on apron.* **Judy** *enters from wings answers it, then sits down.*

Judy Hello?

Sheila (*Holds receiver in one hand, card in the other*) Is that you, Judy?

Judy Of course it's me, Mum. What's wrong?

Sheila Oh, I'm fine. It's just the neighbours.

Judy (*Groans*) Oh no, not again, what is it this time?

Sheila Well, it's most peculiar. They want me to be their grandmother.

Judy Their grandmother? I don't understand.

Sheila For Chinese New Year.

Judy You're not making much sense.

Sheila They need an elderly relative to be at this special dinner and they don't have any. At least, not here, in Australia.

Judy So you're saying they want *you* to fill in?

Sheila Yes. Mrs Lee asked me yesterday and this morning, she sent the kids in with this card.

Judy What card?

Sheila (*Impatient*) The one I'm holding. I'm trying to read it to you. It says: 'DEAR MRS WALKER' – oh, and they don't know how to spell Walker.

Judy (*Gritting teeth*) Go on.

Sheila 'PLEASE WILL YOU BE GRANDMOTHER NEXT TUESDAY. COME TO DINNER HALF PAST AFTER SEVEN.' And it's signed: Danny and Susie – they're the kids.

Judy How nice of them! So, you're going?

Sheila Do you think I should?

Judy Of course you should. It would be very rude if you refused.

Sheila But what'll I do when I get there?

Judy Do? What anyone does at a dinner party. Enjoy the food, talk to everyone at the table and generally have a good time.

Sheila (*Pause*) You're sure?

Judy I'm sure.

Sheila But – I won't know what to say to them.

Judy Mum! That's the most ridiculous thing I've ever heard. Since when have you *ever* been at a loss for words?

(*Fade.*)

(*THE END.*)

Drama Activities

APPRECIATING THE PLAY

SCENE 1

1. If you were directing the play, what acting suggestions would you give to the actor playing the role of Sheila?
2. At the very beginning of the play there is tension between Sheila and Judy. Why is this?
3. 'Don't be so racist.' Why does Judy accuse Sheila of being racist?
4. What is Judy's attitude to Greg and his new girlfriend?
5. 'I don't want them next door, not after what they did to your father.' What is wrong with Sheila's reasoning?
6. 'Some of us move with the times.' How has Sheila failed to move with the times?

SCENE 2

7. When Sheila is introduced to Kasumi, how does Sheila react to her?
8. 'And those bastards worked the poor buggers till they dropped.' What emotions does Sheila reveal here?
9. How does Sheila react to the mention of the Cowra breakout?
10. What explanation does Kasumi give for the Japanese prisoners' breakout?
11. 'They hurled themselves at the barbed wire only to be mown down by machine guns.' What is Sheila's reaction to this?
12. What words of Sheila show that she has always been fond of Greg?
13. What evidence can you find to suggest that by the end of Scene 2, Sheila has come to accept Kasumi?

SCENE 3

14. Imagine you are directing Scene 3 (which takes the form of a day dream). How would you create the impression for the audience that it is 'a daydream examination of Sheila's thoughts'?

15 What does this scene show about the relationship between Frank and Sheila?

16 'In the end I just wanted to die.' Why did Frank give up?

17 'Don't live in the past.' Why is this advice important for Sheila?

SCENE 4

18 '*Spotlight on* **Greg** . . .'. Why do you think the screenwriter has included this stage direction?

19 'I'll make you a chocolate cake.' What does this reveal about Sheila's attitude to Greg?

20 What evidence in this scene can you find to show that Sheila has a very positive attitude to Kasumi?

SCENE 5

21 'It's just the neighbours.' Why does Judy groan when Sheila says this?

22 Do you think this scene is a good ending to the play? Why?

ISSUES
WAR

This play examines three main issues: racial prejudice, the futility of war and the dangers of living in the past. Let's look at the first two of these issues.

Carefully read each of these pieces of dialogue and write down what it shows about war.

- 'Darwin, yes. It was bombed, and Townsville too, pretty badly.'
- 'When the time came, they just hurled themselves at the barbed wire only to be mown down by machine guns.'
- 'Our boys would never have shot in cold blood.'
- 'He was killed the first day. He wanted to die. To end his shame.'
- 'She took Grandad's death pretty badly.'
- 'They beat him to death in that camp.'

RACIAL PREJUDICE

Look at each of these pieces of dialogue. Some of them are examples of racial prejudice, while others put forward racial equality. Write down each piece of dialogue and explain what view it gives of life and what it tells you about the speaker.

- 'They're taking over. Suburb by suburb.'
- 'Mrs Lee was hosing her garden when I pulled up. And she's very nice.'
- 'I don't want them next door. Not after what they did to your father.'
- 'You'll never catch me driving a Japanese car.'
- 'Well don't criticise the neighbours. They've done nothing to you.'
- 'Hate drains you, saps all your energy. It eats in like tropical ulcers, festering away inside.'
- 'PLEASE WILL YOU BE GRANDMOTHER NEXT TUESDAY. COME TO DINNER HALF PAST AFTER SEVEN.' Danny and Susie.

WRITE YOUR OWN PLAY

Typically, drama is about people and their problems. If you look around you at school or at home, you'll soon become aware of some interesting situations that can be turned into worthwhile drama.

For example, you may decide to protest to your school principal over the excessive amount of homework being given to you each week. But it is more than a simple protest, it is the protest of an individual against a system. So, in thinking about a central idea for a play, don't hesitate to use some problem that you or a friend have experienced – some problem with a simple local setting that you thoroughly understand.

You are going to write your own play. But first, let's look at some of the things you need to consider.

Here is an example, in play form, of a problem that you may understand and be sympathetic about.

FIGHT! FIGHT!

Tina (*To her friend*)   I just heard all this noise so I looked around the corner of the science block . . .

Sharon   Well, come on, what did you see? Don't keep me in suspense!

> **Tina** Rod and Reg are fighting. My two best friends fighting!
> **Sharon** What are you going to do?
> **Tina** I don't know.

When Tina looked around the corner of the science block, she not only discovered a problem, she also saw and felt conflict. Conflict, which may be physical, verbal or emotional, is the ingredient of drama that captivates audiences. Audiences also like to have the conflict resolved by the end of the play.

STORY OUTLINE

The first step in writing a play is to write down your idea for the story – this includes the problem and the conflict. Then encapsulate each scene in two or three sentences. Here is a sample outline of *Fight! Fight!*.

Scene 1
Tina sees the boys fighting and tells her friend, Sharon. Tina rushes out to stop the fight but the boys refuse to stop until she agrees to ask one of them to the school dance.

Scene 2
A teacher stops the fight but the boys refuse to shake hands until Tina has decided on one of them. This will be difficult and hurtful. Then Tina has a brilliant idea. She asks them not to fight for one moment and rushes off around the corner of the science block.

Scene 3
She returns with her friend Sharon and introduces her to the boys. Reg and Sharon like each other immediately. Tina and Sharon ask the boys to the dance.

Scene 4
The teacher congratulates all of them on being so civilised about resolving their problem.

This story has a beginning, a middle and an end. The beginning is the fight and the reason for it. The middle is when the teacher stops the fight and Tina has her brilliant idea. The end comes when the problem is resolved – Reg and Sharon like each other so the fighting stops and they can all go to the dance.

STORY TO SCRIPT

Dialogue is the essence of drama. Everything in a play, except stage directions, consists of characters speaking. As they speak, they reveal their feelings and motives. Gestures and movements are also important, but, for the audience, true knowledge about the characters comes from the dialogue.

Consider the kind of dialogue that you will use in your play. It must be natural for the situation you choose. In places such as at home and in the school playground, the dialogue will be informal and relaxed – the kind of everyday speech that people use who know each other well.

Formal dialogue is thoughtful, dignified and often serious in its purpose. It is appropriate for ceremonies, formal speeches and in law courts.

So, listen to the conversations that are occurring all around you, on the train, at school, during sport and so on, with the idea of developing an 'ear' for the ways people normally communicate.

Now write and act out the script.

IDEAS

Choose one of the following ideas for a play of your own. To make your effort more manageable, imagine yourself as the main character. Remember your main character has some problem that *must* be solved. Then you need three to four other characters to interact with.

- Queue jumping at the school canteen
- Sports stars in conflict
- In trouble with the law
- A rude waiter
- Pollution in the school grounds
- The takeaway food disaster
- Supermarket trolley trouble
- Gate crashers at the birthday party
- Your impossible next-door neighbours
- Cheating in an exam
- A shock at the hairdressers
- The drama lesson that went wrong
- Road accident
- Late for work
- A troublesome customer

Acknowledgements

The authors and publishers are grateful to the following for permission to reproduce copyright material:

Bill Condon for play *The Cowpokes of Calico*; Vashti Farrer for play *Possible Changes*; Robin George for play *The Hood, the Sad and the Cuddly*; The Barbara Hogenson Agency, Inc. and McIntosh & Otis for *To Kill a Mockingbird* (screenplay) © 1964/1992 by Boardwalk Productions and Brentwood Productions, Inc.; Reed Books UK for extract from *To Kill a Mockingbird* by Harper Lee published by William Heinemann; Thomas Nelson UK for play *Adam's Ark* by Harold Hodgson.

Photographs, cartoons: Auspac Media, p. 169 (Bristow); Austral International, p. 19, 29, 36, 41, 63, 144, 172, 210, 224; Universal City Studios, Inc. 1962, courtesy of MCA Publishing Rights, a Division of MCA, Inc. All rights reserved, p. 2, 5, 48, 59; Centre for Motion Picture Study/Margaret Herrick Library and Film Archive, p. 1, 54.

While every care has been taken to trace and acknowledge copyright, the publishers tender their apologies for any accidental infringement where copyright has proved untraceable. They would be pleased to come to a suitable arrangement with the rightful owner in each case.

Permission to perform
The following plays may be performed without permission or payment of a fee in school-related performances, provided that the playwright is acknowledged: 'The Hood, the Sad and the Cuddly' by Robin George; 'Dracula' by Tom Hayllar; 'The Cowpokes of Calico' by Bill Condon; 'Possible Changes' by Vashti Farrer.

Requests for permission to perform 'Adam's Ark' by Harold Hodgson should be directed to: Royalty Department, International Thomson Publishing Services, Cheriton House, North Way, Andover, Hants, SP105BE, United Kingdom.

See imprint page at front of this book for information about permission to perform the screenplay of 'To Kill a Mockingbird' by Horton Foote.